THE WAR IN NICARAGUA

W.ᵐ Walker

THE

WAR IN NICARAGUA

GEN'L WILLIAM WALKER

With a Foreword by
ROBERT HOUSTON

THE UNIVERSITY OF ARIZONA PRESS
Tucson, Arizona

About the Author

William Walker (1824–1860), a freethinker, early champion of women's rights, abolitionist, and socialist of a sort, abandoned a promising career as a muckraking newspaper editor to lead an army of American mercenaries in an abortive invasion of western Mexico in 1853. The adventure was a failure, but Walker soon turned his attention to Nicaragua, invading that nation in 1856. Defeated in 1857, Walker attempted to seize control of Nicaragua twice more. Captured by a mixed force of Hondurans and English sailors, Walker was executed in Trujillo, Honduras, on September 12, 1860.

The text of *The War in Nicaragua* is a direct photographic reproduction of the first edition, published in 1860 by S. H. Goetzel & Co. (Mobile, Alabama), and is reproduced courtesy of the Special Collections Division of the University of Arizona Library, Tucson.

THE UNIVERSITY OF ARIZONA PRESS
First Printing 1985

Library of Congress Cataloging in Publication Data

Walker, William, 1824–1860.
The war in Nicaragua.

Reprint. Originally published: Mobile:
S. H. Goetzel, 1860.
1. Nicaragua—History—Filibuster War, 1855–1860.
I. Title
[F1526.27.W28 1985]   972.85'04   84–22224
ISBN 0–8165–0882–8

To My Comrades in Nicaragua

I dedicate this effort to do justice to their acts and motives : To the living, with the hope that we may soon meet again on the soil for which we have suffered more than the pangs of death—the reproaches of a people for whose welfare we stood ready to die : To the memory of those who perished in the struggle, with the vow that as long as life lasts no peace shall remain with the foes who libel their names and strive to tear away the laurel which hangs over their graves.

W. W.

CONTENTS.

CHAPTER 1.

THE VESTA AND HER PASSENGERS.

CHAPTER II.

RIVAS, JUNE TWENTY-NINTH, 1855.

CHAPTER III.

VIRGIN BAY, SEPTEMBER THIRD, 1855.

CHAPTER IV.

GRANADA, OCTOBER THIRTEENTH, 1855.

CHAPTER V.

THE ADMINISTRATION OF RIVAS.

CHAPTER VI.

THE COSTA RICAN INVASION.

CHAPTER VII

THE DEFECTION OF RIVAS.

1*

CHAPTER VIII.

THE WALKER ADMINISTRATION.

CHAPTER IX.

THE ADVANCE OF THE ALLIES.

CHAPTER X.

THE RETREAT FROM GRANADA.

CHAPTER XI.

OPERATIONS ON THE SAN JUAN.

CHAPTER XII.

THE DEFENCE OF RIVAS.

PREFACE.

No history is so hard to write as that of our own times. Few, if any, can free themselves from the fashions of thought and opinion which control the daily life of their neighbors, and every one inhales to some extent the vapors and miasms floating in the air he hourly breathes. The task is even more difficult if a man attempts to narrate events in which he has taken part. As the soldier, warmed by the heat of battle, dimly sees through the dust and smoke of a well-fought field, the large movements which decide the issue of the conflict, so he who has mingled in the struggles of parties or the contests of nations, may not be as well fitted as others to speak of facts moulded partially by his own will and hand. But if the memoir writer be fair and discreet, he may contribute materials for future use, and his very errors may instruct after ages. The author of the following narrative does not expect to attain perfect truth in all things ; he merely asks the reader to give him credit for the desire to state facts accurately, and to reason justly about the circumstances attending the presence of the Americans in Nicaragua.

March 1st, 1860.

FOREWORD

The strange career of William Walker. It's a phrase used time
and again by journalists, historians of Central American affairs,
and biographers — even by Ripley's "Believe It or Not." In one
sense, it's an accurate phrase: that a thin little Tennesseean,
something of an intellectual, who was barely thirty, with no
military experience to speak of, could become dictator of
Nicaragua in a period of less than a year *is* strange, given what
our age knows of the world and its possibilities.

But the mid-nineteenth century admitted to no such limited
possibilities, and its scruples (at least public scruples) about
what chunk of the earth rightfully belonged to whom were far less
certain than ours. Almost any sort of adventurism was acceptable
to a large part of the thirty million Americans, as long as it could
be somehow justified by our messianic duty to spread democracy. If now we address our rhetoric to fighting communism, then
we addressed it to fighting ignorance, colonialism, the shameful
inability of "effete and decadent" races to govern themselves
properly—anything that stood in the way of Progress.

Reading this book should make both the parallels and the
differences between our two ages clear. The ironies that have led
us along a path from Nicaragua in the 1850s through the
Spanish-American War, through our habitual occupation of one
Central American country or another, through Vietnam and to
Central America again in the 1980s, speak for themselves. There
is no need for neon arrows to point them out. They will find you
by themselves.

The book in which I first discovered William Walker was
written by an Englishman, who adopted the traditional British
view that Walker was a joke, a little man who was eventually

[1]

"dealt with" as he should have been by the English, who considered Central America their sphere of influence in the 1850s. Nonetheless, I was fascinated by the sheer adventure of the story itself. More than four years later, after research that took me from the Library of Congress to the jungle rivers of Nicaragua, I published a novel on Walker, *The Nation Thief* (Pantheon, 1984).

In the course of those four years, my fascination with the incredible story grew, as did my puzzlement with the man himself. Eventually I decided the only honest course was to allow my readers to judge for themselves whether Walker was hero, monster, or joke (although I find it hard in any case to consider a man responsible for the deaths of twelve thousand people—by his own vice-commander's estimate—a joke). I can do no more now. His book, this book, gives part of the story. My job is to sketch briefly the rest, and allow you to do the judging. Whether William Walker's career was strange, or whether it goes to the very heart of the American historical experience—an experience crowded with angels of light, angels of darkness, forever soaring and falling on wings of money—you will decide.

Most accounts give Walker's birthdate as May 8, 1824. His father was a strict, proper Scot who had settled in the rough frontier town of Nashville and had done well as a banker and merchant. Walker and his two brothers and sister were raised in comfort, very religious, and part of a household that refused to own slaves. Portraits of him as an adolescent show a thin, dreamy-eyed boy; later pictures show those eyes hard and distant, the eyes that newspapers latched onto for their description of him as "the Grey-eyed Man of Destiny." Most writers of the time couldn't leave those eyes alone, in fact. "Hypnotic," they were called. "So large that they almost seemed pointed [*sic*]." And later, the Nicaraguan Indian legend of the gray-eyed god who would return to lead them back to power and glory did Walker's cause no harm.

Aside from the eyes, however, there was nothing arresting about him: lank, sandy hair and freckles on an unsmiling face (his brother remembered that Walker believed smiling was a sign of weakness, and there is a single recorded instance of his laughing). His features were sharp and hard, features we now associate with Southern hill-country faces. He spoke rarely, dressed like a down-at-the-heels undertaker much of the time, and lived quite happily in a bare room on cheese and bread. Withal, he was an "insignificant little man," as one writer who met him put it.

Much has been made of Walker's childhood. It was centered upon a constantly ill mother to whom he was hugely attached, and with whom he would spend hour after hour reading aloud (Scott, Byron, and other fashionable romantics, appropriately enough)—a "monastic" childhood, one biographer called it, in which imagination and dreams of grandly heroic deeds from pseudomedieval romances were no doubt his best escape. His schoolmates called him "honey" or "missy," and one friend of his mother's wrote afterward that he was "very intelligent and as refined in his feelings as a girl. I used often to go to see his mother and always found him entertaining her in some way," (quoted by Frederic Rosengarten, Jr., in *Freebooters Must Die!*, 1976).

In those days of pre-Freudian innocence, such devotion to his mother was considered commendable. Later writers—notably A. Z. Carr—have seen it differently, of course. No material I've encountered has mentioned the word "homosexual" in relation to Walker, though there is sufficient evidence at least strongly to suggest the possibility. Throughout his brief life, his strongest attachments—with the exception of those to his mother and one other woman—were to other men, and he avenged wrongs against his favorites with a passion that often went beyond common reason (you'll find those in this book).

But the evidence is and must remain inconclusive. Some of his men, for example, insisted that he went to brothels with them in Nicaragua, though that may or may not mean anything. One Guatamalan general, on the other hand, suggested he was probably asexual or impotent, that he loved only "the sensuality of power."

The Freudians are best left to settle the question. What matters ultimately is that he grew up serious, unlovely, and probably incapable of ordinary love; that in the end he did show himself truly to love most "the sensuality of power," and it was a fatal love.

By the age of fourteen he had graduated from the University of Nashville. By sixteeen, he had an advanced degree from the same university, concentrating chiefly in classics. By nineteen, fully grown now at five-four and a hundred and twenty pounds, he was granted a medical degree from the University of Pennsylvania. From there he went for advanced medical studies at the Sorbonne, and spent two years in Europe, intermittently studying and traveling, and generally disliking what he saw as European decadence.

He never practiced medicine, however. A. Z. Carr (*The World and William Walker*, 1962) theorizes that somehow he had a romantic notion that he would come home the only one able to heal his dying mother, and when he failed, he gave up medicine. Whatever the reason, after his mother's death he headed south to New Orleans where he began to work toward what had always been his greater passion: politics. (". . . there have been times when I thought the last vestige of such an idea had disappeared," Rosengarten quotes from a letter to a friend, "but often it reappears to me, in my waking dreams, leaving me uncertain whether it be an angel of light or an angel of darkness.")

By twenty-two, he had read law and been admitted to the bar, studying in the office of a man who figures prominently in this book and in Walker's future career, a handsome, charismatic, slightly older lawyer named Edmund Randolph. And in the revolutionary year of 1848, he became one of the editors of what was then considered a radical newspaper, *The New Orleans Delta*, where an unknown poet named Walt Whitman worked for a time under him.

Things began to happen for him quickly. He was invited back to Nashville that year to give a commencement address at his alma mater, an address on art in which he claimed, by reference to his admired Byron, that war in a just cause was an aesthetic act. But in New Orleans, his editorials kept him in disfavor with the movers and shakers: with great historical irony, he exposed a plot to take over Cuba and make it a slave-holding territory of the United States. He supported Kossuth's cause in Hungary, and even hinted that this new European idea called Socialism might not be such a bad proposition. He took a position in favor of the gradual abolition of slavery, and in support of women's rights.

And he fell in love, a love as unlikely as most things in his life. Through Randolph, he met Ellen Martin, the beautiful daughter of an aristocratic New Orleans family who would surely have been one of the city's prize catches long before Walker met her, but for one flaw. She was a deaf-mute. Walker learned sign language for her, however, and they became engaged. In my novel, I fantasize that he was attracted to her because "not even the carnality of speech" could come between them. True or not, it serves as an emblem for the idealism, the eternal and ironic passion for "purity" in the man. Years later, when he stood in front of a Honduran firing squad, he still wore the small gold cross she'd given him.

But within a year, that promising life in New Orleans had fallen apart. Ellen died in an epidemic of cholera, a disease that would constantly stalk Walker as enemy and as friend, as *The War in Nicaragua* shows. He turned taciturn, gloomy—apparently experienced all the fine nuances of Romantic Melancholy, and set off in search of Desperate Adventure.

Gold Rush San Francisco was his first stop, where he followed Edmund Randolph less than a year after Ellen's death. With Randolph's help, he found work as a newspaper editor again, and again stepped into trouble. He took on the corrupt judiciary of

San Francisco this time, and found himself fighting duels and getting to know the inside of San Francisco's jail, until Randolph made him a cause and public demonstrations freed him. A local hero now, but possibly in danger, Walker left San Francisco for Marysville, California, and dabbled in conventional politics, which he soon found to be too slow and tame for him.

Given who and where he was, and the times, it was probably inevitable that he would try his hand next at "filibustering." That he would find a place in history as "King of the Filibusters" would have been far harder to predict.

The most commonly accepted origin of the word "filibuster" is the Dutch for "freebooter." Filibustering was the rage in those days after we took half of Mexico in an easy war and our Manifest Destiny was to grab and hold whatever lands we could. American civilization had a right and duty to expand itself, and if the government wouldn't do that, there were plenty of private citizens who would. The expedition to Cuba that Walker had spoiled was one example of filibustering. There were others—two in particular to the state of Sonora in northern Mexico which ended disastrously. But such disasters didn't deter Walker. There were still people to be liberated in Sonora, and great silver and gold mines to work, great cattle estates to be founded. There were American colonists suffering from Apache raids and corrupt "greaser" government. (A word in general use even then, very possibly coming from the practice by Mexican soldiers of greasing their bayonets with rancid pig fat—and probably having little to do with tonsorial preference, since *yanquis* greased their hair abundantly, too.) And there was glory to be won.

So in 1853, with forty-five men and financing from bonds to be repaid in Mexican land, "Colonel" William Walker set out in a brig from San Francisco to become a president for the first time. It was an adventure as quixotic as could be imagined by the maddest Spaniard. To avoid being stopped for violating the U.S. Neutrality Laws, Walker's ship had to slip out of San Francisco in such a hurry that it left most of the party's ammunition and food behind. At the last minute, Walker decided it would be wiser to conquer Lower California first, since it was isolated and relatively undefended, so he put in at Cabo San Lucas and then at La Paz, tiny, dusty places where he managed at least to capture both the outgoing and incoming governors and proclaim himself President of the Republic of Lower California. (The first of many proclamations he was to issue over the next seven years: he was a master of proclamations.)

In spite of a lack of supplies, mutinies, and a population who showed little enthusiasm for being liberated, Walker moved north to Ensenada, closer to the overland route to Sonora, and proclaimed Sonora a free state, too. There, boxed in by both the Mexican and United States navies, he decided to head inland toward Sonora and stir up an insurrection among the oppressed.

The trip was a nightmare: two hundred miles of wasteland to the Colorado River, deserters being summarily shot, boots wearing through, clothing turning into rags. Yet Walker forced his men on, showing for the first time the almost superhuman determination that marked his political career. Only when they lost their cattle—their only real food supplies—trying to cross the Colorado on rafts, did they quit, and then only because a large part of Walker's force managed to desert north toward Fort Yuma. Walker himself led his remaining men back the way they had come, planning to rescue a garrison he'd left behind near Ensenada. He was too late. He found them massacred by a Mexican bandit leader.

Limping, in a single ragged boot, Walker rallied his half-starved men into a last desperate charge to safety past the bandits at a place called Tia Juana, and surrendered himself to the U.S. Army at the border. It was his thirtieth birthday.

Some historians have suggested that the Gadsden Purchase, which gave southern Arizona (including Tucson) to the United States, may have resulted from the Mexican government's belief that they were better off selling what they stood a good chance of losing to Walker anyway. If that's true, it is the only tangible result of Walker's first "filibustering" campaign. Less tangible but ultimately more important was the taste for war, the military experience, and the reputation for determination that Walker came away from his Lower California debacle with. Only a year later, he was off again, in another leaky brig heading south. But this time he was heading for Nicaragua, for his true appointment with his "destiny," as he forever called it.

And that's what this book is about. You might want to read it now before you come back to the rest of this essay.

Much has been written about this book. That it is well put together and remarkably free from the rhetorical excesses of much of the nineteenth-century journalistic tradition Walker knew, is true—though to a contemporary reader, the rhetoric often is still somewhat lush. That, all things considered, it is a surprisingly objective evaluation of Walker's career in Nicaragua also has a reasonable amount of truth to it. Of course it is partisan, but Walker is no apologist for himself. And that's part of the puzzlement about the man: within his own defined bounds, he maintained a degree of strange integrity that belies those who see him *only* as a power-mad little dictator. His courage under fire was attested to by his supporters and enemies alike, and even the most hostile of his biographers slip into a sneaking admiration of him from time to time. He could be stubbornly (sometimes suicidally) loyal, as he was to Edmund Randolph and other friends. He was erratically brilliant, swinging between moments of military genius and military idiocy. He could convince his troops that they were going straight into heaven or history books, and they would follow him into utter hells. No matter how twisted his vision became in his attempts to win the favor of the South by legalizing slavery, he never gave in to the kind of common greed and cynicism most others in his position would have. He never became a Batista or a Somoza, never had any Swiss bank accounts, though the effects of his acts in Nicaragua were no less disastrous for the Nicaraguan people. Yet many of them willingly remained loyal to him until the end, believing that somehow they were still better off under Walker than their own aristocrats.

What matters at last is this: all over Central America, William Walker is remembered as the pattern and paradigm for American intentions. There's not a schoolchild who doesn't know his name and his story. Parents for generations have been frightening children to sleep with his name. He has become the core around which their national myths have been created (and all countries define themselves by their national myths): the heroic and successful struggle of the people of Central America against the arrogance and power of the North Americans—as they see it—has sustained them through all the years of other American interventions since Walker's first and "unofficial" one. Whoever their internal enemies are, they know for certain from which direction their external enemy has traditionally come.

The War in Nicaragua was written over a period of only months in 1859 and early 1860, partly to finance Walker's final expedition to Central America. After his defeat in April of 1857, he had returned to the United States to a hero's welcome, though that soon faded when the remnants of the common soldiers in his army put into port with their stories of Walker having abandoned them to the long march across the country at the mercy of the Central American Allies. Nonetheless, by the end of 1857, he was back in Nicaragua again with a new force, going for Vanderbilt's Transit Route again. This time, however, a U.S. warship stopped him before he even got off the beach at San Juan del Norte, though an advance party had had success in making its way up the river toward Lake Nicaragua. He was brought back to New Orleans, tried for violating the Neutrality Act—and acquitted.

He was rapidly using up his political capital. The new railway across Panama was making Vanderbilt's hazardous Transit

Route less and less of a prize (it never did return to full operation, and there is doubt that Vanderbilt seriously considered the canal project beyond his first enthusiasm). Another attempt to send men south resulted in a disastrous shipwreck and the ignominious return of Walker's men aboard a British warship. By now, there was little doubt that a war between the states was brewing, and the country's attention was turning toward that new excitement. Only in the South, among the pro-slavery people, did Walker still find his needed support, which explains his convoluted chapter devoted to proving that he was always a slavery supporter (not true, based on his earlier writings). He desperately needed to find a way to keep his cause alive, and this book, which became a best seller after its publication in Mobile in 1860, was his solution. (He was to the end a man who understood the power of the press and the value of manipulating it.)

In June of 1860 he set sail with about a hundred men from Mobile on his last voyage south. He had been given a contract by the English settlers on the Bay Islands, off the Honduran Coast, to lead them in a revolution against the Honduran government when the British government turned the islands over to the Hondurans, as planned, in July of that year. Walker of course had grander schemes. In Honduras, he would link up with Trinidad Cabañas, whose plea for aid he had spurned in his Nicaraguan heyday, would defeat his old enemy the Butcher, and march south to retake Nicaragua.

After a series of disasters that would have turned anyone but William Walker back to Mobile, he did manage to capture the port of Trujillo, Honduras, and set up his last provisional government. He was a president again for a little while, issuing proclamations, making speeches, drilling troops. But not for long. Seven hundred Honduran troops set up camp around Trujillo, and a British warship (appropriately named the *Icarus*) steamed into port shortly afterward. The captain trained his guns on Walker's position, demanding his surrender and the customs duties from the port that had been pledged to the queen as repayment of a debt, money Walker didn't have.

In the night, instead of surrendering, Walker plunged into the jungles with his sixty-odd remaining men in the desperate hope of finding Cabañas. For days, pursued by Honduran troops, eating nothing but bananas, sick with coast fever, he drove his men through the endless jungle rains in the direction he had been told Cabañas's troops had last been seen. The British caught up with him again in the empty trenches Cabañas had abandoned weeks before. He had barely a dozen starving men left, and was holding off an entire Honduran army across the river.

His arrogance—or pride—held to the last. On board the British warship, the captain offered safe passage back to New Orleans for all American citizens. But when Walker was asked his citizenship, he answered, "I am William Walker, President of the Republic of Nicaragua."

In Trujillo, the captain handed him over to the Butcher's troops as a Nicaraguan citizen.

He was held in chains in Trujillo only long enough for a messenger to be sent to the capital of Tegucigalpa and return with the Butcher's execution order. It is reported that he spent those last few days in prayer and meditation, writing a few last protests to the "civilized world" about British treachery and Honduran injustice, and talking to an American correspondent from the *New York Herald*. He told a priest that he had no fear of death. "If my political career is over," he is supposed to have said, "it is right that I die." He had created himself in Central America, had embraced that "waking dream" of his boyhood and had found the angel in it to be truly of darkness at last. But he had long before given up any other identity, any other possible self. If his options were to die or to become nobody once more, it was clear which option held the greater terror for him.

On the morning of September 12, at the age of 36, he was shot on the beach at Trujillo in front of an old adobe wall. Some witnesses say he tried to make a last speech in Spanish before the firing squad shut him off. Others claim he went quietly and in prayer. When he had fallen, the captain of the firing squad blew his face away with pistol.

He was buried in a ten-peso wooden coffin, in a weedy gravesite, under a plain, small stone on which his name is misspelled.

ROBERT HOUSTON

For Further Reading

Allen, Merritt Parmalee. *William Walker, Filibuster.* Harper, 1932.

Carr, A. Z. *The World and William Walker.* Harper & Row, 1963.

Doubleday, C. W. *Reminiscences of the "Filibuster" War in Nicaragua.* Putnam, 1886.

Gerson, Noel B. *The Sad Swashbuckler.* Thomas Nelson, 1976.

Greene, Laurence. *The Filibuster.* Bobbs-Merrill, 1937.

Houston, Robert. *The Nation Thief.* Pantheon, 1984.

Jamison, James C. *With Walker in Nicaragua.* E. W. Stephens, 1909.

Roche, James J. *The Story of the Filibusters.* Unwin, 1891.

Rosengarten, Frederic, Jr. *Freebooters Must Die!* Haverford House, 1976.

Scroggs, William O. *Filibusters and Financiers.* Macmillan, 1916. (Reissued 1969.)

Original source materials, such as diaries, journals, manuscripts, and editions of Walker's newspaper *El Nicaraguense*, may be found in the Manuscript Collection, Rare Book Room, and Latin American Collection of the Library of Congress; in the National Archives; and in the Tennessee State Historical Society, among other places.

THE WAR IN NICARAGUA.

Chapter First.

THE VESTA AND HER PASSENGERS.

On the 5th of May, 1854, a number of native Nicaraguans who had been exiled by the existing Government of their Republic, landed at Realejo, and thence proceeded to Chinandega with a view of organizing a revolution against the acting authorities of the country. Among them were D. Maximo Jerez, D. Mateo Pineda, and D. Jose Maria Valle, leading citizens of the Occidental Department. They had sailed from Tiger Island on a vessel commanded by an American, Gilbert Morton, and were about fifty-four in all when they surprised the garrison at Realejo. After the revolutionists reached Chinandega, they were joined by large numbers of the people, and they proceeded with little delay to march towards Leon. On the road thither they met the forces of the Government at several points, each time routing them; and the President, D. Fruto Chamorro, seeing the temper of the people, and unable to resist the revolution about Leon, fled alone, and without an escort, to Granada. He did not reach the last named city for some days after leaving Leon, having gone astray in the woods and hills about Managua, and his partisans had almost despaired of ever again seeing him, when he rode into the town where his principal adherents resided.

After the revolutionists, headed by Jerez, reached Leon, they organized a Provisional Government, naming as Director, D. Francisco Castellon. This gentleman had been a candidate for the office of Director at the preceding election in 1853 ; and his friends asserted that he had a majority of votes, but that Chamorro had obtained the office by the free use of bribes among the members of the electoral college. Chamorro was installed in the office, and soon found pretexts for banishing Castellon and his chief supporters to Honduras. In that State, General Trinidad Cabañas held executive power ; and favored by him, Jerez and his comrades had been able to sail from Tiger Island with the arms and ammunition requisite for their landing at Realejo.

While his political enemies were in Honduras, Chamorro had called a constituent Assembly, and the constitution of the country had been thoroughly revised and changed. The constitution of 1838 placed the Chief Executive power in the hands of a Supreme Director, who was elected every two years ; the new constitution created the office of President, who was to be chosen every four years. In all respects the new constitution placed more power in the Government than had been trusted to it by the previous law ; hence it was odious to the party styling itself Liberal, and acceptable to those who called themselves the party of order. The new constitution was printed on the 30th of April, 1854; and its partisans say it was also promulgated on that day. The opponents of the new constitution say it never was promulgated. At any rate, the revolution, made professedly against this constitution, was started on the 5th of May, before the new law could have been promulgated in the towns and villages distant from the capital.

The Leonese revolutionists styled their Executive Provisional Director, and asserted their resolution to maintain the organic act of 1838. They took the name of Democrats, and wore as their badge a red ribbon on their hats. Chamorro was called by his friends President—they thus declaring their adhesion to the new constitution ; and calling themselves Legitimists, they mounted the white ribbon, in opposition to the red of the Democrats.

During the month of May the Provisional Government was accepted by all the municipalities of the Occidental Department, and by some of the other towns ; and the democratic army, as it was called, marching southward, reached Granada in the early part of June. The delay of the Democrats at Leon and at Managua had given Chamorro time to organize his force, and though his numbers were small, he repulsed Jerez and his followers (for these latter could not be called a force) when they attempted to carry Granada by assault. After the first repulse, Jerez sat down before the town, and affected to lay siege to the place. The rabble at his heels were, however, busier in plundering the shops of the suburbs than in defeating the plans of their enemies. The arrival of some officers and soldiers from Honduras assisted Jerez in his efforts to organize the "democratic army," and was a proof of the readiness with which Cabañas had recognized the Provisional Government.

For some months Jerez remained at Granada, vainly attempting to get possession of the chief square of the city, known as the Plaza. All the towns of the State had in the meanwhile declared for Castellon, and his friends held the lakes as well as the San Juan river, by means of small schooners and bungos. The schooners were under the command of a physician—an American or Englishman who had resided in the United States, and bore the name of Segur, although his real name was Desmond. In the month of January, 1855, Corral succeeded in taking Castillo, as well as the lake schooners, from the Democrats; and soon thereafter Jerez broke up his camp before Granada, and retreated in a rapid and disorderly manner towards Managua and Leon. The flight of the Democrats from Rivas followed almost immediately the retreat from Granada; and in a few weeks the turn of affairs was visible by the adhesion of many persons of property to the Legitimist party.

It was well for the Democrats that Chamorro, worn out by long disease and anxious thought, died a short time after they left the Jalteva. He was buried in the parish church, on the main Plaza of Granada, and his death was kept carefully concealed from the enemy. His name was strength to the Legitimists and a terror to their foes; and had he lived, a far more vigorous hand than that of Corral would have driven the flying Democrats back to the square of Leon. After the death of Chamorro, Corral remained in command of the Legitimist army, and the Presidency fell, under the constitution of 1854, to one of the Senators, D. José Maria Estrada.

In the meantime, causes at work outside of Nicaragua were destined to influence very materially the fate of the Provisional Government. President Carrera, of Guatemala, being friendly to the principles of the party led by his countryman Chamorro, had determined to act against the Government of Cabañas, in Honduras. In view of this fact, Alvarez and the Honduras contingent received orders to return from Nicaragua, and this dampened the spirit of the Democratic leaders. Honduras, threatened by the much greater power of Guatemala on the north, not only had need of all the resources she could control, but she could hardly hope, without foreign assistance, to resist the strength of Carrera and his Indians. Not even the Nicaraguans themselves could blame Cabañas for the course he took, and the friendship between Castellon and the President of Honduras remained unaffected by the policy the latter was forced to pursue. The alliance between the Governments at Leon and at Comayagua continued, and they seemed to be linked together for a common fate. But closely as the cause of Castellon was bound to that of Cabañas, it was not in Honduras, nor yet in Guatemala, that its destiny was being determined. The very day which witnessed the most signal triumph of the Nicaraguan Democrats was destined to behold the overthrow of the Cabaña administration; and to ascertain the cause of such a strange result we must leave Central America and consider events in California.

Three days after Jerez and his comrades landed at Realejo—that is on the 8th of May, 1854—a novel scene was enacted on the boundary between Upper and Lower California. On that day a small band of Americans marched from the Tia Juana country-house to the monument marking the boundary between the United States and Mexico, and there yielded their arms to a military officer of the former power. These men were poorly clad, but even at the moment of their surrender they—I speak not of their leader—bore themselves with a certain courage and dignity not unworthy of men who had aspired to found a new State. They were the last of what has been called the expedition to Lower California; and some among them had seen the flag of Mexico lowered at La Paz to give place to another made for the occasion. They had passed through much toil and danger; and most of them being altogether new to war had taken their first lesson in that difficult art by long fasts, and vigils, and marches across one of the most inhospitable regions of the American continent. The natural obstacles of Lower California, the scarce subsistence, the long intervals between watering-places, the rugged sides of the mountains, and the wide wastes of sandy desert, would make war in that territory not a pastime even to a well-appointed force. And when you add to these natural difficulties an enemy who knows the country well, and who is always able to muster larger numbers than your own, some idea may be form-

ed of the trials of those engaged in the Lower California
expedition. When, however, these men crossed the line,
they gave no sign of failing spirit, but looked the foe
which hung about their rear and flanks as resolutely in
the face as if they had just left a field of triumph and
victory. Such a fact is itself sufficient to prove that the
vulgar ideas of this expedition are false ; and as several
of the persons with Colonel Walker in Lower California
afterward acted in Nicaraguan affairs, it is not irrelevant
to ascertain the motives which guided them in their first
enterprise, so little understood by the American people.

The object of these men in leaving California was to
reach Sonora ; and it was the smallness of their numbers
which made them decide to land at La Paz. Thus
forced to make Lower California a field of operations
until they might gather strength for entering Sonora,
they found a political organization in the peninsula requisite. It was the intention of their leader to establish
at as early a time as possible a military colony—not
necessarily hostile to Mexico—on the frontier of Sonora,
with a view of protecting that State from the Apaches.
The design of such a colony first took form at Auburn,
in Placer county, California, early in 1852. A number
of persons there contributed to send two agents to Guaymas for the purpose of getting a grant of land near the
old town of Arispe, with the condition of protecting the
frontier from the Indians. These agents—one of whom
was Mr. Frederic Emory—arrived in Sonora just after
Count Raousset de Boulbon had agreed to settle several hundred French near the mine of Arizona; and the
State Government of Sonora expected the French to do

the work the Americans desired to attempt. Mr. Emory
and his companion, therefore, failed in their object; and
the Count de Boulbon soon afterward going to Sonora,
the Auburn plan was abandoned. The Government of
Arista, or rather persons attached to that administration,
became hostile to Raousset de Boulbon on account of
their interest in a conflicting claim to the mine he contracted to work ; and by the intrigues of Colonel Blanco
the French were driven into revolution, and afterward,
during the illness of their leader, into an agreement to
leave the country.

At the time the news of their departure from Sonora
reached California, Mr. Emory proposed to Mr. Walker,
to revive the Auburn enterprise ; and Walker, together with his former partner, Mr. Henry P. Watkins,
sailed for Guaymas, in the month of June, 1853, intending to visit the Governor of Sonora, and try to get such
a grant as might benefit the frontier towns and villages.
Walker was careful to provide himself with a passport
from the Mexican consul at San Francisco; but this
availed him little when he reached Guaymas. The day
after his arrival there the Prefect ordered him to the
office of police, and after a long examination forbade him
to leave for the interior, refusing to countersign his passport for Ures. Seeing the obstacles placed in his way
at the outset, Walker determined to return to California ;
and after he went aboard the vessel for that purpose the
Prefect sent him word the Governor, Gandara, had
ordered his passport to be countersigned in order that he
might go to the capital. The same courier who bore the
order from Gandara to the Prefect, Navarro, also brought

news that the Apaches had visited a country-house, a few leagues from Guaymas, murdering all the men and children, and carrying the women into a captivity worse than death. The Indians sent word that they would soon visit the town " where water is carried on asses' backs"—meaning Guaymas ; and the people of that port, frightened by the message, seemed ready to receive any one who would give them safety from their savage foe. In fact several of the women of the place urged Walker to repair immediately to California, and bring down enough Americans to keep off the Apaches.

What Walker saw and heard at Guaymas satisfied him that a comparatively small body of Americans might gain a position on the Sonora frontier, and protect the families on the border from the Indians ; and such an act would be one of humanity, no less than of justice, whether sanctioned or not by the Mexican Government. The condition of the upper part of Sonora was at that time, and still is, a disgrace to the civilization of the continent ; and until a clause in the treaty of Guadalupe Hidalgo was rescinded by one in the Gadsden treaty, the people of the United States were more immediately responsible before the world for the Apache outrages. On none more immediately than on the American people, did the duty devolve of relieving the frontier from the cruelties of savage war. Northern Sonora was, in fact, more under the dominion of the Apaches than under the laws of Mexico ; and the contributions of the Indians were collected with greater regularity and certainty than the dues to the tax-gatherer. The state of this region furnished the best defence for any American aiming to settle there

without the formal consent of Mexico ; and although
political changes would certainly have followed the
establishment of a colony near Arispe, they might be
justified by the plea that any social organization, no
matter how secured, is preferable to that in which indi-
viduals and families are altogether at the mercy of
savages.

But the men who sailed for Sonora were obliged to
sojourn, for a time, on the peninsula ; and their conduct
in Lower California may be taken as the measure of
their motives in the enterprise they undertook.   Where-
soever they went they sought to establish justice and
maintain order, and those among them who violated law
were summarily punished. An instance occurred at the old
mission of San Vincente, illustrative of the character of the
expedition, and of the persons who directed it. Several of
the soldiers had formed a conspiracy to desert and to pillage
the cattle-farms on their way to Upper California.   The
plan and purposes of the conspirators were revealed by
one of the confederates, and the parties to the plot were
tried by court-martial, found guilty of the charge, and
sentenced to be shot.   A military execution is a good
test of military discipline ; for no duty is so repulsive to
the soldier as that of taking life from the comrade who
has shared the perils and privations of his arduous service.   On this occasion, too, the duty was more difficult,
because the number of Americans was small, and was
daily diminishing.   But painful as was the duty, the
men charged with the execution did not shrink from the
performance of it ; and the very field where the unfortunate victims of the law expiated their offence with

their lives, was suggestive of comparison between the
manner in which the expeditionists - and the Mexican
Government severally performed the duties of protection
to society. The expeditionary force, drawn up to vindicate law, by the most serious punishment it metes out
to the offender, stood almost in the shadow of the ruins
of the church of the mission fathers. The roofless buildings of the old monastery, the crumbling arches of the
spacious chapel, the waste fields which showed signs of
former culture, and the skulking form of the half-
clothed Indian, relapsing into savageism from which the
holy fathers had rescued him, all declared the sort of
protection Mexico had given to the persons as well as
the property of the Peninsula. In the vital functions
of government, the expeditionists may safely chal-
lenge a comparison of their acts with those of Mexico
in Lower California ; and the ruin and desolation which
followed the unwise no less than unjust measure of
secularizing the missions, were sufficient to forfeit the
claim of the Mexican Republic to the allegiance of the
peninsula.

The main fact for us to know is that those engaged in
the Lower California expedition gave proof of their desire
not to destroy, but to re-organize society wherever they
went. They were all young men, and youth is apt to
err in pulling down before it is ready to build up. But
they were men, also, full of military fire and thirsting
for military reputation ; and the soldier's instinct leads
him to construct rather than to destroy. The spirit of
the soldier is conservative ; the first law of military
organization is order. Therefore, these men, though

young, were not ill-fitted to lay the foundations of a new
and more stable society than any they might find either
in Sonora or Lower California. They failed, however;
whether through the actions of others more than of themselves, it imports not our present purpose to determine.
Suffice it to say that the last remains of the expedition
reached San Francisco about the middle of May, 1854.

The leader of the expedition—William Walker, or, as
he was then called, Col. Walker—after returning to
Upper California, resumed the occupation of editor of a
daily paper. One of the proprietors of the paper he edit-
ed was Byron Cole, whose attention had been for several
years directed to Central America, and more particularly
to Nicaragua. Cole, in frequent conversations with
Walker, urged him to give up the idea of settling in Sonora, and to devote his labors to Nicaragua; and soon
after he heard of the revolution undertaken by Jerez and
Castellon, Cole sold his interest in the paper at San
Francisco, and sailed for San Juan del Sur. He left for
Nicaragua on the steamer of the 15th of August, 1854,
being accompanied by Mr. Wm. V. Wells, whose attention was fixed on Honduras. From San Juan del Sur,
Mr. Cole, after numerous delays and vexations, succeeded
in getting to Leon, and there obtained from Castellon a
contract, by which the Provisional Director authorized
him to engage the services of three hundred men for
military duty in Nicaragua, the officers and soldiers to
receive a stated monthly pay, and a certain number of
acres of land at the close of the campaign. With this
contract Cole returned to California early in the month
of November, and forthwith sought Walker for the pur-

pose of getting him to take an interest in the enterprise. As soon as Walker read the contract he refused to act under it, seeing that it was contrary to the act of Congress of 1818, commonly known as the neutrality law. He, however, told Cole that if he would return to Nicaragua, and get from Castellon a contract of colonization, something might be done with it. Cole accordingly sailed a second time for San Juan; and on the 29th of December, 1854, Castellon gave him a colonization grant, under which three hundred Americans were to be introduced into Nicaragua, and were to be guaranteed forever the privilege of bearing arms. This grant Cole sent to Walker, and it reached the latter at Sacramento early in the month of February, 1855.

A few days after receiving this contract. Walker went to San Francisco with the view of providing means, if possible, for carrying two or three hundred men to Nicaragua. He there met an old schoolmate, Mr. Henry A. Crabb, who had just returned from the Atlantic States; and Crabb having passed through Nicaragua on his way from California to Cincinnati, gave a glowing report of the natural wealth and advantages of the country. While crossing the Transit Road, Crabb heard of the events then transpiring in the Republic—of the revolution at Leon and the siege of Granada; and he also ascertained that Jerez was anxious to obtain the aid of Americans for the campaign against the Legitimists. This suggested the idea of getting an element into the society of Nicaragua for the regeneration of that part of Central America; and while in the Atlantic States Crabb had secured the co-operation of Mr. Thomas F.

2

Fisher, formerly and now of New-Orleans, and of Captain C. C. Hornsby, who had served in one of the regiments known as the Ten Regiments, during the Mexican war.   The three, Crabb, Fisher, and Hornsby, left New-Orleans together in the month of January, 1855 : and on the way to San Juan del Norte they found aboard the steamer Mr. Julius DeBrissot, bound, as he said, for the Gallipagos Islands.   DeBrissot joined the party; and he, together with Hornsby and Fisher, remained in Nicaragua, while Crabb proceeded to San Francisco.   When Walker met Crabb at the latter place, he was awaiting advices from Fisher, who stopped on the Isthmus for the purpose of visiting Jerez and obtaining from him authority to engage Americans for the service of the Democratic army.

Not many days elapsed before Fisher himself came to California, bringing with him authority to enlist five hundred men for Jerez, and with a promise of the most extravagant pay, in both money and lands, to the officers and men who might engage in the service.   It seems Fisher, Hornsby, and DeBrissot, found the newly-arrived United States Minister, John H. Wheeler, on the Isthmus ; and as His Excellency was anxious to visit the Democratic camp in the Jalteva, as well as Chamorro, in Granada, before deciding what authority he would recognise, Fisher and his party went as an escort to the Minister, and under the protection of the American flag, into both camps.   From Jerez, however, Fisher obtained at this time the contract he bore to San Francisco ; while Hornsby and De Brissot, after leaving Granada, went to Rivas, and entered into a Quixotic agreement with D. Maximo Espinosa to take Fort Castillo Viejo and the San Juan river from the Legitimists, who had lately driven the Democrats from the stronghold at the Rapids. These two gentlemen, however, were soon glad to manage their escape from San Juan del Sur aboard of the steamer for San Francisco; and not long after Fisher's arrival, Hornsby and De Brissot both appeared in California.

Crabb and Walker had known each other from childhood, and their views were similar in regard to the state of Central America, and the means necessary for its regeneration. Therefore, Crabb generously proposed to give Walker the whole benefit of the contract Fisher had made with Jerez; and Crabb, in view of certain political movements then occurring in California, decided to remain in that State. Walker, however, while thanking Crabb for his offer, refused to have anything to do with the Jerez contract, preferring to act under the Castellon grant to Cole, not only because of its entire freedom from legal objections, but also because it was more reasonable, and had been given by an authority competent to make the bargain. Hornsby and De Brissot embarked in the enterprise with Walker; and it will be seen hereafter that they, as well as Fisher, held commissions under the Republic of Nicaragua.

In the meanwhile, Walker had taken care that no show of secrecy should bring suspicion on his undertaking, either as to its illegality or its injustice. He took the Cole grant to the District Attorney of the United States for the Northern District of California, Hon. S.

W. Inge, and that gentleman after examining it declared no law would be violated by acting under it. At
that time, too, General Wool, commanding the Pacific
Division, was supposed to have special power from the
President for suppressing expeditions contrary to the
Act of 1818. His headquarters were at Benicia, and
the General was in the habit of reading to many persons the letters addressed by him to the then Secretary
of War, Colonel Jefferson Davis, defending the course he
took in reference to the Lower California expedition.
Among others, he read these letters (which the old gentleman seemed to think models of logic and style) to
Walker, the very person about whose acts the discussion
had arisen between himself and the Secretary. From
these letters Walker was led to infer that the common
impression about the powers vested in the General, under the Act of 1818, was correct ; and, therefore, when
he heard of General Wool being in San Francisco, he
sought him out, and found him on the wharf only a few
minutes before four o'clock, the hour for the departure
of the Sacramento steamer. The General was about to
leave in the boat for Benicia ; and after hearing Walker's statement as to the nature of the grant made to
Cole, and of his intention to act under it, the old man,
shaking him heartily by the hand, said he not only
would not interfere with the enterprise, but wished it
entire success. Thus having secured the sanction of the
proper Federal authorities, Walker proceeded in his
efforts to provide means for carrying colonists to Nicaragua under the Cole contract. He soon found that it
would be impossible to get more than a pitiful sum of

money, and that his arrangements would have to be made on the most economical scale.

While engaged in these preliminary preparations, Walker received an injury in the foot, which kept him in his chamber until the middle of April; and, in fact, the sore was not wholly healed when he sailed from San Francisco. Thus confined to the house, he was able to do little more in the way of means than to obtain a thousand dollars from Mr. Joseph Palmer, of the firm of Palmer, Cook & Co. At this gentleman's house he had met with Colonel Fremont and talked with him about the enterprise in Nicaragua ; and the Colonel, who had passed across the Isthmus the previous year, thought well of the undertaking. It is due probably, to both Colonel Fremont and Mr. Palmer, to state that they were not fully aware of all the views Walker held on the subject of slavery ; nor, indeed, was it necessary at that time for those views to be expressed. Besides the assistance given by Mr. Palmer, Walker was much aided by two friends—Mr. Edmund Randolph and Mr. A. P. Crittenden.

After much difficulty, a contract was made with one Lamson for the passage of a certain number of men, aboard the brig Vesta, from San Francisco to Realejo. The agreement had been made through a ship-master, McNair, and it was considered that he would sail in command of the Vesta. But, after the cash payment on the charter party had been made to Lamson, he and McNair fell out, and the former was obliged to employ another captain for his vessel. The provisions and the passengers were all aboard the brig about the 20th of

April; and when it was thought she was on the point of
leaving, the Sheriff seized the vessel by attachment at
the suit of an old creditor of the owner, Lamson.   The
evening, too, after the attachment, there were some
signs of the brig getting under way for sea; and therefore the Sheriff sent down a posse of eight or ten, armed
with revolvers, for the purpose of preventing an escape.
A sort of scuffle, more in jest than in earnest, occurred
between some of the posse and their acquaintances
among the passengers; and the new captain, frightened
out of his wits, jumped over the rail to the wharf, taking with him the papers of the ship.   A few days afterward the United States Marshal served a writ on the
brig for the price of the provisions; and the revenue
cutter W. L. Marcy was hauled astern of the Vesta,
with orders to keep her from going to sea with the
Deputy Marshal aboard.   To make assurance doubly
sure, the Sheriff had the sails of the brig unbent and
put in store.   The owner seemed to be entirely without
means to satisfy the claims against the vessel, and
everybody thought the chance very small for the departure of the vessel on her proposed voyage.

Walker, however, advised the passengers to remain
aboard, and all except a few followed the advice.   Soon
he found a captain for the Vesta, in the person of Mr.
M. D. Eyre, who professed some knowledge of navigation.
The holder of the claim against Lamson, under which
the attachment issued, happened to be a friend of Crabb,
from Stockton; and he was induced by good will for the
voyage the Vesta was bound on, to grant easy terms for
the release of the brig.   Lamson really controlled the

action of the merchants who sold him the provisions; and when he was told it might not be safe for him to keep the passengers in San Francisco, he rather hesitatingly agreed to have the libel dismissed. But the sheriff's costs had run up, by the employment of the posse, and other extraordinary expenses, to more than three hundred dollars; and Walker having expended nearly the last dollar, it seemed as if this trivial amount might stop the whole enterprise. The costs of the sheriff were very large, if not illegal; but, as he had the sails in store, he seemed to have the Vesta in his power. Walker managed, however, to get an order from the sheriff on the store-keeper for the sails; and as the sheriff was kept in ignorance of the dismissal of the libel, he supposed the cutter would detain the brig in port if she tried to go out. Besides this, he had a keeper aboard; and the keeper having been a member of a California Legislature, was supposed to keep a sharp look-out for any suspicious movement. The captain of the cutter was informed a little before dark that the Vesta was out of the marshal's hands, and arrangements were made through one of the Marcy's officers, for her sailors to come aboard about ten o'clock, in order to bend the sails of the brig. The United States sailors came at the appointed time, and the passengers managed to get the sheriff's keeper into the cabin, where he was detained for several hours. Swiftly and silently the work of bending the sails went on; and shortly after midnight, on the morning of the 4th of May, 1855, the steam-tug Resolute came alongside the Vesta, and hitching her on, towed her from the wharf, through the shipping, into the stream, and out by the Heads to sea. The sheriff's keeper was sent to the Resolute, the towlines were cast off, and the Vesta put to sea, to the great joy of the passengers, who had been for two weeks alternating between hope of her departure and fear of her detention.

When the brig got to sea, it was found that there were fifty-eight passengers bound for a new home in the tropics. Among them were Achilles Kewen, who had commanded a company under Lopez, at Cardenas, in 1850 ; Timothy Crocker, who had served under Walker throughout the Lower California expedition ; C. C. Hornsby, whose previous adventures in Nicaragua have been alluded to ; Dr. Alex. Jones, who had lately been to the Cocos Islands in search of a buried treasure ; Francis P. Anderson, who had served in the New-York regiment in California during the Mexican war ; and others, whose names will hereafter appear in the course of this narrative. They were most of them men of strong character, tired of the humdrum of common life, and ready for a career which might bring them the sweets of adventure or the rewards of fame. Their acts will afford the best measure both of their capacity and of their character.

The voyage of the Vesta was rather long and tedious. In crossing the Gulf of Tehuantepec she encountered a gale which tested her timbers—twenty-nine years in her sides—to the utmost. The bow of the old brig would open to the waves as they roared around her, and at times her decks were swept clear by the huge billows passing over her. She was worked by men detailed from the passengers ; and after living through the storm off

Tehuantepec, the crew had little to do until she reached the Gulf of Fonseca. More than five weeks had been consumed since leaving San Francisco before the volcano of Coseguina—the first Nicaraguan land—was seen looming in the distance. The want of wind detained the brig for some hours at the mouth of the gulf, while a boat was sent in to the port of Amapala, on the Island of Tigre. Captain Morton, the same American who had carried Jerez to Realejo, in May, 1854, was at Amapala with instructions from Castellon, awaiting the arrival of the Vesta. The captain was gladly welcomed aboard the brig, as the skipper who had brought the vessel from San Francisco knew nothing of the Central American coast. After taking Morton aboard, the Vesta proceeded on her way, and on the morning of the 16th of June, she came to anchor within the port of Realejo.

I have been somewhat minute, and it may be tedious, in narrating the earlier incidents of the enterprise whereby Americans were introduced as an element into Nicaraguan society, because we may often judge best of events by seeing clearly the origin of them. The father ceases to have any direct influence over either the mind or the organization of the child after the moment of conception; and yet how often we trace not merely the features of the father, but even the delicate traits of his character, in his offspring. The fine cells which determine the nature of organic structure, have been minutely studied by the physiologist, and the manner of their development has opened to him some of the hitherto hidden laws of life. If, then, you desire to understand the character of the late war in

Nicaragua, do not despise the small events which attended the departure of the fifty-eight from San Francisco. From the day the Americans landed at Realejo dates a new epoch, not only for Nicaragua, but for all Central America. Thenceforth it was impossible for the worn-out society of those countries to evade or escape the changes the new elements were to work in their domestic as well as in their political organization.

The state of native parties in Nicaragua on the 16th day of June, 1855, was quite different from that existing on the 29th of December, 1854—the day on which Castellon made the grant to Cole. When the Vesta dropped anchor in the port of Realejo, the Provisional Government was confined almost entirely to the Occidental Department. The Legitimists held all the Oriental and Meridional Departments, and most of the towns and villages in Matagalpa and Segovia were subject to their sway. The ally, too, of the Provisional Government, Cabañas, sat less firmly in the executive chair of Honduras than he had on the previous Christmas. A force organized by the aid of Guatemala, and commanded by a General Lopez, had invaded the Department of Gracias; and while Lopez was sent into the north of Honduras, General Santos Guardiola—whose name was itself a terror to the towns of both States—sailed from Istapa for San Juan del Sur, aboard the Costa Rican schooner San José, with the intention of engaging in the service of the Legitimists for a campaign in Segovia, close to the confines of Tegucigalpa and Choluteca. Guardiola arrived at Granada only a few days before Walker reached Realejo; and the latter found the people about Chinandega trembling at the name of one who, whether properly or improperly it is hard to say, had acquired the epithet of the " Butcher" of Central America. After the retreat from Granada Jerez had fallen into disgrace with his party—at least they denied him all claim to military capacity, no doubt glad to place on the shoulders of their leader the blame of all the misfortunes which had followed their entire want of military virtue. In place of Jerez, Castellon put at the head of the " Democratic Army" General Muñoz, who had at that time more reputation as a soldier than any man in Central America. He had been invited to Leon from Honduras, whither he had retired several years previously in consequence of having failed in a revolution against the Government of D. Laureano Pineda; and it was only by much entreaty and grave concession that Castellon had prevailed on him to take the command of the army of the Provisional Government. Since assuming the command Muñoz had acted wholly on the defensive, devoting his time to drilling the men pressed into the service of Castellon ; and it was widely whispered among the people, especially among the blood reds of the Democrats, that Muñoz was anxious for a compromise between the two contending parties, thinking more of maintaining himself in power than of the success of the principles for which the revolution was begun.

Walker was not ill pleased to hear from Morton on the way from Tiger Island to Realejo, the condition of affairs in Nicaragua. He felt that the more desperate the fortunes of the Castellan party were, the more deeply would they be indebted to the men who might rescue

them from their danger, and the more thoroughly would
they be committed to any course or policy the Americans might propose. Far from being depressed by the
news, which to some might have appeared gloomy, he
saw in the very straits to which the Democratic party
was reduced, the cause no less than the presage of the
success of his companions. The anxiety, too, with
which Castellon evidently awaited the arrival of the
Vesta, was cheering. He had sent Morton to Tiger
Island for the express purpose of boarding the brig and
of bringing her as speedily as possible to Realejo; and
when the vessel appeared off the Island of Cardon, the
collector of the port and a special officer, sent by the
Provisional Director, Col. Ramirez, came out to the Vesta
in order to welcome her to the waters of Nicaragua.
On the evening of the 15th of June—the day before
the Vesta was able to enter the harbor—these two officers came aboard the brig, and Colonel Ramirez informed
Walker that he was ordered from Leon to see all proper
arrangements made for the reception of the Americans.
Quarters had been prepared for them at Realejo, and the
Director was anxious to see Walker as early as possible.

As soon as the brig came to anchor, the passengers
got ready to go up the river to the town which lies four
or five miles from the harbor. Several bungos were secured for the purpose; and a little past noon the native
boatmen pulled away from the brig, the Americans
taking with them their clothes and blankets as well as
their arms and ammunition. Each of them carried a
rifle, and many of them had revolvers. The bungos
entered the river, and silence was rarely broken save by

the plashing of the oars in the water, or the harsh cry of a macaw screaming its discordant note from the boughs overhanging the stream. The deep gloom of the tropical forests was more impressive from the ocean of sunshine which surrounded it; and the stillness of all nature affected the beholder with an awe which commanded silence and reflection. After pulling a short distance, however, the native boatmen, whose senses long use had blunted to the peculiar impressions of the scenery, began to talk about the different objects they passed; nor did they fail to point out the stones used by Morgan as ballast, and which he threw from his vessel in order to receive the precious freight he pillaged from Realejo. The distance of the present town from the harbor is due in fact to the dread the Spaniards had of the buccaneers of the seventeenth century.

It was near 4 o'clock in the afternoon when the Americans drew up at the wharf of Realejo and leaped ashore for the first time in Nicaragua. The guardhouse was near the landing-place, and as Walker passed, the officer, a light, active young fellow, with a bright red short-cloak thrown gracefully over his left shoulder, turned out the guard, and saluted. The soldiers all wore the red ribbon with the words "Ejercito Democratico" printed on it; and although without uniform or any music except that made by a very indifferent drum, they had a good military carriage, and their step, unimpeded by shoe or sandal, was excellent. As the Americans passed up the street to the quarters assigned them, the women, with their best dresses and most pleasing smiles, stood at the doors and windows saluting with much

natural grace the strangers who had come to find a home
in their midst, and to share the fortunes of the party
with which their husbands and lovers, and fathers and
brothers, were identified.

Early the next morning, Walker and Crocker,
accompanied by Col. Ramirez and Capt. Doubleday, an
American who had served in the Democratic army during the siege of Granada, started for Leon. As they
entered the town of Chinandega the church bells rang a
welcome peal, and at all the villages on the road they
received marks of good will and hospitality. The road
from Chinandega to Leon, by Chichigalpa and Posultega,
passes through a country for which nature has done
much and man little ; and the effect of even what little
man had done was marred by the constant signs of
revolutionary violence. Under the shade of the magnifi-
cent ceiba might be seen halted a company of soldiers
with their trowsers rolled above their knees ; but on
close observation you could perceive that the sergeants
and corporals were keenly watching lest some of their new
recruits might take advantage of the halt to slip away
for a moment, and so escape the hated service. It was
a relief to turn from man and his works to the nature
brilliant with beauties in her tropical aspects. As the
travellers approached Leon they beheld spread out before
them a vast plain which seems almost boundless in
extent as you look toward the south ; while gazing
northward, you perceive the lofty line of volcanoes—
Viejo on one flank and Momotombo on the other—
stretching from the Gulf of Fonseca to the Lake of
Managua. It is only when you ascend the tower of the

cathedral within the city, and are able to distinguish to the westward the ocean through the break in the coast range of hills, that you see the southern wall of the plain made by the mountains around the town of Managua.

But it was not to muse over nature or to admire her vast and grand proportions in these southern latitudes, that the companions of the swarthy Ramirez had come to Central America. The sight of the picket on the outskirt of the town, though at least three quarters of a league from the Plaza, was more suggestive of the objects they had in view ; and riding rapidly through the lanes and streets they soon reached the house of the Provisional Director. Castellon received the new-comers with frank cordiality, and expressed the lively pleasure he felt at their arrival. It did not require many minutes to see that he was not the man to control a revolutionary movement, or to conduct it to a successful issue. There was a certain indecision, not merely in his words and features, but even in his walk and the general motions of his body ; and this trait of character seemed to be aggravated by the circumstances about him. A short conversation revealed his anxiety that Walker should meet Muñoz ; and Castellon said at once that he needed the military assistance of the Americans to secure the success of the Provisional Government He said he wished them to enter the service as a separate corps, and proposed to call them *La Falange Americana*—the American Phalanx.

During the evening Muñoz called at the house of the Director, and Walker was presented to him. The contrast between the manner of the Executive and that of the General was striking. Castellon was modest, gentle, almost shrinking in his address ; Muñoz had an air of conceit which affirmed a feeling of superiority on his part, to all around him. It was not difficult to see that they disliked each other ; though Castellon concealed his feelings and opinions better than Muñoz. The General, soon after saluting Walker, began to talk in the most ridiculous style about the comparative military merits of General Scott and General Taylor, exposing his ignorance in every sentence, and showing the weakness of his character. Muñoz let the American perceive that the new element Castellon proposed to introduce into the war did not have the approval of the commander-in-chief; and after the General took leave, Walker told Castellon that if he and his comrades entered the service of the Provisional Government, it was with the distinct understanding they were not to be put under the orders of Muñoz. Walker found that the Director was not at all averse to have some one with him to lighten the burden he had been obliged to bear in the person of the commanding general.

The next day Walker determined to return to Chinandega, to let the Americans know that Castellon wished their services as soldiers ; and before leaving, he proposed to the Director, in case they enlisted, to immediately march on the town of Rivas, with a view of occupying the Meridional Department. This movement, if successful, would furnish money to the Government, which was now obliged to overtax and thereby to create disaffection among the people of the Occidental; and the occupation of the Transit Road would place the Americans in a position to increase their numbers from the passengers across the Isthmus. The Director said he would place the proposition before his Minister of War, D. Buenaventura Selva, and advise Walker of the decision in the matter.

The Americans were delighted, on Walker's return to Chinandega, where he found them, to hear that Castellon wished them to engage in the service, and that in a few days they might be called on to march against the enemy. On the 20th of June, Walker received a commission as Colonel in the Democratic army, and the Secretary of War informed him that commissions would be issued to other officers among the Americans as he might suggest. Achilles Kewen was appointed to the rank of Lieutenant Colonel; Crocker was made Major; and the *Falange* being organized into two companies, two captains were named, the senior being C. C. Hornsby By the constitution of 1838, a simple declaration of intention made any native-born citizen of an American Republic a naturalized citizen of Nicaragua, and under this clause most of the *Falange* became Nicaraguans.

At the same time the Secretary of War sent Walker his commission, he informed him that the Director desired him to organize a force to act against the enemy in the Meridional Department; that Col. Ramirez had been ordered to raise two hundred natives, and to report with his command to Col. Walker as soon as he was ready to march; and that the civil and military officers at Chinandega and Realejo had been ordered to give him any assistance he required in the way of supplies and transportation for the force intrusted to his charge.

Chapter Second.

IMMEDIATELY after receiving the dispatches of the Government placing him in command of an expeditionary force to act against the Legitimists at Rivas, Walker began to prepare the *Falange*, as the Americans were henceforth called, to march to Realejo whence they were to sail on board the Vesta for a point in the Meridional Department. The stores, both commissary and ordnance, were sent by ox-carts to Realejo and thence by bungos to the brig anchored off Point Ycaco. On the 23d, three days after the order reached Chinandega, the force was aboard ready for sailing. Ramirez had been backward in his movements and showed little disposition for the enterprise, deeming it hazardous and ill-advised. He was evidently influenced by the words of Muñoz, whose disapproval of the expedition to Rivas was well known. So much did the opinion of his superior, Muñoz, control his conduct, that he made small effort to enlist the number of men—two hundred—the Director assigned as the strength of the native force. When the Vesta was ready for sea, not many more than one hundred natives mustered on her decks. Among the officers with Ramirez

was Mariano Mendez, a pure Indian who had been engaged in revolutions and counter-revolutions from his
youth upward. With violent passions and uncontrolled
desires he had a courage and experience which made
him at times useful to the men who were in the habit of
attempting political changes for personal objects; and
when active service was reqnired, they would put the old
chief on a good horse with a stout lance in his hand, and
reasonably expect from him the most hazardous enterprises. Utterly unfit for civil life and incapable of being
subjected to the rigid rules of military law, he was a
dangerous tool and an unreliable friend. He would not
serve under Ramirez, and obeyed no orders except those
from Walker himself. Aboard of the Vesta his principal
amusement was to spread his blanket on the deck and
gather a crowd of soldiers about him for his favorite
game of Monte. Once the money of the bettors was on
Mariano's blanket, it mattered little, so far as the fate
of the cash was concerned, whether the cards ran for or
against him; It was honor enough, so Mendez thought,
and so some of the men seemed to think, for a soldier to
bet with a Colonel of Lancers, as he claimed to be; and
to lose his money was, with the soldier, a pleasant mode
of paying for so signal a distinction. Muñoz was no
doubt glad to get Mendez out of Leon; and the Colonel
of Lancers was glad for awhile to exchange the aguardiente of Subtiaba for the chocolate of Rivas, especially
with the prospect of being able to slip a few ceroons to
Leon for sale among the Indians of his neighborhood.

Nor had Castellon failed to provide for a civil organization in case the expedition got a foothold within the

Meridional Department. D. Maximo Espinosa, the owner of a valuable cacao plantation near Rivas, was authorized by the Minister of Relations, D. Francisco Baca, to act as Prefect of the Department, and also as Commissioner to collect the revenue so necessary for the sustenance of the Provisional Government. Espinosa was an old man, upward of seventy, with a Don Quixote cast of features, and the dark lustreless eye, full of melancholy, so characteristic of his race. A ruling passion with him seemed to be hatred to D. Juan Ruiz (one of Estrada's Ministers), whose lands touched those of Don Maximo. Indeed it is probable that an old feud about limits between Don Juan and Don Maximo determined the latter to espouse the cause of the Democratic army. Having lived all his life near Rivas, Espinosa was thought to be well informed as to the roads and places near the town. His nephew, who accompanied him, was also familiar with the Meridional Department; and his services as guide were useful to the expedition.

Morton was placed in charge of the Vesta; and although he knew the coast well and took all advantage of the winds, it was not until four days after leaving Point Ycaco that Walker was enabled to land. On the evening of the 27th of June, about sunset, boats were let down for landing the force at a point known as El Gigante, a short distance above Brito and some six leagues to the north of San Juan del Sur. The boats were few and small, and De Brissot who, by his desire to produce an effect was often taking false steps, ran a whaleboat he had charge of against the rocks the first trip she made to the shore. It was nearly midnight before the whole force, consisting of about fifty-five Americans and one hundred and ten natives, was landed on the coast. When the disembarkation commenced the moon was shining brightly; but by eleven o'clock the sky was overcast. The clouds continued to grow thicker and darker, and before the force was formed in marching order, drops of rain, precursors of a heavy shower, began to fall. Espinosa and his nephew found the trail which led over the coast range of hills to Rivas; and about midnight the Americans in front, Ramirez and his command in the rear, and a few native soldiers detailed to carry the ammunition covered with ox-hides in the centre, the column took up its march for the interior. The men carried nothing but their arms and blankets with two day's provisions in their haversacks, so that they marched with as much rapidity as the damp, muddy nature of the ground would permit; but before they had gone more than half a mile the rain came down in torrents. Then Espinosa and his nephew lost the trail; the old man complained of colic, and the young one seemed to be afraid to venture further. A halt was ordered; several were sent out to search for the trail; and in the meanwhile the main body got what shelter it could under the heavy foliage of the large dark-looking forest trees. In a few minutes, however, the rain ceased, the trail was found, and the command resumed its march. At dawn the little force had somewhat recovered its spirits, and had got over the drenching of the night previous; and marching briskly through the thick forests, they avoided all habitations, designing if possible to surprise the enemy at Rivas the night of the 28th. About nine o'clock they came to an old deserted adobe house, and halted several hours for breakfast and rest.

The encampment that morning was quite gipsy-like. The felt hats of the *Falange* showed, in their drooping brims, the effects of the night's rain; and thick, heavy beards gave to most of the body a wild and dangerous air. As soon as the sentries were posted, the Americans began to dispose of their crackers and cold meat, washed down in some instances by a draught from a liquor canteen; while the native soldiers opened their supplies of cheese and tortillas, winding up with a little tiste—a mixture of chocolate, sugar, and corn meal, diluted in water—from the fantastically carved jicaras they carried tied with a string run through the button-holes of their jackets or trowsers. After breakfast and several hours' sleep, the force was well prepared to renew its march, and the disagreeable impressions of the night were completely forgotten in the balmy effects of the soft, mild air, which seemed a fluid altogether different from the atmosphere of northern climates. You felt as if a thin, and vapory exhalation of opium, soothing and exhilarating by turns, was being mixed at intervals with the common elements of the atmosphere. By night, however, the clouds began again to gather; and soon after dark a steady rain set in. The weather interfered so much with the march that Walker saw he could not reach Rivas, as he had expected, before morning; and as the natives carrying the ammunition began to complain of their burden, it became an object to secure pack-horses for the command. Besides this, many of the Americans, tired and foot-sore, lost some of the alcirty requisite for action.

At the little village of Tola there was a small body
of horsemen, sent out by the commandant at Rivas, to
watch the approach of Walker, whose departure from
Realejo had been already communicated to Corral at
Granada. Report said the news of this fact was carried to the Legitimists by a German who received a
passport to leave Leon from Muñoz. The story is not
improbable, and was confirmed by so many circumstances, that it is not singular the Americans adopted it as a
well-authenticated fact. The Legitimists themselves
said, the first news they got was from this German; and
it is certain he passed through Pueblo Nuevo with a
passport from the commanding general of the Democratic
army. On receipt of the news of Walker's sailing from
Realejo, Corral sent Colonel Bosque with a force to
Rivas; and after his arrival at the latter place, Bosque
began to build barricades, and to press the men of the
town into the ranks as soldiers. He had sent out horsemen to scour the country between Rivas and the sea-
coast; and twenty of these were, according to the
information Walker received from some Democrats near
Tola, quartered in the village the night of the 28th.
As the expeditionary force approached Tola, the rain
fell fast; the roads became filled with water, and the
men found it almost impossible to keep their ammunition dry. About half a mile from the village, some
twenty men were sent on in advance to attack, and, if
possible, capture the enemy there. The detachment
marched briskly forward, the main body following at a
short distance. As Walker reached the outskirts of the
village, he heard, between two claps of loud thunder,

the sharp crack of the American rifles, then all was still. The detachment had found the hostile party in the corridor of one of the principal houses of the town ; and so little did the Legitimists expect an enemy in the midst of the storm, that they were, without a sentry posted, playing at cards. Several of them—among others the officer in command—were wounded ; the rest escaped, and carried the news of the approach of the Americans to Rivas. After securing the horses of the Legitimist troopers, sentries were posted by the Democrats, and they halted for the night. Orders were given to the surgeon, Dr. Jones, to look after the wounded prisoners—much to the dissatisfaction of some native officers, who thought they ought to be shot.

A little after eight o'clock next morning, Walker marched for Rivas, which lies about nine miles to the eastward of Tola. The day soon became clear and bright ; and the *Falange*, eager for a fight, pressed forward briskly. Mendez having found a horse and taken a lance from one of the enemy, was in a fine flow of spirits, and kept near the head of the column, sometimes pressing the advance-guard to let him pass. But Ramirez hung back, and even checked his men as they stepped close after the Americans. Every now and then market-women, with fruit-baskets on their heads, and just from Rivas, would gayly greet the soldiers, nodding familiarly to some acquaintance among the natives, and much wondering at the strange figures of the men from California. Nor were the Americans less amused at the new faces and forms they met on the road ; and such of them as spoke any Spanish, would waste all the terms of endearment they could muster on the girls, who seemed pleased with the compliments of the men from the land of gold. When, however, the command reached the summit of a hill, about four miles from Rivas, a scene of beauty and of splendor burst upon their vision, and for a while drew them from everything else, even from thought of the eager strife in which they expected soon to mingle.

As the advance guard reached a turn in the road it seemed to halt for a moment, involuntarily, and though the order was to march in silence an exclamation of surprise and pleasure escaped the lips of all. Mendez, the red streamer flying from the lance which rested on his stirrup, was up with the advance and uttered the single word " Omotepe." To his eye the scene was familiar, but to the Americans it appeared a vision of enchantment. The lake of Nicaragua lay in full view, and rising from it, as Venus from the sea, was the tall and graceful cone of Omotepe. The dark forests of the tropics clothed the side of the volcano, which seemed to repose under the influence of the soft sunshine around it. The form of the mountain told its history as if written in a book ; and the appearance of the volcano was so much that of a person enjoying a siesta, the beholder would not have been surprised to see it waken at any moment and throw the lava from its burning sides. The first glimpse of the scene almost made the pulse stand still ; and the Falange had scarcely recovered from its effects when the command was halted opposite a country-house a few hundred yards from Rivas, in order to prepare for the attack on the town.

3

About a mile from Rivas Walker had fallen into the road leading to Granada, so that he might enter the former place from the north. He took this course with a view of securing the houses either of the Maleaño or of the Santa Ursula estates—two cacao plantations on the edge of the town furnishing good positions to a force either attacking or defending the place. Halting his troops, then, less than half a mile from the first houses of the town, Walker called the principal officers, American and native, around him, explaining his plan of attack, and assigning to each his separate duty. Kewen and Crocker were ordered to drive the enemy, if possible, from the streets, keeping the Americans advancing at a quick step until they reached the Plaza ; while Ramirez and his command were to follow close after the Americans, protecting, as much as they could, their flanks and rear. A few moments sufficed for these orders, and all declared their full understanding of the several places assigned them. Then Kewen and Crocker ordered their men to advance. As they got within sight of the first houses, a body of the enemy opened fire ; the reply of the rifles was sharp and deadly, and the shout of the Americans as they rushed forward proclaimed their eagerness for the strife. The Legitimists fell back rapidly toward the Plaza ; the hill of Santa Ursula was gained by the Falange, and driving in the panels of the gates and doors with the butts of their rifles, the soldiers soon had possession of the houses on the summit. Walker rode past just as the houses were entered ; and seeing Crocker a short distance in advance, he called out to know how far the men had got toward the

Plaza. Crocker was panting with excitement ; his chin was bleeding from the graze of a bullet, one arm hung useless, being shot through near the shoulder, while in the hand of the other side he carried his army revolver, with half its barrels discharged. But the rage of battle was on him ; and heedless of wounds he was trying to drive the men toward the enemy. As soon, however, as he saw his commander, he sank his voice, and said in a low tone, " Colonel, the men falter ; I cannot get them on." Then Walker, looking to the rear, saw that the natives were not yet in sight. The pack-mules and horses with the ammunition were slowly coming on ; and Mendez, with a few natives near him, was to be seen a little to the right. Passing to the front, Walker saw it was too true, as Crocker said, that the men could not be brought to advance. At the same time a brisk fire was opened on the left flank of the Americans by Colonel Manuel Arguëllo, who had just arrived with a force from San Juan del Sur. Then the Americans were concentrated in a large adobe house near the hill of Santa Ursula, and in some small houses on the opposite side of the street ; the ammunition was unpacked, and the whole force was, as far as possible, placed under cover, in order to get a breathing time before future action.

The enemy seeing Raminez did not press forward to aid the Americans, got in between the two bodies ; and Madregil, as the Leonese colonel was called, marched off with nearly his whole command toward the Costa Rican frontier, thinking, doubtless, that the Falange would be destroyed. The Legitimists, too, noticing the disap-

pearance of Ramirez, began to press the Americans on
all sides, making several efforts to charge the houses,
where the rifles did good execution. The white ribbons
were strewed thickly about the streets, and the Americans had several killed and wounded early in the conflict. But the spirits of the latter did not droop until
first Crocker and then Kewen was reported killed.
Even after these losses, however, the men were brought
to a charge in order to drive the enemy from an old
gun, a four-pounder, they were trying to get to bear
on the houses the Americans occupied. The charge was
successful, and the enemy were unable to use the piece
during the action. Then the Legitimists tried to fire
the houses held by the Democrats, and they so far succeeded as to get one of the roofs in a blaze. By this
time upward of fifteen of the Americans were killed or
wounded, not more than thirty-five of them remaining
for action. The fight had begun at twelve o'clock, and
it was near four when orders were issued to prepare for
retreat. Several of the wounded had to be left; but
those who could march at all were notified of the intention to abandon the houses, so that they might be ready
to move when the order was given. The enemy, protected by the thick undergrowth, had crowded in some
force close to the houses when the order was given to
sally. At the moment of leaving the house, a shout was
raised by the sallying party; the nearest of the enemy
turned and fled in confusion; and the main body of the
Legitimists, paralyzed, as it were, by the offensive
appearance of the American movement, waited, expecting
everywhere an attack. Thus the Falange escaped from
its difficult position with the loss of only one man killed.

When the Democrats attacked Rivas, the Legitimists
had probably five hundred men in the town ; and they
were re-enforced soon after the action commenced by
Arguëllo, with some seventy-five or eighty men. There
were, according to the best accounts, at least seventy of
the Legitimists killed, and as many wounded. The
Americans lost six killed and twelve wounded ; and five
of their wounded left behind were barbarously murdered by the enemy, and their bodies burnt. After such
a day, the Legitimists were not much in the humor of
pursuing those who had taught them a first lesson in
the use of the rifle.

But it was not by numbers that the loss of the Americans was to be computed. The chivalrous spirit of
Kewen would have weighed against a host of common
men ; and the death of Crocker was a loss hardly to be
repaired. A boy in appearance, with a slight figure, and
a face almost feminine in its delicacy and beauty, he
had the heart of a lion ; and his eye, usually mild and
gentle, though steady in its expression, was quick to
perceive a false movement on the part of an adversary,
and then its flash was like the gleam of a scimetar as it
falls on the head of the foe. With little military experience and less military reading, he was a man to
lead others where danger was to be met ; and none who
knew him feared he would get a command into any position from which his courage and address would be unable to extricate them. To Walker he was invaluable ;
for they had been together in many a trying hour, and
the fellowship of difficulty and danger had established a
sort of freemasonry between them.

There had been with the Americans during most of the day, at Rivas, two natives, one of them a boy, the other a man, familiar with the country about Rivas. Under the guidance of the latter the little band retreated through cacao plantations, seeking some road which might lead them toward the Transit. Their march was of course slow, and they were obliged to wait often for the wounded to come up. Among those most seriously hurt were De Brissot and Anderson (afterward Colonel Anderson), the former having a wound through the fleshy part of the thigh, and the latter, in addition to a wound in the thigh, having a scratch in the scalp and a cut in the foot. Capt. Doubleday, a volunteer in the expedition, was useful by his knowledge of native character and the modes of native warfare; and although having a painful wound in the head, he did not for a moment lose his spirits or presence of mind. Two or three times in their wanderings through plantations, the retreating party came upon native laborers, who are accustomed to fly at the sight of armed men, through fear of being pressed into military service; and once overtaking a slow, cautious old man who, after some hesitation, half opened his jacket, to show a red rose under it, they were amused by seeing a white rose at the same time fall to the ground. After a doubtful day in revolutionary times, the poor fellow thought it best to have the white emblem for the Legitimists as well as the red for the Democrats. Nor were the Americans themselves altogether lacking in such prudence; for many of them had torn the red ribbon from their hats, in order to escape the notice of hostile parties. This, however, was a vain precaution, since their tongue, as well as their dress and manners, plainly told the race, and therefore the party, to which they belonged.

It was nearly dark when the guide succeeded in striking the road from Rivas to St. George, about half way between the two places. As the Falange approached the high road the bells of Buenos Ayres were ringing in the distance, and Doubleday thought it was for the victory of the Legitimists, though it was probably for the usual vesper prayers. Marching briskly on, the remains of the expeditionary force passed, about dark, the outskirts of San Jorge, all the doors being closed, as usual when a battle has been fought in the neighborhood, and all the dogs of the village seeming to bark at the tread of the retreating Americans. Walker ordered Mayorga, the guide, to take the command by as quiet a path as possible to the Transit; and he soon led the party by a trail to the right of the road between Rivas and Virgin Bay. The ground was muddy and difficult, the men at times sinking into it over their shoes and half way up to the knee. And if the march was trying to well men, how much more so was it to Anderson and De Brissot, with the muscles of their thighs bored through by musket-balls. The rear guard, however, did its duty well, and kept the column closed up, while maintaining the coolness and firmness requisite for meeting the enemy in case of a pursuit. But there was no sign of pursuit; and about midnight the wornout soldiers of the Falange halted, and camped until morning at a deserted hut on the top of a hill, some two miles from the Transit road.

A little sleep and a hearty breakfast revived the exhausted spirits of the command; and before nine o'clock on the morning of the 30th, they were again toiling along the muddy trail. Soon they got a glimpse of the white Transit road, between two and three miles from Virgin Bay. It looked American, and the very sight of it refreshed the Falange and put new life even into the wounded. Not many minutes after they got on the Transit, Walker heard, at a distance ahead, the tinkle of a mule-bell, and the guide said it was the treasure train, the passengers having crossed from San Juan del Sur to Virgin Bay the day before. As the train was usually accompanied by an escort, Walker was apprehensive of a collision between the treasure guard and his force, and of the misrepresentations which would necessarily arise from such an event. Hence he hastily ordered the men to be hid on the side of a hill they were then passing; and he was relieved at seeing the whole train pass by with none but the muleteers in charge of it. The march was then resumed, and near the Halfway House a man named Dewey, formerly a gambler in California, rode up, and informing Walker he was just from San Juan del Sur, told him some of the native Democrats, Mendez among them, had passed through town the night before, on their way to Costa Rica, but that no Legitimists had been there since the departure of Arguëllo, early on the morning of the 29th, for Rivas.

A few minutes after sunset, the people of San Juan del Sur beheld about forty-five men, several of them wounded—some without hats, others without shoes—all of them travel-stained and clinging to their rifles, defile through the streets of the town and take up their quarters in the barracks near the beach. The appearance of the Falange at that moment was not imposing; but he who knew how to read men might see from the looks of these, that they bore with firmness the blows of adverse fate. There was no hesitation in their march or in their movements. A few men—you could not style them a detachment, scarcely a detail—were ordered to take possession of all the small boats in the harbor and keep them under guard. The Costa Rican schooner, San José, cast anchor in the harbor just as the Falange entered the barracks; and, before any of her officers or crew had got ashore, a file of Americans were aboard and held her for further orders. Walker expected to hear something of the Vesta, as Morton had been ordered to cruise off and on near San Juan del Sur, until he saw a certain signal from the shore. But no one at San Juan, although many there were friendly to the democrats, could give any news of the Vesta. Several of the residents of the town did all they could for the wounded and destitute soldiers; and even in that moment of adversity, an Irishman, Peter Burns, and a Texan, Henry McLeod, had the hardihood to link their fate with that of the Falange. It was encouraging for the soldiers to find that some, besides themselves, did not regard their fortunes as altogether desperate; and small as was this addition to their numbers, it gave increased moral as well as material strength to the command.

Hearing nothing from the Vesta, Walker determined to press the San José for the service, and go in search of the brig, or in default of finding her, sail for Realejo. Accordingly the wounded were first sent to the schooner,

3*

and soon afterward the whole command followed. They
found the owner of the vessel, one Alvarado, of Punta
Arenas, aboard the San José, which had formerly been
a pilot-boat out of San Franscisco. Alvarado received
the command courteously, and Walker assured him the
schooner should not be used for the democratic service
longer than was absolutely necessary ; and as this same
vessel had brought Guardiola, a military person of importance, from Guatemala to Nicaragua, with the avowed
object of making war against the Provisional Government at Leon, the owner thought it well to act civilly,
lest a libel might be filed against the schooner on her
arrival at Realejo. In what may be termed minor diplomacy, the Central Americans are not surpassed by
any race on the continent.

The tide was coming in, and there was little or no
wind when the Americans went aboard of the San José;
hence the vessel remained at anchor waiting for the
turn of the tide and for the morning breeze to spring
up. Most of the soldiers, fatigued by their toils and
exitement during the last three or four days, at once
threw themselves on the decks and were asleep almost
the moment after they touched the planks. Walker,
however, with Captain Hornsby and a few others, kept
awake, watching anxiously the shore for any signs of
movement there, and as keenly regarding the waters
and the heavens, in order to catch the faintest signal of
the ebbing tide or of the expected breeze. With all
their senses on the stretch, they suddenly saw the
flames burst forth from the barracks near the beach,
and in an instant the blaze seemed to their startled view

to spread over half the town. Immediately a boat was sent off to gather the meaning of the fire. The flames, on close observation, seemed to be confined, and owing to the calmness of the night the fire did not spread. In a few minutes the boat returned with the news that the barracks had been set on fire by Dewey and a sailor named Sam : the former being an American, who had lived for a while on the Isthmus, and the latter being the owner of a small launch running between Realejo and San Juan del Sur, and which had followed the Vesta on her voyage to El Gigante. These two men had some private hatreds against certain legitimists about the Transit: and taking advantage of the times, they determined to wreak their revenge by this act of destruction. It may be, too, that the thirst for plunder and the hope of satisfying their avarice during the confusion of the fire partly prompted the act : for Dewey was a desperate man who had fled from California to escape the punishment of his crimes. Their act had jeoparded the whole town ; for all the houses being built of wood, a light wind would have borne the flames to most of the property of the place.

It became important for Walker to get possession of these men and punish their offence ; otherwise the whole responsibility of the act might fall on the Americans in the democratic service, and the enemies of these last would say that, in revenge for their repulse at Rivas, they had attempted, like savages, to burn up an inoffensive town. He therefore sent an officer with a few men—their arms concealed in the bottom of the boat— to attempt to get Dewey and Sam aboard the San José.

Half by stratagem and half by force, Sam was brought to the schooner ; but Dewey, doubtful of the result, refused to venture aboard, and took, as he thought, the safer course of getting to Sam's launch, which was luckily hitched astern of the pilot-boat. Sam had no sooner crossed the taffrail of the San José than he came reeling (for he was drunk) to where Walker stood, and openly boasted that he and Dewey had set fire to the barracks, and that they considered it an act of right against the legitimists. After these declarations of Sam, there could remain no doubt of his guilt, and as little of Dewey's, since Sam had made similar statements in the presence of and uncontradicted by his accomplice. The refusal, too, of Dewey to come before Walker, implied guilt. Sam was, therefore, ordered to be tried : and after a short consultation with Capt. Hornsby and John Markham (afterward Colonel Markham), who had shown much discretion at Rivas and during the march thence, Walker determined to send the criminal ashore in order to have him executed there. Riflemen were also placed at the stern of the schooner to watch the launch and prevent Dewey from cutting the lines which held it to the San José.

The prisoner was sent ashore in charge of Capt. Hornsby and a few select men, with orders to shoot him and place on his body a memorandum stating the offence, and by whose command he had been executed ; for haste was necessary, it being far past midnight and Alvarado's skipper was expecting every moment to be able to weigh anchor and set sail. The duty was disagreeable ; and therefore, the Colonel commanding had himself chosen the men for the performance of it. Hornsby was an upright honorable soldier ; but, then, his ability to fulfil the order might depend on the disposition of those who were to carry it into execution. He was almost the only commissioned officer left to Walker ; yet, he was without the large views requisite for perceiving the great importance of clearing the Americans from any participation in the arson which had been committed. Therefore, the commander took aside those who were to go with Hornsby and strove to impress on them the urgent necessity for faithful and conscientious conduct on their part. Hornsby and his detail took the prisoner off in a small boat ; in a short time Walker heard the crack of the rifles, and soon afterward the rubbing of the oars against the rowlocks as the boat approached the schooner. Hornsby came back to report that the prisoner had escaped ; that while the men were in the act of untying Sam he had broken away, and the rifles being fired at random in the dark, it was not known whether he had been hit or not. It was afterward ascertained that he escaped unhurt to Costa Rica.

The escape of Sam gave an air of connivance at his crime to the action of the Americans. This was the impression certain to be made on the natives of the country, unless some means were found to counteract it. Indeed, when the Costa Rican merchant, Alvarado, who was watching the events as they happened, heard Sam had not been shot, he seemed, by his air, more than by his words, to intimate that the Americans were not over-anxious to punish the offender. Hence, it became necessary to guard against Dewey's escape ; for such an

event would tend to strengthen the inference enemies
might draw from the failure to execute the sentence of
his accomplice. Throughout the night, therefore, which
seemed to Walker as if it would never end, strict guard
was kept over Sam's launch. The wearying wretched-
ness of that night's watch may be imagined when it is
considered that the future character of the Americans
in Nicaragua depended, to a great extent, on their ability
to punish Dewey's crime.

At last day broke, and about sunrise the breeze sprung
up off shore. The skipper of the schooner weighed anchor and the vessel put to sea, towing the launch astern.
Walker ordered the San José to be kept two or three
leagues from the land, steering for Realejo, and watching in-shore for the Vesta. A native woman of Chinandega, Sam's mistress, and who sailed with him on his
voyages, managed the rudder of the launch. Three or
four hours passed thus; the riflemen in the stern with
their eyes constantly on the launch, and with orders to
shoot Dewey if he attempted to cut the lines by which
she was towed. The small hold of the boat enabled
Dewey to keep out of sight, and as he had a couple of
army revolvers with him, and was a remarkable shot, it
was necessary for the men watching him to keep themselves covered. It was a contest between crime and
law after the fashion of the Indian. After a while
Dewey rose stealthily from the hold, and managing to
place the woman between himself and the riflemen, was
evidently preparing to make a desperate effort to cut
loose from the schooner. The woman was warned in
Spanish to keep clear from Dewey, and was told that

death would be the result if she attempted to aid him in his plans. But the poor creature was unable to get away from the man. The order was given to the riflemen to watch their opportunity and shoot Dewey when they could do so without endangering the woman. The discharge of a couple of rifles, almost at the same instant, told that the opportunity had been found. Dewey dropped into the hold, shot through the body ; but the ball, passing entirely through him, had, unfortunately, inflicted a painful and dangerous wound on the woman. The woman was brought aboard the San José ; her wound was dressed by the surgeon, and she recovered in a short time her usual health. Dewey's body was sewed up in canvas and buried at sea.

I have minutely narrated the circumstances attending Dewey's death, because they made a deep impression on the native mind, and gave a certain and decided character to the Americans in the democratic service. The Nicaraguans conceived from these events a respectful idea of American justice. They saw that the men they had been taught to call " filibusters," intended to maintain law and secure order wherever they went; that they had the will to administer justice, and would, when they had the power, protect the weak and the innocent from the crimes of the lawless and abandoned. And it is this sentiment stamped deeply on the people of Nicaragua which makes the evil-doers of that land dread the re-appearance of the Americans in the country. The anarchy and license of thirty-five years of revolution have unfitted the political leaders for subjecting

their lawless passions and unbridled impulses to the
fixed rule of unchanging and unswerving duty.

Late in the afternoon of the same day the schooner
left San Juan, her passengers recognized the Vesta at a
distance bound northward, and apparently for Realejo.
After the brig saw the schooner, her movements became
mysterious and uncertain ; in fact she did not know
what to make of a vessel showing Costa Rica colors, and
clearly looking out for, and in chase of the Vesta.   The
San José, however, soon overhauled the brig, and in a
few moments the Falange was again aboard of their
old acquaintance.   The wind was favorable ; the Vesta
kept on her course for Realejo, and the schooner followed close in her wake.   Alvarado, no doubt, thought
it was fair, and by his civility he had made it safe for
him to carry on a little smuggling, and pay himself out
of the pockets of the Leonese for the services he had
rendered their friends.   Early the next morning, it being the first of July, the Vesta again found the volcano
of Viejo bearing due north, and letting her cable slip, she
stood at her former anchorage opposite Point Ycaco.

A few stragglers from the force of Ramirez, taking the
coast trail from Rivas to Chinandega, had already reached
the latter place, and reported some of the incidents of the
march and action on the 29th.   Therefore the Vesta had
been but a few hours in port, when three or four of the
principal Democrats of Chinandega came down to get the
news of the expedition to the Meridional Department.
On their return with the flood-tide—for whenever a
boat was sent up the river to Realejo, it was generally
on the incoming tide—one of these gentlemen bore to

Castellon the written report of occurrences at the south. In his report, Walker stated his impression that Muñoz had acted in bad faith, and that the conduct of Ramirez was due to the inspiration, if not orders, of the commander-in-chief; and the report concluded by informing the Director that, unless the course of Muñoz was inquired into, and cleared of the suspicions hanging about it, the Americans would be compelled to leave the service of the Provisional Government, and seek elsewhere than in Nicaragua a field for their faculties and enterprise. The next day Dr. Livingston, an American, long resident in Leon, brought Castellon's reply to Walker aboard of the Vesta. The Director complimented the Americans on their conduct at Rivas, thanked them for the services they had rendered the democratic cause, but evaded saying anything in reference to the acts of Muñoz. He urged Walker, however, not to think of leaving Nicaragua, as such an event might be fatal to the Provisional Government; and Dr. Livingston was sent to urge verbally the same views, intimating, too, that the critical position of the democratic party made it inexpedient for the Director to scan too closely the conduct of the commander-in-chief. Walker, however, appeared obstinate, having decided in his own mind to remain some days on the brig for the purpose of allowing the Americans to recover from their fatigues and wounds, and with a view of making the Castellon party manifest as clearly as possible the necessity of the Falange to their cause. So Dr. Livingston went back to Leon, with a report not very encouraging to the Provisional Government.

For some days Walker continued to receive letters from Castellon, entreating him not to give up the democratic cause, and urging him to march the Falange to Leon. In order to bring about the latter result the Director stated that the Legitimists were meditating a movement against his capital, Corral being at Managua with a force of nearly a thousand men, and with arms and ammunition for the supply of a large additional number of recruits. It was also certain that the recruiting of *voluntarios forçados*—forced volunteers—was going on actively in the Oriental Department. Don Mariano Salazar, too, the most energetic man in the democratic party, visited Walker aboard the Vesta, to impress on him the danger of an attack on Leon by Corral, and the necessity of having the American rifles about the residence of the Director. Salazar was the brother-in-law of Castellon; and being a merchant of much shrewdness and sufficient capital, he managed to have a sort of monopoly of the trade in foreign fabrics, imported by the ports of Realejo and Tempisque. Thus he was able and willing to furnish means to the democratic army, and offered to supply the Americans with any ammunition they might need. He, accordingly, sent to La Union, and procured a quantity of rifle powder for the Falange; the powder which the natives used in their muskets not being fit for the arms of the Americans. Walker appeared, however, inflexible, and the friends of the Provisional Government again began to despair.

Some ten days passed in this manner, and the Falange, recovered from the effects of the expedition to Rivas, was beginning to wish for more active exercise

than could be found aboard the Vesta. It was, therefore, decided to march them to Chinandega, as they
were promised good quarters there, and the wounded
would be able to get more delicate diet than was to be
had at Point Ycaco. Accordingly boats and bungos were
procured, and the whole body of Americans was transported to Realejo without previous notice given to the
authorities. Not many minutes after Walker reached
the town he was standing in front of the Collector's
office, and saw the Director, Castellon, and Don Mariano
Salazar, step from the boat. It seems Don Francisco
had left Leon that morning, and passing by the Polvon,
a sugar plantation belonging to two Americans, John
Deshon and Henry Myers, had reached the Vesta only
a few minutes after the Americans entered the river.
He had forthwith followed, in order to persuade Walker
to continue his march to Leon. His anxiety was apparent; in fact it was necessary for him to get back to his
capital before the people discovered his absence, otherwise a panic might ensue, and the effects be disastrous.

In reply to the entreaties of Castellon, Walker affected to be undecided as to his course after reaching
Chinandega, evading a positive reply, by saying he did
not know whether he could safely leave his wounded at
the last-named town, since the Legitimists, if they intended to enter the Occidental Department, would certainly occupy that place, in order to cut off supplies and
communications. The Director told Walker that if he
intended to go to Leon, the sub-prefect at Chinandega
had orders to furnish him with all the supplies and transportation he required. Castellon and Salazar left for

Leon in better spirits, because there appeared a prospect of retaining the Falange in the country; and the Americans proceeded to Chinandega, where they arrived the same afternoon, and found as comfortable quarters as the town afforded. All the officers, civil and military, vied with each other in the efforts they made to satisfy the wants of the Falange; and the women of the place were constantly paying to the wounded those little attentions which take away from the tedium of the soldier obliged to lie idle and inactive, while the bustle of preparation for marching and adventure is going on around him.

The day after reaching Chinandega, Walker made his requisition on the sub-prefect for the horses and ox-carts necessary on the march to Leon; and the Americans were in high spirits at the idea of visiting the old capital of the country, and the second city in size of Central America. The evening before they set out for the seat of the Provisional Government, Byron Cole rode into Chinandega accompanied by Don Bruno Von Natzmer. The former had waited several months after sending his contract to California, expecting each week to hear of the arrival of Americans at Realejo; but as time wore away and the cause of Castellon waned rapidly, he had gone to Honduras hoping to find profit, if not fame, in the gold hills of Olancho. There he met Bruno Von Natzmer, a Prussian, who had resigned his commission in the cavalry of his native country to join Baron Bulow in the colony he proposed to establish in Costa Rica some years ago. Von Natzmer spoke Spanish very well, French tolerably, and English quite indiffer-

ently. Having resided for some time in Central America, and being a man of fine intelligence, Von Natzmer
was well calculated to render much service to the Americans. He and Cole had left Olancho for Nicaragua as
soon as they heard of the arrival of the Vesta at Realejo ; and it will be seen in the course of events that
they were valuable auxiliaries to the Falange.

Leaving the wounded at Chinandega, in charge of the
sub-prefect there, Walker marched to Leon, carrying
the ammunition and baggage in the ox-carts of the
country. It was late at night when he arrived at the
first pickets ; and the strength of the pickets, as well
as the number of sentries, indicated that Muñoz thought
it not altogether improbable the enemy might be in the
neighborhood. A native officer was sent on to inform
the sentries it was necessary to pass of the approach of
the Falange ; though the creaking of the cart-wheels,
easily heard at the distance of a mile, was sufficient
evidence that the party entering the city did not expect
to take it by surprise The white trowsers and jackets
of the sentries, as they paced their posts, enabled a person to distinguish their position, even in the darkness of
the night, while the clothing of the Falange was favorable to secrecy and concealment. Nor were other differences in military habits less striking ; and it was difficult for the Americans to see the advantages of many
pickets where large camp-fires were kept burning, as
the light enabled an enemy not only to discover the position, but also, in some cases, the exact strength of the
picket. It might appear a delicate matter for a force
speaking an entirely different tongue, and with military

habits altogether dissimilar, to enter a friendly camp near
the hour of midnight; but the very difference of language and habits in this case facilitated the task, and
no unpleasant incident occurred to mar the arrival of the
Americans at the quarters which were assigned them.

The day after the arrival of the Falange at Leon,
Castellon expressed a desire for a meeting between Muñoz and Walker, entreating the latter to forget his resentment for the grievances he thought he had suffered at the
hands of the commanding-general. Accordingly they met
at the house of the Director, and both avoided any allusion
to the past, conversing mostly about the prospects of the
advance on the part of Corral. The cholera had broken
out at Managua; and with an adventurous captain this
might have determined him to attack an enemy, hoping
by a movement forward to escape the dreadful scourge,
or if pursued by the plague to scatter it also among the
hostile force, and at least to bring on an action before
his own strength was destroyed by the ravages of disease. But Corral was not of the temper such a movement requires; and his character was sufficient guaranty
that the cholera alone, without other foe, would drive
him back to Granada. Nevertheless, there were constant
rumors of the approach of the Legitimists; and the market-women were frequently seen picking up their trays
and baskets and flying in all directions from the Plaza.
These alarms would sometimes happen at night as well
as during the day; and one of them, soon after the
Falange reached Leon, was near having serious consequences.

Muñoz had invited Walker to visit the pickets with

him, and to observe the condition of the camp after
tattoo. Previous to mounting they had met at the house
of the Director, and they with Castellon were conversing
together when a clashing was heard at the main entrance of the building, and the officer on duty ordered
the body-guard to fall in. The general-in-chief, the Director, and Walker, all advanced rapidly toward the
gate in order to ascertain the cause of the movement;
and on getting into the street, they found the Americans
with cartridge-boxes on, and their rifles in their hands,
mingled with the officers of the general's staff, some
mounted, others dismounted, some with their swords
drawn, and others with their pistols out of their holsters.
As soon as the Americans saw Walker they at once retired toward their quarters; and then the cause of the
disturbance became manifest. Two of the officers of
the general's staff had got to quarrelling at the door of
the Director, and had drawn their swords intending to
fight out the quarrel on the spot. In the effort on the
part of others of the staff to prevent this, a certain noise
and confusion ensued; and as the quarters of the Falange were near the Director's house, and the Americans
knew that Walker was there with Muñoz, the idea occurred to some of them that treason was being practised
on their leader. They rushed to the house demanding admission, and were about to force the door when
Walker appeared. The difference of language added, of
course, to the misunderstanding; and in the confusion
of the moment the report spread among the people that
the enemy had secretly entered the town, and were
already at the house of Castellon. The alarm continued

for some moments ; but at length quiet was restored, and the officers proceeded to make the tour of the camp.

The ride that night would have furnished amusement and interest to the general observer, no less than to the soldier. The sentry duty is well done by the natives, and if they fought as well as they do guard duty, or as patiently as they submit to all manner of hardship except when mixed with danger, they would make extremely formidable troops. In riding through the streets at night, it was difficult at times to keep your horse from treading on the soldiers. There they lay on the hard pavements ranged by companies in two files, the feet of the front and rear ranks toward each other, and their heads against the walls of the houses on opposite sides of the street; their arms are at their sides, and their cartridge-boxes with one compartment, and made sometimes of leather, sometimes of hide, turned in front, in order to enable them to lie easily on their back or sides. And if dismounting you enter their quarters and see them, some on the brick or dirt floors, others swinging in hammocks, and bent up almost double in order to keep from falling out, you would not wonder at the horror the whole people have of military service. There is scarcely any labor a Nicaraguan will not do in order to keep out of the clutches of the press-gang ; and their immunity from this dreaded evil by the presence of the Americans in the country, gave the latter much of the moral power they possessed over the native population. The laborers and small proprietors run more risks to escape military duty than they are generally required to meet, if they are so unlucky as to be caught by the recruiting sergeant.

After the Falange had been in Leon a few days reports of the advance of Corral became less frequent, then
ceased altogether ; and afterward there came vague
rumors of terrible ravages by cholera at Managua, and
of the intention of the Legitimists to fall back on
Granada. Then Walker broached to Castellon his real
object in going to Leon. He desired to get an efficient
native force of two hundred men, commanded by a man
in whom he had confidence, to make another effort
against the enemy in the Meridional Department. Castellon appeared uneasy as soon as the subject was
broached, and at length proposed a meeting of Muñoz,
Walker, Jerez, and several others, in order to discuss a
plan of a general campaign. Jerez was at that time
under a cloud ; but Walker sought to bring him forward
inasmuch as he manifested a deep resentment at being
superseded in the command of the army by Muñoz.
Accordingly the meeting was held, and of course without result. The general-in-chief proposed to divide the
Americans by tens, distributing them among the several
bodies of the native troops, and this done he proposed to
march by several directions on Granada. But the
object of his policy was too plain to deceive anybody,
and by proposing such a plan he merely disclosed his
feelings without being able to move a step toward the
accomplishment of his desires. The manner of Castellon
showed Walker that but little was to be done toward
obtaining aid for another expedition to Rivas, although
the Director went so far as to say that Muñoz would
march toward the Department of Segovia in a few days,
and something might be done after his departure in

furnishing force for the Meridional Department. Walker then, to the chagrin of Castellon, determined to countermarch to Chinandega.

Orders were issued to the Falange to prepare for marching, and requisitions were made on the prefect for horses and ox carts, but hours passed and the carts did not make their appearance. All at once a section, consisting (in the Nicaraguan use of the term) of three hundred or three hundred and fifty men, marched into a strong house just opposite the quarters of the Americans. Walker immediately ordered the Falange to be on the alert, standing by their arms and ready for action. At the same time he sent word to Castellon that the movement of these troops was menacing and, unless they were ordered from their new position within an hour, the Falange would consider the force hostile and act accordingly. The native troops were immediately ordered from the building, and they marched out of the house less than an hour after they marched into it. Had Muñoz been able to take the Americans unawares, he would, in all probability, have disarmed them and sent them out of the country. Nor was it long after these troops evacuated the house opposite the Falange, before the carts, required for the march of the latter from Leon, were driven to their quarters. In a little while the Americans were on the road to Chinandega, keeping a sharp lookout to the rear and all the time prepared for any movement which might appear offensive. They arrived, however, at Chinandega without any incident worthy of notice.

Cole had remained in Leon with the view of securing

certain modifications in the contract by which the Americans had entered the service of the Provisional Government. He easily obtained what he sought. The colonization grant was given up, and Walker was authorized to enlist three hundred men for the military service of the Republic, the State promising them one hundred dollars a month, and five hundred acres of land at the close of the campaign. Castellon also gave Walker authority to settle all differences and outstanding accounts between the Government and the Accessory Transit Company. These powers were necessary preliminaries to the effort for securing a position in the Meridional Department; and it was a fixed policy with Walker to get as near the Transit as possible, in order to recruit from the passengers to and from California, and to have the means of easy and rapid communication with the United States. So far as the Falange was concerned it was idle for them to waste their energies and strength on a campaign which did not bring them toward the Transit road.

As soon as Walker received the documents Cole brought from Leon he determined to return to the Meridional Department, whether he was or was not able to obtain aid for the expedition from the Provisional Government. It was necessary, however, to wait on events and choose the most opportune moment for carrying out the designs he had in view.

Chapter Third.

NOTHING tries so much the firmness of men like those constituting the Falange as inaction. The roving and adventurous life of California had increased in them the thirst for action and movement characteristic of the American race ; and as they were engaged in the service of the Provisional Government on mere promises, the value of which depended on success, it is not singular that the garrison life at Chinandega soon became irksome to them. Two of the men, especially restless and unsettled in their characters, abandoned the service ; and their conduct as well as their conversation had a demoralizing effect on many others of the Falange. Walker perceiving the spirit which began to prevail called the men together and addressed them for a few minutes, exhorting them not to look back when once the hand was to the plough ; and his address had the effect of bringing the disaffected to a sense of the duties and responsibilities devolved upon them. In his conversations as well as in his addresses he strove constantly to fill them with the idea that small as was their number they were the precursors of a movement destined to affect materially the civilization of the whole continent. Thus filled with the importance of the events in which they were participating, the Falange became capable of performing worthily the part assigned them.

Nor were other causes for difficulty lacking. The skipper of the Vesta, Eyre, did not know what to do with his vessel. He had brought her out of San Francisco without sailors and it was impossible to engage any in the port of Realejo. Besides, her condition as to sea-worthiness made it unsafe to undertake a long voyage with her. Therefore it was thought advisable for the men who had worked the vessel down from California to bring suit against her for wages ; and the collector intervened also for his port charges. After due notice judgment was rendered against the captain and vessel in favor of the claimants, and the brig was ordered to be sold under execution. She was bought for a little upward of six hundred dollars by the two persons, McNab and Turnbull, who had separated from the Falange.

In the meanwhile, letters were daily passing between Castellon and Walker in reference to the expedition to the Meridional Department. The Director seeing that the commander of the Falange was bent on this enterprise, no longer opposed it directly but strove to delay it promising assistance after the departure of Muñoz from Leon. At length Muñoz marched with six hundred men, the best organized and best equipped in the Provisional service ; but he left few materials either of men or of arms to be disposed of by the Director. The movement of Muñoz was made with the view of acting against Guardiola, who having left Granada with a small force but with a good supply of arms and ammunition was proceeding toward Condega, thereby joining hands with his friends in Tegucigalpa and being thus enabled to act against either Comayagua or Leon as circumstances might require. Guardiola was recruiting industriously in the villages of Matagalpa and Segovia; and his activity together with the terror of his name inspired the people of the Occidental Department with a dread they seemed unable to shake off. The Director himself thought Guardiola intended to strike at Leon; and he therefore desired to have the Falange within easy distance of his capital. The people of Chinandega, too, were anxious to keep the Americans in their town, in order that their property might not fall a prey to the reputed rapacity of Guardiola and his soldiers.

Under these circumstances it was easy for Walker to see that there was small hope of his securing assistance from the Provisional Government for any enterprise outside of the Occidental Department. He went on, however, purchasing all the rifles he could find about Leon and Chinandega, in order to have arms for any recruits on the Isthmus, and continued to replenish his stores of fixed ammunition, almost entirely exhausted by the Rivas expedition. Powder and caps were obtained from La Union; but it was impossible to get lead thence, and the quantity of that metal in northern Nicaragua was extremely small. The cartridges used by the natives in their muskets contained an iron missile, made by cutting into slugs, about an inch long, the gratings of the windows. Leon and Chinandega were searched in order to procure one or two hundred pounds of lead for the American rifles ; and the only supply to be had was from a few pounds of bird-shot and a few pieces of lead sheeting belonging to an Englishman at Chinandega. An officer was sent to buy the metal from him, but he refused to sell. A small guard was then sent with orders to take the lead, paying therefor a reasonable price. Thereupon the Englishman declared to the officer that if the guard entered his house he would run up the British flag and put his house under the protection of the British Government. The officer, uncertain how to act, returned to Walker for orders ; and being told that no foreign resident, except a representative of the sovereignty of his country, had a right to fly a foreign flag, he was ordered to enter the house, and in case the British colors were shown over it, to tear them down and trample them under foot, thus returning the insult offered to the Republic of Nicaragua by their display. The native authorities, accustomed to yield to the wishes of not only British consuls but even of British merchants, were utterly astounded at these orders. On the Englishman, however, the orders produced a wholesome effect ; for he immediately gave up the lead, about one hundred and fifty pounds, for the use of the Americans.

At the same time Walker was collecting the scanty supplies of arms and ammunition the country afforded for the use of the Falange, he was also searching for some native officer who would have the resolution to join in the expedition to the Meridional Department with or without the consent of the Provisional Government. Such a person was found in the sub-prefect of Chinan-

dega, D. José Maria Valle. He was one of those who
accompanied Jerez on his landing at Realejo, in May,
1854, and had risen to the rank of Colonel in the democratic army; but a severe wound in the lower third of
the thigh had endangered his life during the siege of
Granada, and the bone being broken in splinters, he was
left with a stiff knee, and had retired for the time from
active service. Valle had great influence over the soldiers about Leon and Chinandega, and with a certain
rude eloquence he was accustomed to stir the hearts of
the people with a recitation of the wrongs they had
suffered from the Legitimist Government. Almost a
pure Indian, without any education, being unable to
either read or write, he would ride through the streets of
Chinandega and into the hamlets of the neighborhood,
speaking of the generous Americans, who had come to
help them in their struggles against the Granadians.
Nor was his influence confined to the men. When he
took the guitar in hand he would carry the women away
with his songs of love or of patriotism; and the control
he exercised over the women was not to be despised in
a country where they serve to some extent the use of
newspapers, at the same time scattering news and forming opinion.

Since the arrival of the Americans in the country,
Chélon—as Valle was familiarly called—had been their
firm friend; and it was not difficult to secure his co-
operation in the movement toward the Meridional Department. He was, however, a warm adherent of Castellon,
and the latter could scarcely refuse his permission for
Chélon to march with the Falange. But the Director

endeavored to dissuade Valle from the enterprise, trying
to convince him of the danger to Chinandega from
Guardiola, in case the town was left inadequately
guarded. As the devotion of the sub-prefect to his
family and friends was strong, it required an effort for
him to resist the arguments of Castellon ; but his hatred
to the Legitimists, and his desire to avenge the death of
a brother he had lost in the siege of Granada, overcame
the logic of the Director. Valle was, however, one of
those wavering men easily influenced by persons around
them, and it became necessary to fix his determination
by leading him to take some active steps in the enterprise.

Accordingly Walker decided, near the middle of August, to march the Falange to Realejo, and place it
aboard the Vesta. The morning the Americans were to
leave Chinandega, and while they were packing the
carts for the march, an alarm arose and the rumor flew
through the town that Guardiola was a few leagues off
on his way to attack the place. The commandant sent
a couple of drummer-boys through the streets beating
the call to arms ; and although it was Sunday, the
churches were closed, and the whole town wore the appearance of expecting an immediate assault. Walker,
however, thought the alarm was a mere trick, got up by
the government, in order to keep the Americans from
marching. The general impression about the Falange
was that you only had to show them a chance for fighting to secure their presence at the dangerous point.

When the Americans left Chinandega the people who
really imagined Guardiola was near the town, gave up

to despair, expecting soon to find themselves at tne mercy of one their fancies painted as a relentless foe. In a few hours, however, the alarm subsided ; and, although Don Pedro Aguirre, the sub-delegado of hacienda at Chinandega, who had shown much attachment to the Americans during their stay there, followed the Falange as far as Realejo, the news of Guardiola still being in Segovia encouraged the old man to remain ashore rather than proceed to the Vesta. As a consequence of this change in his resolution (for he had brought his trunk along, with the idea of going to the brig) Don Pedro was taken with cholera at Realejo, and died there after a few hours' illness.

The cholera—or colerin, as the natives called it, for the disease was a mild type of cholera—had appeared at Chinandega in the month of July. It had aided the democrats previously by its ravages at Granada and at Managua ; and moving slowly northward had finally reached the Occidental Department. At Chinandega it preyed entirely on the natives, and the Americans escaped it altogether. Nor was this peculiarity of the disease confined to Chinandega. It will be seen hereafter that although natives and Americans were together on the same vessel, with the disease killing off the former in considerable numbers, the latter were entirely free from the malady. Whether the fact arose from the more vigorous life or from the more generous meat diet, or from the greater care in sleeping, which the Americans had, it is dfficult for the unlearned—probably also for the learned—to decide.

In going aboard the Vesta Walker had put out the

report that he intended to leave for Honduras since the Provisional Government would render him no assistance in the expedition to the Meridional Department, and General Cabañas had written letters inviting the Falange to Honduras. In fact, the President of the latter State was beginning to be hard pressed by the invaders from Guatemala; and in some of his letters to Castellon he had inquired whether some of the Americans could not be sent to Comayagua in return for the aid rendered to the Provisional Government of Leon the previous year. Walker, however, had little idea of getting farther off rather than nearer to the Transit: still less did he intend, if he could prevent it, to have the Americans divided up into squads, and thus trifled away for the use of chiefs of contending factions. In his letters to Castellon he spoke of going to Honduras; and the former, despairing almost of keeping the Falange in the Occidental Department, rather favored the plan, sending copies of extracts from letters Cabañas had written on the subject.

The Falange, with all its baggage and ammunition having been put aboard the Vesta, Valle, who had recently performed the duties of commandant as well as sub-prefect for the district of Chinandega, began to recruit his force. He placed on his staff D. Bruno Von Natzmer (afterward Col. Natzmer) who, in his new capacity, was of great service to Valle as well as to the Americans The people immediately began to talk about Chélon's recruiting; and rumors were soon rife of a revolution against the government at Leon. In fact, Valle wished to pronounce and establish a new provisional

government; for he had been used to such proceedings
for the last twenty-five years, and felt at home in them.
But Walker dissuaded him from the idea; and at length
got him to march his force to Realejo, and thence to
send it aboard of the Vesta. Von Natzmer, who wished
Walker to go to Honduras and was doubtful of the enterprise in the Meridional Department, rode up to Leon
and let the Director know what was going on. Castellon,
in great alarm, wrote to Valle, now entreating him as
his old friend, then commanding him as a superior his sub-
ordinate, to desist from joining Walker. But Chélon was
now aboard the Vesta; his course was decided, and the
Director could not turn him from his purpose. Von
Natzmer, on his return to Chinandega, was put in arrest
by Walker; but he had acted with good motives, though
from mistaken views, and being soon after released he
showed himself first, a worthy soldier, and after, one of
the best officers in Nicaragua.

Valle brought down from Chinandega between one
hundred and sixty and one hundred and seventy men;
but while the commissary stores were being taking
aboard the brig numbers died of cholera and several deserted when sent ashore at Point Ycaco to keep the
vessel from being overcrowded while in port. Just before the Vesta sailed a courier came down with letters
from Castellon, informing Walker that there had been an
action between Muñoz and Guardiola, at Sauce; that
the Democrats had won the day, after several hours'
fighting, but that Muñoz had died of a wound received
in the battle. The loss of the Democrats had, however,
been heavy, and the Director, uneasy lest the Legit-

imists, though defeated, might move toward Leon, when they heard of the death of Muñoz, was anxious to keep all the force he could in the Occidental Department. Again he urged Walker to return to Leon, and now, Muñoz being out of the way, all would be well. But the Vesta was ready for sea, and the order was given to weigh anchor, Morton being again in charge of the vessel. And, as the brig was overcrowded, a ketch of Punta Arenas, having a German supercargo aboard, was employed to convey a part of the force bound for the Meridional Department.

The expedition sailed on the 23d of August, and the ketch was ordered to sail for San Juan del Sur. Scarcely had the Vesta passed the mouth of the harbor before she saw the schooner San José making for the port, her decks being apparently filled with men. The schooner passed close to the brig, and some aboard of the latter recognized Mendez among the passengers of the San José. Walker ordered the Vesta to be put about, and leaving her near the mouth of the harbor, he, with Valle, took a small boat and endeavored to overhaul the schooner as she sailed slowly up toward the river; but they were unable to reach her until some minutes after she had come to anchor. On boarding the schooner it was ascertained she was from Punta Arenas, and that Ramirez, who had come passenger, had already taken a boat and started for the town, fearing to meet the Americans after his conduct at Rivas. Chélon easily persuaded Mendez to go aboard the Vesta, but, as they had to wait for the ebb tide, it was nearly dark when they started for the brig. As they passed down the harbor, Valle insisted on saying good-bye once more to his two daughters, whom he had brought as far as Point Ycaco.   The girls, with a younger brother, got into the boat with their father, and went with him some distance down the harbor, the old man promising them presents from Granada when he returned, and the girls as gay as if their parent was going out with a hunting party.   The old revolutionist took his eldest son (not more than fifteen) with him, and telling the yoauger to take care of his sisters, he embraced them as composedly as if he expected to meet them at breakfast the next morning, and saying adieu again and again as he put off for the Vesta, left them, to pass through many a scene of peril and danger before again meeting them.

After getting to sea the cholera was less severe among the troops, and few died between the time of leaving Realejo and the arrival of the brig at San Juan del Sur. The passage was long, and it was the 29th of August before the Vesta made the port.   Two Americans seeing her outside brought Walker the intelligence that all the Legitimist troops had left San Juan as soon as the well-known brig hove in sight.   The ketch had not arrived, nor had she been seen by the Vesta for several days. Some uneasiness was felt on her account, but the calms and contrary winds which had prevailed and the slow sailing of the craft were sufficient to explain her non-appearance.   Soon after dark the Vesta dropped anchor in the port, but it was determined not to land the forces until the next morning.

A short time after the brig came to anchor Walker ascertained that Parker H. French had just arrived in the town from Granada, and was there waiting the next steamer for San Francisco. French had started for California in 1849, but, being engaged in some doubtful transactions in Texas, on his way to the Pacific, his name had ever since been suggestive of unfairness and dishonesty. In California he had been a member of the Legislature, and afterward established a short-lived journal at Sacramento. During the time Walker was trying to get men at San Francisco to go to Nicaragua French had met him and professed to have great influence with C. K. Garrison, the agent of the Accessory Transit Company in California. French's character presented no obstacle to an intimacy of the sort he alleged between himself and Garrison, and French told Walker he had spoken to Garrison in reference to the proposed expedition and its bearing on the Transit Company. Certainly Garrison did nothing to aid the departure of the Vesta from San Francisco, but French intimated that after the sailing of a first party for Nicaragua he would himself follow, and would manage to interest Garrison in the enterprise. Nothing was heard from French until it was reported through the country that the Legitimist government was about to secure the services of a " coto "— one armed man—whose skill as an artillerist was amazing; for French had brought with him from San Francisco a mulatto servant to be used as the vehicle for communicating the most astonishing stories as to his master's skill, bravery and general attainments. At his own desire French was brought aboard the Vesta under arrest. He strove to impress Walker with the idea that he had gone to Granada to observe the strength and defences of the place, and he then proceeded to state what he had observed. Of course Walker attached no importance to his statements, nor did he ever care to examine minutely the real motives of French in going there. The motives of such men are generally so tangled that he who attempts to unravel them is poorly paid for his trouble.

The next morning the force, together with all the stores, were landed, and the Democrats had scarcely taken possession of the town before the steamer from California appeared off the harbor. It was a glad sight for the Falange, inasmuch as it suggested the fact that they were now in communication with the friends of youth and manhood, and that there would now be an opportunity to swell their numbers from the passengers crossing the Isthmus. Some difficulty occurred at first in regard to the conveyance of the passengers across the Isthmus, as the contractor seemed afraid to venture to town with his mules and carriages ; but soon they were all sent to Virgin Bay, and the town settled to its usual quiet condition. About midnight the ketch appeared, and the troops aboard of her were immediately landed. The full force of the command then amounted to near fifty Americans, and one hundred and twenty natives. A number of the latter were on the sick list, and the prevailing disease was the colerin, which generally carried the patient off in two or three days.

The enemy was reported to have five or six hundred men—some said eight hundred, but this was an exaggeration—at Rivas, and in a day or two it was known Guardiola had arrived to take the command. Flying from Sauce after his defeat there, the Legitimist General had hurried to Granada, entering that city with a single attendant. Brooding over his ill-luck in the north, and anxious for a chance to regain his lost fame, he leaped at the opportunity of going to Rivas in order, as he said, to sweep the "filibusters" into the sea. He marched from Granada with some two hundred select soldiers, expecting to make them the nucleus of a force to be organized after his arrival at Rivas. With him marched several officers, reputed to be of skill and courage, and desirous of more active service than was to be had under Corral. French's mulatto man, Tom, who was sent over to Virgin Bay on some errand for his master, reported on his return that Guardiola had come down with a thousand men, and would march at once on San Juan del Sur ; but this story was like that of his master being able to hit a man every shot with a twenty-four pounder at the distance of a mile.

By the morning of the 2d of September, the passengers from the Atlantic side had arrived, and were aboard the steamer ready to sail. French returned to San Francisco with authority to raise and bring down seventy-five men for the service of the Provisional Government. Anderson, who had been wounded at Rivas, also went up on the steamer, hoping, by change of air, to recover his health and the use of his leg. The Vesta sailed for Punta Arenas the same day the steamer left ; and on the afternoon of the 2d, the port had a solitary look. On shore, however, the town wore an aspect of activity. Pack-mules and carts were being collected for a march, and the soldiers in all the quarters were busy preparing for a movement which, it was supposed, might bring them nearer to the enemy.

Owing to the delays of some native officers, it was past midnight before the force was ready to march. The column was formed with the Falange in front, and the command of Valle in the rear, the baggage and ammunition of the Americans being in their charge; while the ammunition of the natives, they having no baggage, was under a guard from their own body. The night was fine and pleasant, the road good, and the spirits of the command high. At the Half-way house a halt was ordered, and the owner of the establishment brought water to the door, the soldiers not being allowed to enter as there was liquor within. The keeper of this house was, perforce, a model trimmer. He was an American; but having witnessed various political changes since his residence on the Isthmus, and his place being often visited the same day by scouting parties belonging to adverse parties, he had acquired the habits of a man born in the midst of revolutions. He had in perfection all the little arts by which a man manages to maintain his neutrality though constantly surrounded by circumstances tending to endanger it.

About day-break the report of a gun was heard in the direction of Rivas; but not much attention was given to it at the time. The march was uninterrupted, and the force reached Virgin Bay about nine o'clock in the morning. A few moments after Walker halted and took quarters in the village, a well-authenticated report was brought to him that Guardiola had marched from Rivas with a strong force the previous afternoon; but the same report stated that he had returned to the town. The pickets were posted; quarters were assigned the several companies, and all prepared for a hearty breakfast after their bracing night march.

Breakfast was just over, and some of the men had already spread their blankets for sleep, when a fire of musketry was heard in the direction of the picket on the transit road. Then the picket of natives was seen retiring slowly and in excellent order, firing, as it fell back with coolness and entire regularity. The conduct of this picket, checking as it did momentarily, the advance of the whole body of the enemy, was admirable; and it gave the Falange time to get ready for the reception of the attack. The picket reached the main body without loss, and they had scarcely got to the first houses of the village before the enemy was seen in large numbers, pressing forward rapidly along the sides of the Transit, and to the right and left of the road, through the thick wood which skirts its edges.

On the right of Virgin Bay, as you stand with your back to the Lake and your face toward the Pacific, is a rising ground, offering advantages to an enemy attacking the place; on the left, the ground is level, though somewhat interrupted by ditches, and covered with fences made of upright stakes, affording defence for a force within the village. Near the lake the ground falls at once to the beach by a steep declivity, thus forming a sort of bank for the protection of riflemen. The building of the Accessory Transit Company, a large wooden storehouse surrounded with palisades, stands on the edge of the village next the lake, and to the

left of the road. A small, trifling wharf then ran a
few yards from the end of the Transit into the lake ;
but it afforded little advantage either for embarking or
disembarking. Thus the democratic force stood with
its back to the lake, and in a few moments its front and
flank were simultaneously threatened by the enemy.
It thus became necessary to fight well or be cut to
pieces ; none, not even the natives under Valle, hoping
or expecting any quarter at the hands of Guardiola.

Walker's first object was to prevent the enemy from
gaining the high ground on his right flank, and for this
purpose he placed some twenty of the Falange along
the slope under cover of the weeds and bushes and of a
few small huts scattered irregularly on that side of the
village. This detachment advanced toward the enemy,
creeping cautiously along, and firing only when it could
do so to advantage. At first the Legitimists came on
quite boldly ; but when they got within thirty or forty
yards of the Americans their hearts seemed to fail them.
The defiant air of the Americans, shouting at the same
time they fired with deadly accuracy, appeared to ap-
pal their assailants ; and the officers of the Legitimists,
marked by their black coats, and many being mounted,
were seen freely using their riding whips and the backs
of their swords in order to drive the soldiers to the use
of the bayonet. But these efforts had little effect, and
Walker seeing the enemy checked on the right, turned
his attention to the other flank, which was being vigorously assailed.

Valle and Luzarraga, with the native force, had steadily resisted the advance of the Legitimists by the cen-

tre on the transit road. At one time the Granadinos had nearly got to a charge against the Leoneses, and one or two of the latter actually received bayonet thrusts from the former ; but the Democrats showing a firm front, the enemy retired, thrown into some confusion and disorder by a fire from the houses on the edge of the village. But it was on the left flank that the Legitimists pressed their opponents the hardest. They appeared to aim at securing a position on the beach, and also at gaining possession of the Accessory Transit Company's house, whence they might assail the rear of the Democrats. Markham, with some fifteen of the Falange, was pouring a well-directed fire from behind the fences and palisades on the left of the village, and a few others were deployed at irregular intervals along the beach to prevent a lodgment there by the enemy. At one time the Legitimists had got within thirty or thirty-five yards of the Company's buildings, but Gay and several others charging with revolvers had driven them back ; then Markham pressed forward toward the wood, skirting the left of the village, and the enemy showed signs of giving way, not only in that direction but on all sides. Soon the firing grew feebler and feebler ; Chélon was seen coming in from the transit road with the ox-carts carrying the enemy's ammunition ; and then a loud shout from the whole democratic force announced that the day had been won by them.

Walker's loss was trifling, and, considering the duration of the action, its heat, and the close distances at which the firing was done, almost inexplicable, unless on the supposition that the Central Americans fight bet-

ter far off than near.   None of the Falange were killed,
though several were wounded.   Small was shot through
the chest, besides being hit in more than one place elsewhere ; Benj. Williamson had a painful hurt in the
groin ; Capt. Doubleday was struck in the side ; and
Walker was struck in the throat by a spent ball, which
knocked him to the ground for a moment, while the letters of Castellon, in his coat pocket, were cut to pieces.
The only wound apparently fatal was that of Small, and
he recovered in a few weeks ; while Williamson's wound,
seemingly trifling, kept him in bed for months.   The
native Democrats had two killed and three wounded.
The loss of the enemy was large.   Upward of sixty
dead were found on the field ; and subsequent reports
stated that over a hundred wounded—many of whom
died of their wounds—reached Rivas, whither Guardiola
retired, almost unattended, after the action.

When the wounded prisoners were examined, it was
ascertained that Guardiola had marched from Rivas the
afternoon of the 2d, with about six hundred chosen
troops of the Legitimist army.   He had camped over
night at Jocote, a farm-house, distant about half a
league from the Half-way house.   His plan was to attack the Americans soon after daylight, at San Juan del
Sur, expecting to find them there.   But on arriving at
the Half-way house he found, probably from the servants
of the establishment, as well as by the signs on the road,
that Walker had just passed toward Virgin Bay.   Immediately facing about, he followed the Democratic force—
probably not more than four or five miles in their rear.
He had with him a six-pounder, with which he expected

to drive the Democrats from the houses ; but on arriving at Virgin Bay, he was unable to use the piece, through some defect in the carriage. Finding he could not use his gun, he decided to attack at once with the bayonet. Rations of aguardiente were distributed to the troops, and the order was given to charge. But either the quantity of liquor was insufficient, or it may have been too great, or it began to die out before the soldiers got close to their adversaries. The empty demijohns which were picked up on the road after the action looked like huge cannon-balls that had missed their mark.

The people of the village were quite relieved when they saw Guardiola driven back to Rivas. When the firing commenced the women and children had sought refuge in the Company's house ; and the agent, Mr. Cortlandt Cushing, had so arranged the trunks and boxes stored in the building as to protect the inmates from the fire of the enemy. Although very much frightened, the women and even the children maintained a silence which might be the result of revolutionary training. After the danger had passed, however, their tongues were unloosed, and the squalling of babies, mixed up with the shrill tones of the mothers, soon brought even the smooth-tempered agent into the open air. Fortunately, none of the poor people were hurt ; and after it became very certain the enemy did not intend to return, they withdrew to their several houses, engaging with as much calmness as if no war existed, in the daily round of their domestic joys and domestic cares.

The troops, both American and native, being fatigued by the night-march as well as by the excitement of the

action, Mr. Cushing undertook to have the dead of the
enemy buried. In the meantime the wounded Legitimists were brought in and carefully tended, the surgeon
of the Falange dressing their wounds as carefully as if
they had been Democrats. This surprised the people of
the village much ; and the poor fellows, who expected to
be shot, were exceedingly grateful for the attentions they
received. Details of the Leoneses were sent into the
neighboring wood to gather up the muskets thrown away
by the retreating foe ; and more than a hundred and
fifty of these were collected. Later in the day Valle
and Mendez, with such Americans as were able to get
horses, scouted the roads for several miles round, to see
if any of the Legitimists yet lurked in the neighborhood ;
but no signs of the enemy were found, and they seemed
to have disappeared as suddenly as they had appeared.

Walker's object in marching to Virgin Bay had not
been to occupy the place, but to prevent the enemy, as
well as the people of the Department, from supposing he
intended to remain entirely on the defensive, by keeping
his force shut up at San Juan del Sur. His own force
would acquire confidence by seeing its ability to pass
through the country without the fear of an attack from
the enemy ; and he had scarcely hoped for so fortunate
a circumstance as the march of Guardiola to Virgin Bay.
The action of the 3d of September secured the Democrats for a time from being troubled by the Legitimists,
and gave them time to gather up the friends they had in
the Meridional Department. On the afternoon of the 4th,
therefore, Walker marched back to San Juan, carrying
with him his wounded, and the arms and ammunition

taken from the enemy. Early the next morning the column was seen pouring over the hill back of San Juan, and in a short time the whole force was again quartered within the town.

Despatches were immediately sent to the Provisional Director informing him of the incidents at Virgin Bay, and requesting, if possible, new supplies of men and provisions, with a view to offensive operations. The bearer of despatches arrived in Leon just in time to see the Director die. Within an hour after the official news of the victory reached the capital, Castellon breathed his last, yielding to the fatal cholera which was then slaying so many scores of his countrymen and adherents. He had fulfilled his task—an important one it was—of introducing a new element into Central American society; and his amiable spirit—the body worn out, probably, by the toils and troubles ill-suited to his gentle nature, and offering an easy prey to the fearful pestilence—had gone forth to give an account of the deeds done in the flesh. Much as his friends and neighbors loved and respected him, their estimate of his character will rise yet higher if they live long enough to see in maturity the fruits of the policy he inaugurated. Leon deeply mourned his death, and time will yet develop the fact that, soft as his nature seemed, he was destined to have a far wider, and a far deeper, and a far more enduring effect on the fate of Nicaragua, than was left by his stern, unyielding rival, Don Fruto Chamorro, who preceded him only a few months—but how fruitful—to the grave.

The despatches to Castellon were answered by the new Provisional Director, D. Nasario Escoto, who succeeded

5

to the office in virtue of being the Senator of the Republic designated for the place by the constitution of 1838. The Senator-Director warmly thanked the expeditionary force, native and American, for the services it had rendered, and he further wrote that the Provisional Government would use all diligence to forward supplies from Realejo to San Juan del Sur. The cholera, according to Don Nasario, was making much havoc about Leon, and hence it was difficult to command labor, much less men for military service. Besides this Walker wanted only volunteers from the natives, and refused the forced levies by which the ranks of all factions, and parties, and governments, are generally filled in Central America. The Director promised to send only these, and stated the circumstances to account for the fewness of the number.

In the meanwhile the little force at San Juan del Sur was swelling its numbers from another source. Soon after the news of the action at Virgin Bay spread through the country, the men of San Jorge—always democratic in their feelings and now irritated by the arbitrary acts of the Legitimists at Rivas—began to come with the red ribbon on their hats, asking to receive arms and be admitted into the democratic ranks. Those, too, who had fled to Guanacaste when the Granada Government got possession of the Meridional Department, now returned and joined Walker with the hope of once more getting back to their families and friends. Among these last were Dr. Cole, an American, who had married some years previously into a family residing near Rivas, and the three Cantons, Tranquillino, Clemente, and Daniel. Soon, also, Don Maximo Espinosa—who had been hid in the neighborhood of his plantation since the 29th of June—made his appearance, and then came his son-in-law, Don Ramon Umaña. After Espinosa's arrival at San Juan del Sur he was charged with organizing the civil administration of the Department in virtue of the authority given him by the Provisional Government in the month of June previous.

Nor were deserters from the enemy's ranks wanting. Almost every day the men from Rivas, forced into the service by the Legitimists would manage to escape from the barricades, and come down to San Juan del Sur to report the numbers and situation of the enemy, and even to take up arms to avenge the injuries they had sustained. As Walker would not permit the native democratic officers to follow their old habit of impressment, the people from the neighboring farms, men as well as women, came in daily with their supplies of fruits and provisions for the soldiers. It was difficult at first to check this inveterate habit of catching a man and tying him up with a musket in his hand to make a soldier of him, but seeing the good effects of the policy the officers afterward desisted from a practice which seemed to have become almost a second nature to them.

Soon after returning from Virgin Bay Walker had, in order to raise means for the support of his troops, resorted to a military contribution on the principal traders doing business at San Juan del Sur. Among others, John Priest, the United States consul, who kept an inn and drinking-house, was assessed at the same rate as others of his calling. Priest refused to pay, on the ground that he was a foreign consul, showing thereby an intelligence more akin to his inn-keeping than to his consular character.   He talked largely about having an American man-of-war brought into port for the purpose of enabling him to sell grog quietly to soldiers and sailors without being obliged to pay taxes for the support of a government which could not claim him as a citizen.   But as he had on a former occasion complained loudly at the outrages said to have been practised on his person and property by the Legitimists, but had, when the United States sent a sloop-of-war to inquire into his grievances, made the commander of the ship appear very ridiculous by demanding compensation for Priest, when the latter had really signed a paper fully exonerating the Chamorro government, the consular inn-keeper's threats carried little weight with them.   For his contumacy, he found a native guard placed in his house, with orders not to permit any one to pass in or out until the assessment was paid.   Not many hours elapsed before the inn-keeper forgot his consular dignity, and came forward with the money to pay the contribution.

There were, in fact, few sources of revenue at San Juan.   Most of the lots in the town are held by the occupants at a monthly rent, to be paid to the State; and in addition to this there were the customs and the monopoly of the sale of beef.   These revenues, small as they were, could not be honestly collected through means of native functionaries.   One of the Leoneses, acting as collector, was caught taking bribes from a merchant for smuggling; and the complaints against Mendez for killing cattle and selling beef in fraud of the revenue were almost daily.   The habit of cheating the State, prevail-

ing in all parts of Central America, leads to the mal-
administration which produces revolution; and the
habit of revolution in turn reacts and increases the disposition of officers to make as much as possible for themselves at the public expense, since the tenure of their
offices must, necessarily, be short. It is difficult to say
which is cause and which effect; and it may be that
they are both common effects of a radically bad social
organization. Nor can reforms in revenue, either as to
the method of raising or of collecting it, be well attempted
in the midst of war. The taxes to which the people are
accustomed, being those most readily collected, must be
resorted to in times when the demand for money is
urgent.

Walker soon had evidences that the Legitimists found
the question of revenue as difficult as did the Democrats.
Near the 20th of September the steamer Sierra Nevada
arrived at San Juan, having on board D. Guadalupe
Saënz, who had been sent to California for the purpose
of raising means to aid the government at Granada.
Don Guadalupe seeing the red-ribbons on shore did not
venture to land, but a detail was sent to the steamer
and searched the vessel thoroughly without, however,
being able to find the Commissioner of Estrada. His
papers, less fortunate than his person, fell into the hands
of the Democrats, and showed that he had sold to one
Body of California some brazil-wood belonging to Mariano Salazar, but then in the possession of the Legitimists,
and that he had made a contract with the same Body
for the establishment of a mint in Nicaragua. The private papers of Don Guadalupe also disclosed that while

acting for the Government he had not failed to take care
of himself; and they proved that Body had probably
made good bargains, as his partner in the contracts was
no less a person than Commissioner Saënz himself. The
diary, too, kept by Don Guadalupe, revealed the singular sensation he had when he first tasted a sherry cob-
bler, and recorded his deliberate opinion as to the superiority of such a beverage over the tiste of Nicaragua.

The Sierra Nevada was not able to get coal at San
Juan, and had to go to Realejo for that purpose. It was
consequently some days after her arrival before she got
off for San Francisco. A few recruits for the Falange
were obtained from the passengers for California; and
they, together with some residents of the Isthmus, who
enrolled themselves in the body, swelled its numbers to
nearly sixty effective men. The strength of Valle's
force, in spite of losses from cholera, reached over two
hundred. In the meantime the Legitimists had been
recovering from the effects of Virgin Bay. Guardiola,
made more moody than ever by his late defeats, was not
sorry to yield the command to Corral, who came from
Granada with a view of directing the operations against
the Democrats in person. With more amenity of manner than the Hondureño, the legitimist commander-in-
chief, was able to conciliate many the other had repelled; but he lacked decision and was more fertile in
perceiving difficulties than in defying or overcoming
them. Not having been defeated like Guardiola—for
his skill consisted rather in avoiding action than in
bringing the enemy to blows—he was better suited to
restore order to the disorganized troops he found at

Rivas, and to infuse spirit into the adherents of his party residing in the department

There were constant reports coming to San Juan of Corral's intention to advance against the democratic force. But the rainy season made the roads difficult to pass, and swelled the water-courses so bodies of men could not cross them with ease, unless having more facilities than are to be found in Central American armies. A report, however, that Corral had actually marched, coming with some probabilities of truth, induced Walker to march out to meet him, and, if possible, bring him to action unexpectedly. A day or two, therefore, after the steamer sailed, the Falange, accompanied by Valle's command, was marched late at night to the hill, a little over a league distant from San Juan, on the transit road; and on the side of the hill next to Virgin Bay the whole force was placed in ambush to await the approach of Corral. The night was dark and dismal, the rain falling now slowly and like a heavy mist, then rapidly and in drops nearly as big as a revolver bullet; but the men stood to their places, sheltering themselves under the large trees which cover the sides of the hill, and being careful to keep their cartridge-boxes dry, drawing them, for this purpose, to the front part of the belt, and bending over so as to protect the precious powder with their bodies. Such situations have their excitements and pleasures as well as their discomforts; and although, when the morning came, and no enemy appeared, the force looked wet and weather-beaten, it marched at a brisk and cheerful pace to the Half-way house, where a ration of liquor made the men as fresh and lively as if they had passed the night in a palace.

Hearing no tidings of the enemy from mine host at the Half-way house, who always ran off to another subject when the news was asked or talked of, Walker determined to continue his march to Virgin Bay. There he heard that Corral had actually left Rivas with nearly his whole force; but on reaching the river Lajas, the Legitimist general hearing the Democrats had marched from San Juan, and fearing they might attack the chief town of the Department while it was comparatively undefended, hastily counter-marched and withdrew within his barricades. Thus Walker, by the march to Virgin Bay, ascertained that he had only to leave San Juan del Sur, apparently for Rivas, in order to paralyze any advance movement his opponent might make. Besides this, however, he obtained other useful information which hereafter materially affected the operations against the enemy. The day he reached Virgin Bay he intercepted despatches and letters from the *Mayor General*—literally Major General, but really performing the duties of Adjutant General — of the Legitimist army, D. Fernando Chamorro, to Corral; and they disclosed to the democratic officer the destitute condition of the government at Granada and its inability to assist its commander-in-chief at Rivas with more men. The letters also indicated that Granda itself was almost entirely undefended; that the spirit of its people was drooping: and that the chiefs of the party began to despair of maintaining the war much longer if vigorously pressed by the democratic forces.

After reading these letters and despatches, Walker sent them to Corral with a note stating that he had taken the liberty to read them, thus making the Legitimist general feel that his condition and prospects were not unknown to his adversary. Walker also intimated in the note that the country needed repose, both parties, so far as the native forces we're concerned, having nearly exhausted themselves in the long struggle. To this note Walker soon received a reply acknowledging the receipt of the letters and despatches from Granada, and within Corral's answer was a small slip of paper containing some cabalistic signs the democratic colonel did not understand. Supposing these signs to be masonic—for it was known Corral was a mason—Walker showed them to Captain Hornsby, who, although a mason, seemed ignorant of their meaning. Then they were shown to De Brissot, who, according to Hornsby's statements, was of high standing in the mystic order. De Brissot said the signs were masonic, and that Corral desired by them to know whether he could communicate confidentially with Walker. Here the correspondence ended ; and it had served the purpose of showing that Corral was not indisposed for peace even in the then condition of affairs.

Remaining only a few hours at Virgin Bay, Walker returned with his whole force to San Juan del Sur. Even had the condition of the roads allowed a march to Rivas, he did not have sufficient strength for an attack on that place. Besides this, his views were now directed elsewhere ; and the reports he received almost daily from Granada confirmed the statements of the despatches he had intercepted. A musician by the name of Acevedo, imprisoned at Granada for being a democrat, escaped to

5*

San Juan and gave a full account of the state of affairs there, saying, among other things, that there were more than a hundred democrats working in the streets with balls and chains about their legs.

On the morning of the 3d of October the steamer Cortes from San Francisco came into port, and soon the news spread that Colonel Charles Gilman, one of the companions of Walker in Lower California, was aboard with some thirty-five men. In a short time they were all ashore, each of them carrying a rifle, and being well supplied with ammunition. Gilman was a man of strong mind, with all the sentiments of a soldier, and having a good store of military knowledge. He had lost a leg in Lower California, and the wound from which he suffered long and cruelly before the amputation of the limb, having kept him abed for many months, his intellect seemed to have ripened rapidly during his confinement. With him were also several others of excellent capacity. Captain George R. Davidson, who had served in the Kentucky Regiment during the Mexican war, was one of the company ; as were also Captain A. S. Brewster, afterward Major ; John P. Waters, afterward Colonel Waters, and John M. Baldwin, afterward Major Baldwin. They had scarcely landed ere they were sent on service, being ordered to guard the specie train across the transit road to Virgin Bay.

The Falange, now numbering nearly a hundred men, was at once organized into three companies, and called a battalion. Captain Hornsby was placed in command of it with the rank of colonel, and Colonel Gilman was appointed lieutenant-colonel. The three captains were

Markham, Brewster, and Davidson. Lieutenant George R. Caston was made adjutant, and Captain William Williamson, quartermaster. While, however, the Americans were thus gaining strength in Nicaragua, they also suffered some losses. Captain Doubleday, who had served for some time under Jerez, and had diligently performed the duties of commissary of war under Walker, asked and obtained leave to return to the United States. Industrious and exact in the performance of his duties, and having from his long residence in the country a knowledge of the language and manners of the people, he was much missed after his departure. He left at this time because having, without invitation, stated to Walker his opinion about certain movements being made, the commander remarked, that "when his commissary's opinion was required it would be asked for." At the time the remark was made, it was of the first necessity for the force to feel that it had but one head. Captain Doubleday afterward returned to the country and engaged in its service with credit to himself and benefit to the cause.

The same day Colonel Gilman with his comrades arrived at San Juan, a small vessel came in from Realejo, having on board a democratic officer, Ubaldo Herrera, with some thirty-five Leoneses. These, with the recruits who had been daily dropping in to fill the places of those cut off by disease, raised the force under Valle to upward of two hundred and fifty men. It became necessary, at the same time, to get rid of Mendez. His offences were daily; and his cruelty to his men, together with his petty peculations, destructive of discipline and order, made it expedient to send him to Leon. He went away telling Walker he would learn that the Nicaraguans were to be governed only with silver in one hand and the whip in the other.

Besides the increase of numbers about this time, the democratic force was somewhat strengthened by a small brass two-pounder brought from Leon, and a new iron six-pounder obtained from Captain Reed of the clipper ship Queen of the Pacific, then in port with a cargo of coal. Some days were passed in mounting the six-pounder, and preparing ammunition for it; and during this period, the organization and discipline of the whole force were being improved. Finally all was ready for a march, and on the morning of the 11th Walker moved with his whole force to Virgin Bay, and arrived there a little after dark of the same day.

Chapter Fourth.

IT was expected that the steamer La Virgen, belonging to the Accessory Transit Company, would arrive at Virgin Bay the evening of the 11th, and the democratic force had scarcely got into quarters before it was announced that she was in sight. A sentry had been previously posted near the wharf with orders to prevent any boat from leaving the village without permission; and as soon as the steamer appeared, Colonel Hornsby was ordered to go aboard when she cast anchor and take possession of her. He executed the order without Capt. Joseph N. Scott, who was on the Virgin, knowing his object until he had accomplished it. Both Mr. Cushing, the agent of the company, and Capt. Scott, protested against the use of the vessel for military purposes, as well as against the forcible possession. Mr. Cushing said he had the assurance of the United States Government, that it considered these vessels of the Accessory Transit Company American property, under the American flag; but he had been in the diplomatic service of the United States, and was too familiar with the first principles of public law, to imagine that persons acting under the authority of Nicaragua would regard any such interpretation of her rights of sovereignty. The Accessory Transit Company was a creature of the government of Nicaragua ; and its vessels were by the very terms of its charter under the Nicaraguan flag. Even, however, had the property been that of a neutral, and not of a subject, it would have been permissible to use it temporarily for the purpose of transporting troops. It is not at all true, as has been sometimes asserted, that the steamer was there by concert between Walker and the agent of the company ; on the contrary, the latter had always resisted the idea of permitting the vessels of the corporation to be used in any manner by the belligerents, and the former, to disarm Mr. Cushing of any suspicions he might entertain, had always protested that he knew of no way in which the steamers could aid the objects he had in view.

From the time the steamers appeared the camp was doubly guarded, and no one was allowed to leave the village. Thus the enemy was kept in ignorance of the fact, that the Virgen was in the possession of the democratic force. The next day preparations were made for embarking the whole command aboard the steamer ; and by four or half-past four in the afternoon, the last boat-full of men was alongside. Soon the order was given to weigh anchor, and the prow of the steamer was turned toward Granada. When the natives saw whither the force was moving, their joy was extravagant. It became necessary, however, to keep them quiet, and as much concealed as possible, in order not to attract attention from the shore, as the scouts of the enemy could be plainly perceived at intervals along the beach. On approaching Granada the lights on the steamer were extinguished, the canvas curtains were let down from the roof of the upper deck, and the boat was kept off from the fort, so as not to be seen by the sentries stationed there.

Near ten o'clock at night the steamer was anchored near the shore, about three miles to the north of Granada. A line was made fast to a large tree on the beach, and the disembarkation was effected by pulling an iron launch from the steamer by means of the cable fastened ashore. It was about three o'clock in the morning when the last body of men landed; and the horses which had been brought up for the use of Valle and Gilman made a great noise at the last trip of the launch. No doubt the noise appeared greater than it was to those who were anxious to keep their movements quiet and secret. After all had landed, the column was formed with some difficulty owing to the darkness of the night, the thickness of the forest trees, and the entire ignorance of the officers and soldiers in regard to the nature of the ground. At last the order to march was given, the Falange in front, the native force in the rear. Ubaldo Herrera, a native of Granada, undertook to act as the guide. While it was dark the march was perplexed and difficult; but as soon as day broke Herrera seemed to know precisely where he was, and in a few minutes the column reached the road running from the city to Los Cocos. One or two market-people whom he met informed Walker that all was quiet in the city, nobody expecting an attack, or apprehending the approach of an enemy.

The Democrats had got to within half a mile of the town, and the first rays of the rising sun had begun to warm the eastern heavens, when suddenly all the bells of the city were heard ringing a quick and joyful peal. Some of the Americans thought the bells were a signal of alarm, and that their tone showed confidence on the part of the enemy, as if welcoming an attack. But the ringing was really to celebrate a triumph Martinez had over the Democrats at Pueblo Nuevo, two days previously. The bells were yet pealing, when the advanced guard of the Falange reached the first huts on the outskirts of the town. Then the Americans seeing, from the startled air of the people in the suburbs, that the Legitimists were completely taken by surprise, threw off their coats and dropped their blankets, rushing forward with a shout to gain the first barricades. The gaunt form of Hornsby in the van served as a sort of guide for those behind. On they pressed, and the first shots of the enemy were from the old convent of San Francisco; but these were few and straggling, and scarcely checked for amoment the impetuous march of the Falange. A shout from the advance announces that the Plaza is won, and the last few shots were fired from the gallery of the government house as Walker entered the square. Then the streets leading from the Plaza were searched in vain for the flying enemy. In fact, the Legitimist force in the town had been trifling, and the encounter between it and the Democrats could scarcely be dignified with the name of an action. Two or three of the Legitimists were killed, and a drummer-boy under Valle was the whole loss of the Democrats. As Norris, the drummer of the Falange afterward said, when asking to be excused from serving as drum-major, " In every battle scene you see a drummer-boy lying dead by the side of his drum."

When the Democrats entered the town all the doors and windows were closed and the several national flags were flying from the houses of the foreign residents—a flag being a very useful piece of furniture to foreigners of equivocal character and doubtful nationality in Central American countries. As soon, however, as the confusion of the collision was over, the houses and doors began to be cautiously opened. The house of the American Minister was about the first to unclose its portals; and its saloon and chamber and court yard presented a curious spectacle. Eighty or a hundred women and children were huddled together seeking safety under the folds of the American flag. There was the gentle dame who thought the Democrats were all robbers and murderers because they made war on the old aristocracy of the land and the humble servant-girl who imagined the Leoneses would kill her because her father or brother had followed the fortunes of his legitimist master rather than take up arms in defence of the rights of his class. In their fancies a filibuster was a sort of centaur with far more of the beast than of the man in his nature; and their surprise was great to hear the Americans speak mildly and conduct themselves quietly after the noise of the fray was over.

Walker had gone for a moment to the house of the Minister in order to answer some of the demands made on his attention there and was returning thence across the Plaza toward the Government House, when he saw several of the native soldiers heavily laden with merchandise trotting hastily along the opposite side of the square. On approaching them they did not halt until ordered, nor did they seem to imagine they were doing aught to anger their chief. It was clear from their manner that they thought the town was to be given up for sack. But Walker, placing his sword at the breast of one of them, called the guard and ordered the offenders to be arrested and the goods restored to their owners. The order was immediately given to the Falange to remain under arms in order to protect the property of the citizens. There were some murmurs among the native soldiers, especially among those who had themselves suffered either in their property or their persons or in those of their families ; but the co-operation of Valle was soon obtained and the disorders were to a great extent arrested.

But on another point Valle was less yielding. In the course of the morning D. Dionisio Chamorro and D. *Toribio* Jerez had presented themselves to Walker under the assurance of their persons being respected, and they had been consigned to the charge of M. Bernard, a French subject, in whose house they resided and with whom they were connected by marriage. As the two well-known legitimists were passing the streets on their way home they caught the eye of Valle, and the old democrat immediately ordered them to follow him to Walker's quarters. By the time Chélon arrived at the quarters he was in a sort of frenzy rhapsodizing about his losses, the death of his brother, the death of his friends, and the cruelties of the Legitimists, and declaiming against all who showed mercy to the hateful Granadinos. A little brandy for which he had a keen relish, no doubt added fuel to the flame of his feelings and inspired some of the eloquence which rolled rapidly from his lips. In vain Walker tried to soothe his irritation ; soft words seemed oil to the fire of his passion. Then changing his tone Walker assumed the language of authority, reminded Chélon that he was his superior and that any disobedience of orders would be summarily punished. Dismissing the legitimists to their house under the escort of Americans, he informed Valle that any one interfering with their persons would do so at his peril. The fierce old democrat retired muttering something about the Granadian bullet in his leg ; but he got over his wrath, and in the evening was as ready as ever for a serenade or a charge, according as the circumstances called for one or the other.

A prisoner of consideration was made in the person of D. Mateo Mayorga, the secretary of relations under Estrada. He was placed on his parole in the house of the American Minister. Other leading legitimists presented themselves in the course of the day, and were put under the protection of the American rifles.

Nearly a hundred prisoners were released from their chains by the capture of Granada. They had been arrested for political offences, and some of them were under sentence of death. Among them were D. Cleto Mayorga, son-in-law of D. Patricio Rivas and cousin of D. Mateo Mayorga, the Minister of Relations ; an American by the name of Bailey, confined, as he said, on suspicion of favoring the democratic cause ; and a youth by the name of Tejada, brother to D. Rafael Tejada, commissioner under Estrada to settle the differences between the Republic and the Accessory Transit Company. All these prisoners asked for arms and were incorporated into the democratic forces, so that before the night of the 13th the aggregate of the troops occupying Granada amounted to near four hundred and fifty men.

A short time after entering the city, on the morning of the 13th, Walker met, on the Plaza, D. Carlos Thomas, a foreign merchant, long resident in the place, and D. Fermin Ferrer, a landholder of Chontales, but who resided at Granada, and was familiar with the routine of public business. Ferrer was appointed prefect, and entered immediately on the discharge of his duties. Thomas rendered much service to Walker, by his knowledge of men and things in Granada ; and among other functions he performed was that of writer of proclamations. He spoke and wrote English, French, and Spanish, with equal facility, and probably equal elegance, his English being, however, more Johnsonese than idiomatic, and his French and Spanish being probably tinged with the same fault. The swell of his sentences was perfectly Ciceronian, when, with a glass or two of brandy in his head, he began to dilate on the grandeur of the present crisis in Nicaragua ; and the exuberance of his feelings overflowed in a proclamation he wrote out for Walker, and had published, somewhat to the annoyance of the latter, when he saw his signature appended in print to an address teeming with the rhetoric which characterizes Spanish-American productions. The proclamation, however, though offensive to taste, did some good ; for the purport of it was, that protection would be given to all interests, and that none need refuse to return to their homes through fear of political persecution.

For a short time after entering the city, Walker took up his quarters at the house of a woman of middle age, called generally, by the people, Niña Yrena. Her family name was Irish, and she was probably the descendant of an Irish officer in the Spanish service, sent to the colonies before the independence. A quick and minute observer, with all the gravity and apparent indifference of the native race, she had rendered much service to the legitimist party in days past ; and even the stern nature of Fruto Chamorro owned her sway, and yielded to her influence, when all others failed to move him. The private relations which it is said, and probably with truth, existed between her and D. Narciso Espinosa, a leading man among the Legitimists, enabled her to breathe her spirit into the party after the death of Chamorro had taken away the unity it before possessed. The Niña was fertile in resources for sending intelligence to her friends ; and hence the headquarters of the force occupying Granada were soon fixed at the government house on the Plaza.

The 14th was Sunday, and at the eight o'clock mass Walker, with a number of other officers, attended, the curate of the city, Father Vigil, preaching a sermon, in which he exhorted to peace, moderation, and the putting away of revolutionary passions. Sketching rapidly the history of Nicaragua, since her independence, he dwelt on the miseries which had flowed from the civil license of the period, and pointed out the necessity to the country of a force strong enough to curb the political passions which had hitherto rent asunder families, and friends, and neighborhoods. None could object to the good Father's sentiments, and the effect of his sermon on the people was excellent and decided. Nor were Father Vigil's labors in the cause of peace confined to the pulpit; he warmly co-operated with Walker in his efforts to make such an arrangement between parties as would put an end to the civil war; and the thorough knowledge of men and things he had, from long practice of the duties of parish priest at Granada, made his counsel valuable in the negotiations which followed the 13th of October.

The chief object Walker had in view, when he marched on Granada was, by securing the main depots of the enemy, to place himself in a position to make the best terms possible with Corral for the advantage of the democratic party, and especially for the policy Castellon adopted, of introducing an American element into Nicaraguan society. Corral had already shown Walker that he was not unwilling to treat for terms; but, of course, it was more advantageous for the latter to treat at Granada than on the Transit, though the possession of the Transit was intrinsically more important to the Americans than the occupation of a town forty or fifty miles from the line of travel across the Isthmus. Hence he did not contemplate, at first, the permanent occupation, regarding his possession of the place merely as a means of getting good terms from Corral, in case a treaty could be negotiated.

Accordingly, as soon as order was established, steps were taken for communicating with Corral. The municipal authorities met and requested Walker to take the Presidency of the Republic. This he declined, suggesting, however, that if Corral were placed in the Executive,

after proper terms were agreed on between the contending parties, he would undertake, as commander-in-chief,
to maintain order within the State. On the part, then,
of the town, commissioners were appointed, the principal being D. Hilario Selva and D. Rosario Vivas, to go to
Rivas and urge on Corral the expediency of an arrangement between the two parties which divided the Republic. At the same time these commissioners proceeded
by land, D. Juan Ruiz, Minister of War, under Estrada,
and Hon. Mr. Wheeler, the American Minister, would go
by the steamer to San Jorge with a view of placing
the same subject before Corral. Mr. Wheeler was
urged to this course by the Legitimists themselves.
The families of the town insisted that he should go with
Ruiz, supposing the weight of his position might influence Corral to treat with Walker, and thus get rid of
the hated Leoneses.

Mr. Wheeler accordingly took the steamer, and in
company with D. Juan Ruiz proceeded to Rivas. When
he arrived there he found that Corral had marched
north on the afternoon of the 14th; and D. Florencio
Xatruch, the friend and comrade of Guardiola, was in
command of the Legitimist troops in the Meridional
Department. The Minister and his secretary were kept
under guard by Xatruch for two days, and they only made
good their escape—for so it may be called—by the
spirit and resolution of Mr. Wheeler. After his arrival at
Virgin Bay, on his return from Rivas, the minister received a note from Corral, dated at his headquarters, the
17th of October, informing Mr. Wheeler that he would
not be responsible for his personal safety, and that he

had communicated an account of his conduct to Mr. Marcy, the Secretary of State, and to the New-York papers. The Minister returned to Granada without seeing Corral, and D. Juan Ruiz failing to keep his parole, fled to Costa Rica.

Selva, Vivas, and the other commissioners who went by land toward Rivas, met Corral, on his march northward, near Nandaime. From that place they sent a communication to Walker, saying that it was impossible to get Corral to treat on any terms; but the next morning Walker got a note from the Legitimist commander, complaining of some Democrats firing on a party of his troops while commissioners were in his camp asking for peace. As no cessation of hostilities had been agreed on, or even proposed as preliminary to the negotiations, the note of Corral showed his anxiety to keep up a correspondence and suggested the inference that he was desirous of an arrangement with Walker. The reply of the democratic commander was to the effect that no armistice having been agreed to, he should continue to carry on the war as vigorously as possible. Though the reply called for no answer, the Legitimist general wrote to say that Walker could scarcely expect any peace to be made on the principles held and enunciated by the native Democrats in his camp. To this, of course, no reply was made, and the negotiations ceased until other events brought them to a speedy and a favorable termination.

On the 17th of October the steamer Uncle Sam arrived at San Juan del Sur, having on board Col. Birkett D. Fry, Parker H. French, and about sixty other Ameri-

cans for the service of the Provisional Government.
They were all armed with rifles and well supplied with
ammunition. On landing they were organized in two
companies commanded respectively by Capt. S. C. Asten
and Capt. Chas. Turnbull. Edward J. Sanders acted as
major, and French had, without authority, promised the
rank of colonel to Fry. A brass six-pounder, with some
ammunition for it, was obtained from the steamer; and
then a most irregular march, considering the presence of
the enemy at Rivas, was made across the Transit to
Virgin Bay. There they found the steamer waiting to
convey the California passengers to the Toro Rapids.
French urged Fry to take the steamer, the passengers
being also aboard, and proceed to San Carlos with a view
of taking that place from the enemy. It was a most
foolish if not criminal act, to take the passengers on the
boat destined for such an expedition, and no benefit could
be expected to result from an undertaking commenced
under such circumstances. On arriving opposite San
Carlos the works appeared too strong for their force; it
was suddenly discovered that the supply of caps was
insufficient, and the Virgin was wisely put about and
steamed over to Granada. Fry's recruits were landed,
and the passengers for the Atlantic States returned to
Virgin Bay.

The existing circumstances made it necessary to over-
look the acts of Fry and French. At the conduct of
the latter Walker was not much surprised; but he had
been led by the opinions of others to expect from Fry a
more discreet and regular course. The reputation of
the latter, as a soldier, had been gained by service in

6

the Voltigeur Regiment during the Mexican war; and the friends of the Nicaraguan cause in California had considered him a valuable accession to the enterprise. Amiable in manner and honorable in sentiment, he had many qualities to conciliate esteem; but a lack of firmness and decision made him too often yield to the evil and inconsiderate suggestions of others. As he had left California under the impression that he was to receive the rank of colonel, it was given to him; and at the same time Sanders, who had much more energy of character, was made major. French was made commissary of war, with the hope that his industry might be useful in the office, while, being under the control of another, his imprudence, to say nothing of more serious defects, might be prevented from doing harm.

After the passengers from California returned to Virgin Bay from Granada, and while they were waiting at the former place for an opportunity to pass down the river to San Juan del Norte, a body of soldiers from Rivas entered the village, and firing indiscriminately, killed three of the passengers (American citizens), and wounded several others, rifling at the same time the pockets of those who were killed. The house of the Accessory Transit Company was broken into and plundered; and the agent, Mr. Cushing, was taken a prisoner to Rivas, whence he was released only after the payment of a fine of two thousand dollars.

Nor were the passengers from New-York less unfortunate than those from California. The Legitimist commandant at San Carlos fired a twenty-four pound shot into the steamer as she passed from the river to the lake, killing a woman and her infant, and taking away the foot of another child. In such a state of affairs it was foolish, of course, to attempt to pass into the river with the California passengers. They, therefore, returned to Granada until some means might be found for passing safely to San Juan del Norte ; and at the same time news was brought to Walker of the events of Virgin Bay and on the lake.

Such conduct on the part of officers, acting under color of the Legitimist government, called for retaliation and punishment in order to prevent its recurrence. Accordingly, early on the morning of the 22d, and soon after the news of the murders at Virgin Bay and on the lake reached Granada, Walker ordered D. Mateo Mayorga to be shot on the main Plaza. Mayorga was a member of the cabinet of Estrada, and was, therefore, morally responsible for the outrages and barbarities practised by those holding a military commission from the Legitimist authorities. He was executed soon after the order was given to the officer of the day, Ubaldo Herrera, and a file of Leoneses were detailed for the duty. All the native democratic officers approved the act, and they then remarked the Americans would hereafter learn that their mercy to the Legitimists was injustice to themselves.

In the meantime, Corral had reached Masaya and was there behind barricades with a large proportion of the Legitimist strength ; while Martinez, who had driven the Democrats from Pueblo Nuevo, on the 11th of the month, falling back on Managua after the surprise of Granada, was again assailed by an irregular body of Leoneses under General Mateo Pineda and Mariano Mendez. This was the position of affairs when, on the morning of the 22d, D. Pedro Rouhaud, a French subject long resident at Granada, went to Masaya, in order to inform Corral of Mayorga's execution and the causes for it, and also to say that all the Legitimist families of the city would be held as hostages for the future good conduct of Estrada's officers toward American women and children, and toward non-combatants generally. This message naturally produced a deep effect, not only on Corral but on all the officers at Masaya, since most of them had families or relatives then in Granada. Accordingly it was resolved that Corral should go to Walker's camp with full powers to treat for peace, and D. Pedro Rouhaud returned late on the evening of the 22d with the gratifying intelligence.

Col. Fry, with a mounted escort of Americans, was immediately ordered to the neighborhood of Masaya, to meet the Legitimist general, and accompany him to Granada. A little after nine o'clock on the morning of the 23d, it was announced that Corral, with the escort, had reached the powder-house, just outside of the city, on the Masaya road ; and Walker, with a number of the democratic officers, rode out to meet him. The commanders of the two forces, after saluting each other, rode side by side through the main street leading to the Plaza. As they passed, the doors and windows of the houses were filled with women and children, dressed in the bright colors affected by the people of the country, and smiling through tears at the prospect of peace. On the Plaza the whole democratic force was drawn up to receive the commanding-general of the Legitimists ; and arms were put into the hands of many of the California passengers, and they were drawn up in as good array as possible, to impress Corral with an idea of the American strength of the democratic army. Then the two commanders retired to the government house, in order to open negotiations.

Corral produced his authority from Estrada, empowering him *omnimodamente*—in all respects—to treat for the Legitimist government without the necessity for ratification, thus beforehand making his acts the acts of the government. Walker had no powers from the government whose commission he held ; and Corral treated with him simply as colonel commanding the forces occupying Granada—it being understood that, in case a treaty was agreed on, it should be sent to Leon for ratification. The Legitimist general seemed disposed to take the lead in the negotiation, and Walker permitted him to develop freely the terms he desired, saying little by way either of objection or amendment. After some consultation, the outlines of a treaty were agreed on, and Corral undertook to draw it up for signature.

The treaty, therefore, as signed, was nearly altogether the work of Corral. By it peace was established between the contending parties, and a Provisional Government was established, with D. Patricio Rivas as executive, for the space of fourteen months, unless an election was previously called. Walker was to be placed in command of the army, and all officers of both sides were to retain their respective ranks and rates of pay. All debts contracted during the war, by either party, were to become debts of the Republic; and to provide for the liquidation of these claims, a Minister of Public Credit was to be added to the usual Cabinet officers. At Corral's suggestion, the Americans were to be retained in the military service of the State ; and the only clause in the treaty inserted at Walker's instance, without a previous suggestion from Corral, was that by which the articles of the Constitution of 1838, concerning naturalization, were to remain the law of the land. All badges of previous parties were to be thrown aside, and the troops of the Republic were to wear a blue ribbon with the device, " Nicaragua Independiente." The foreigners, principally French, who had been in the Legitimist service, were to remain in the army or not, at their choice ; and the contracts made with them as to pay and lands, as well as those made with the Americans by Castellon, became obligations of the State. Martinez was to remain in command at Managua, and Xatruch at Rivas.

On the afternoon of the 23d, Corral and Walker were together, at the house of a merchant of the city, when news came that a steamer was in sight, apparently from San Carlos. The Americans, as well as the native Democrats, were suspicious of bad faith, and apprehended an attack might be made on them while the enemy was appearing to treat. These suspicions turned out to be groundless, as the vessel was the Central America, which had come from Toro Rapids with the news that the Legitimist garrisons at San Carlos and at Castillo had disappeared, thus leaving the river open for the safe passage of those going to the Atlantic side. Thus the props of the Legitimists seemed to crumble and give way under the influence of the loss of Granada.

The treaty having been signed Corral at once returned to Mayasa, with the understanding that he would enter Granada at a time to be hereafter agreed upon between himself and Walker. The Transit passengers then in Granada left the same day, and Capt. Joseph N. Scott carried to Don Patricio Rivas the news of events at Granada, and the offer to bring him immediately to the capital by the Company's steamer. Valle and Ferrer were despatched to Leon with the treaty, and with the request from Walker that the democratic force be withdrawn from the attack on Managua.

In the meantime, means had been provided for setting the Provisional Government in motion as soon as Rivas arrived. Among the passengers by the Cortes, arriving on the 3d of October, was Mr. C. J. Macdonald, a Scotchman, who had been for some time resident in California. He was introduced to Walker by Col. Gilman, with the assurance from the latter that he possessed the confidence of Garrison, the agent of the Accessory Transit Company at San Francisco. Macdonald was at Granada when the treaty was signed, and proposed to advance twenty thousand dollars of the treasure in transit from California to New York on the faith of the new government. French, being Commissary of War, brought the proposition to Walker, and the latter refused to take advantage of it without knowing Macdonald's authority to act. Accordingly a power from C. K. Garrison to Macdonald, vaguely drawn, but still constituting him a general agent in Nicaragua, was shown, and, after asking Gilman particularly about the relations between Macdonald and Garrison in California, so as to be able to interpret the power fully, Walker acceded to the proposition. The bars were landed from the steamer under protest from Scott, and Macdonald drew on Charles Morgan in New-York for the value of them. Obligations were given by the Commissary of War pledging the State to repayment with interest, and securing the debt by pledging dues from the Accessory Transit Company. It may be worth while to state that the drafts of Macdonald on Morgan were duly honored.

This amount was of signal service at the time, for the governments of both Leon and Granada were then entirely without means. Soon after the Democrats occupied Granada, a contribution had been levied by the prefect on the Department, but little had been collected under it. The treasurer of the Fund of Public Instruction should, according to all accounts, have had some thousands of the public moneys in his possession; when, however, he was called on to produce the fund with a view of placing it,' for a time, in the general fund, he paid over to the Treasurer of State only a few hundred dollars. To show the utter destitution of the Legitimists it is only necessary to state that the day after the treaty was signed, Corral drew on Walker for five hundred dollars to pay the daily expenses of the force at Masaya and Managua.

A day or two after the treaty was signed a general order was read forbidding the use of the red ribbon, and commanding the democratic force in Granada to mount the blue ribbon, with the device " Nicaragua Independiente." There were loud murmurs on the part of the

Leoneses when the order was published, and some of them absolutely refused to take the red ribbon from their hats. Several were punished before the order could be enforced, and afterward some of the ardent Democrats would tie a narrow piece of red about their musket barrels. It is possible that Corral had some of the same difficulties in substituting the blue for the white; but the Legitimists were far more orderly and submissive to authority than were the Democrats.

On the 28th it was agreed between the two commanders that Corral and his troops should, on the next day, enter Granada. At an early hour the hum of preparation was heard in the city, and about eleven o'clock it was announced that the Legitimists were on the edge of the town. The democratic force, American as well as native, was drawn up in line of battle on the western side of the Plaza, and Corral marched in by the street from the Masaya road. Thus, in case of any hostile movement—and there were many suspicions of such—on the part of the Legitimists, the Democrats would have been able to act with advantage from the public square down the streets leading to it. The accidental discharge of a single musket or rifle would have led to serious consequences, for each party was suspicious of the good faith of the other. Fortunately no disagreeable or untoward incident occurred. The two commanders approached each other near the centre of the square, and, after embracing, dismounted, walking arm in arm to the church on the east side of the Plaza. Attended by numerous officers, both Legitimist and Democratic, they were met at the door of the church by Father Vigil

6*

and conducted toward the high altar. A Te Deum was sung, and then Corral and Walker passed from the church to the government house, on the opposite side of the square. The troops marched from the Plaza toward the several quarters assigned them, with orders to the officers to keep the soldiers out of the streets and away from the liquor-shops during the day, so that no affray might arise to disturb the general peace of the city.

D. Patricio Rivas having arrived on the 30th, it was decided that his inauguration should take place immediately. The Cabildo was the scene of the ceremony, and a table was prepared within the railing which separates the raised portion of the public chamber from the part occupied by the people. A crucifix with an open copy of the Gospels was placed on one end of the table, and Father Vigil took his seat to put in form the procés verbal recording the installation. The formal record being completed, D. Patricio Rivas knelt on a cushion before the crucifix swearing to observe the treaty of the 23d of October, and to perform the duties of Provisional President in accordance with its stipulations. Then Corral, by a slight gesture, intimated to Walker that they both were to take an oath on the occasion. No agreement of the sort had been made on the subject, and it is possible that Corral had no sinister purpose in thus attempting to take Walker by surprise. But the American did not appear to hesitate. Kneeling in the same manner with the President, he swore on the Holy Gospels to observe, and cause to be observed, the treaty of the 23d, and Corral took the same oath, the form of it being prepared in his own handwriting. After the oath had been taken and recorded, all retired to their several quarters, Corral and the President abiding together at that time.

In fact, for two or three days Corral seemed to have the new executive in his keeping. The afternoon of the 29th he clearly thought the Legitimists had gained the advantage over the Leoneses ; for passing by the house of Niña Yrena, who stood at the door to ask the general what he thought of the turn affairs had taken, he replied in the language of the cock-pit, " We have beaten them (the Democrats) with their own cock." The Niña shook her head incredulously, but Corral was in high spirits, and would not listen to her doubts.

Rivas had been collector of customs for the port of San Juan del Norte, resident at Castillo, or San Carlos, under the Legitimist government ; and although moderate in his political opinions, was naturally disposed to take part with the Granadinos against the Leoneses. Corral was forthwith made minister of war and also minister general ; and nothing was said to Walker about the formation of a Cabinet. On the 30th, a decree from the ministry appointed Walker commander-in-chief; and the minister intimated to him that it would be necessary to take an oath of office. When Corral, on the morning of the 31st, invited Walker to the executive chamber in order to administer the oath, he remarked that it was a mere form, but in accordance with usage. Although Walker had been educated a Protestant, he had no objections to kneeling before the crucifix—the symbol of salvation to all Christians—and if the Legitimist expected to gain a point by the refusal of the American to take the oath, he was, as in the case the day before, disappointed.

On the 31st, Jerez, with a number of the leading citizens of Leon arrived at Granada, bearing the news of the ratification of the treaty by the Provisional Director, D. Nasario Escoto and his cabinet. At the same time Walker received decrees of the government at Leon, issued some days previously, promoting him first, to the rank of brigadier-general, then to the rank of general of division. The appearance of the Leoneses evidently annoyed Corral; and he had not expected so ready a ratification of the treaty. Their presence was, on the contrary, very acceptable to the new commander-in-chief; for there were previously no native Democrats at Granada, sufficiently familiar with public business to take part in the administration.

Carlos Thomas had been much worried by the course of the new President before the arrival of Jerez and the Democrats. He had signified to Don Patricio that matters would go badly if he continued to remain entirely in the hands of Corral. The brother of Don Carlos also, D. Emilio Thomas, a man of excellent sense, and of most honorable character, perceived the error of Rivas in trusting implicitly to the counsels of the minister of war, and did what he could to change the course affairs seemed to be taking. The President saw that it would be necessary for him to rely on some others than Corral, if he expected to bring the Democrats to the support of his administration; and, therefore, he came to consult with Walker in reference to the formation of a cabinet.

As the Legitimists were represented in the cabinet by their former commander-in-chief, it was only fair that the Democrats should insist on the appointment of Jerez to the Ministry of Relations. Walker suggested this ; but when it was mentioned to Corral, he evinced the most bitter opposition to the proposal. He thought it would be impossible for himself and Doctor Jerez—as he insisted on calling the general, D. Maximo—to act together in the same cabinet. The principles of Jerez were, according to his opinion, disorganizing and de- structive of all civil society. The name of D. Buena- ventura Selva was also mentioned ; but he was, if pos- sible, more unpalatable, than Jerez. To D. Fermin Ferrer, as Minister of Public Credit, no serious objection was made ; and as French was ambitious of a seat in the cabinet, it was agreed in the struggle between the two parties, that he should be appointed Minister of Hacienda. The main difficulty was concerning the Minister of Relations ; and Rivas, seeing Walker insist on the appointment of Jerez, finally overcame or silenced the objections of Corral, and the cabinet was completed with the name of the chief the Leoneses.

The government, then, of President Rivas being fully organized, under the treaty of the 23d, by the appoint- ment of Jerez. Minister of Relations, Corral, Minister of War, Ferrer, Minister of Public Credit, and French, Min- ister of Hacienda, the first step was to establish the army on a peace footing. With this view all the natives in Granada who desired discharges obtained them. The desire of the soldiers to go to their homes was universal, the military service being distasteful to most of them. On the 4th of November the Legitimist troops who had marched in from Masaya were entirely disbanded, and not many of the native Democrats remained in the service. Thus one of the first results of the treaty was to release more than fifteen hundred men from the ranks of the army, sending them forth to supply the demand for labor then existing generally throughout the State.

The Americans thus remained the chief military defence of the government, and all parties looked to them for the maintenance of peace and order. It was through their instrumentality that the treaty was made; not a treaty, as has been often said, made by two military chiefs, but sanctioned and ratified by two contending governments representing the parties into which the whole people of the country was divided. The act of the twenty-third of October was, therefore, in the fullest sense of the word, the act of the sovereignty of Nicaragua; and therefore no party had the right to say that the Americans were domiciliated in the State and engaged in its military service without its consent. The contract of Castellon was acknowledged by the Legitimist authorities as the contract of the Republic. Both Democrats and Legitimists expressed gratitude for the services the Americans had already rendered; and the new Provisional Government, whose orders were now recognized and obeyed throughout the whole State, looked to them as its tower of strength and bulwark of defence.

But in the midst of the general joy for peace there suddenly arose a voice to disturb the public repose. On the morning of the 5th of November Valle brought to Walker a package of letters which had been given him by a courier Martinez despatched from Managua to the

Honduras frontier. The courier, it seems, was a democrat who had been imprisoned at Managua, as he alleged, for political offences ; and Martinez-had given him his liberty in order that he might carry the letters intrusted to him as far as Yuscaran. After getting away from Managua, however, the democrat suspecting there was something wrong in the package of papers given him, turned his steps toward Granada, and on arriving there delivered the letters to Valle. Walker found one of the letters addressed, in the handwriting of Corral, to D. Pedro Xatruch at Tegucigalpa, and another in the same handwriting to the Señora D. Ana Arbizu also at Tegucigalpa. Another of the letters was addressed to the same Doña Ana in the handwriting of Martinez ; and as the Señora Arbizu was known to be a friend of Guardiola, the letters were opened and the two from Corral were sufficient to amaze any one who had heard him a few days before solemnly swear to observe the treaty of the twenty-third.

The letter addressed to D. Pedro Xatruch read as follows :—" Friend Don Pedro : We are badly, badly, badly off. Remember your friends. They have left me what I have on, and I hope for your aid. Your friend, P. Corral." That addressed to the Señora Arbizu was marked " private," and read : " Granada, November 1st, 1855. General D. Santos Guardiola : My Esteemed Friend : It is necessary that you write to friends to advise them of the danger we are in, and that they work actively. If they delay two months there will not then be time. Think of us and of your offers. I salute your lady ; and commend your friend who truly esteems you and kisses

your hand, P. Corral. Nicaragua is lost; lost Honduras, San Salvador and Guatemala, if they let this get
body. Let them come quickly if they would meet auxiliaries."

In order to fully understand these letters it is necessary to remember that just after the treaty was signed
Guardiola and D. Pedro Xatruch had left Masaya for
Honduras, by way of Segovia, they having there heard
of the entrance of Lopez into Comayagua on the morning of the 14th of October, and of the flight of Cabañas
to San Salvador. The letter of Corral to Guardiola
shows that the latter had made offers of assistance and
letters from D. Florencio Xatruch, contained in the same
package placed in Valle's hands and forwarded by Martinez, showed his desire to return with his brother and
friend to Honduras, but that he had been detained at the
urgent entreaties of Legitimist comrades. Hence the
insertion by Corral in the treaty of the clause leaving
Managua in the hands of Martinez and Rivas in the
hands of Xatruch. And the plot was clearly against
the Americans; for the "if they let this get body"
could refer to none else.

As soon as Walker read these letters the guard was
strengthened, and orders were given to let none pass
out of the town. Officers were sent to the houses of
the principal Legitimists, requesting their presence at
Walker's quarters, and the President and members of
the Cabinet were invited to attend at the same place.
When all had assembled the letters of Corral were produced, and the commander-in-chief charged him with
treason, by inviting the enemies of the State to invade

Nicaragua, and conspiring with them for the purpose of overturning the existing government. The minister of war admitted that he wrote the letters ; most of those present knew his handwriting, and every one saw their genuineness. All appeared surprised at the contents of them, none more so than D. Patricio Rivas ; and a general stupefaction appeared to pervade the Legitimists. Among the Democrats there was an expression of suppressed pleasure, and the energy of Jerez was especially observed. He suggested at once that Martinez should be ordered to Granada, and a new commandant be appointed for Managua. Accordingly the orders were made out by himself, Pascual Fonseca, the sub-prefect, being put in command of the troops in place of Martinez. The latter, however, had in the meanwhile heard of events at Granada, and taking a boat, with a few followers, he crossed the lake to Segovia, thence flying to Honduras.

The leading Legitimists at Granada were placed under guard ; and charges were made out against Corral for treason and conspiracy to overturn the government of the Republic. A court martial was ordered to try him, on the charges and specifications : for there was no existing civil tribunal before which to arraign him, and besides, being a military officer, he could, according to the laws of the country, be called on to answer only in the military forum. The court consisted of Americans, for there were few other officers of the army in Granada ; and Corral, far from objecting to the court, preferred the naturalized to the native Nicaraguans as his judges. Colonel Hornsby was president of the

court ; Colonel Fry, judge advocate ; and French acted as the counsel for the prisoner.   D. Carlos Thomas
was sworn as interpreter of the court.

The court martial met on the 6th, and the testimony
was short but conclusive.   The accused scarcely denied
the charges ; he asked only for mercy.   The condition
of his family was brought before the court, in order, if
possible, to enlist its sympathy.   The prisoner was
found guilty on all the charges and specifications, and
the sentence was " Death by shooting" ; but the court
unanimously recommended him to the mercy of the
commander-in-chief.

The general-in-chief, however, considered that in this
case mercy to one would be injustice to many.   Walker
had solemnly sworn, with bended knee and on the Holy
Evangelists, to observe and have observed the treaty of
the twenty-third of October ; and he was responsible
before the world, and especially to the Americans in
Nicaragua—as well as before the throne of Heaven—for
the faithful observance of his oath.   How could the
treaty continue to have the force of law if the first violation of it—and that too by the very man who had
signed it—was permitted to pass unpunished ?   As an
act of right and justice, none could reasonably impugn
the sentence of the court, and Walker considered the
question of policy as clear and unequivocal as the
question of justice.   Not only did duty to the Americans
in Nicaragua demand the execution of the sentence, but
it was politic and humane to make their enemies feel
that there was a power in the State capable and resolved to punish any offences against their interests.

Mercy to Corral would have been an invitation to all the Legitimists to engage in like conspiracies, and would have involved them in future difficulties, which many of them managed to escape. It was after such reflections as these that Walker determined to approve the sentence of the court, and Corral was, accordingly, ordered to be shot at mid-day on the eighth of November.

As soon as the sentence was published, the sympathy of the people for the prisoner was everywhere shown. His mild and gentle demeanor had conciliated the friendship of those among whom he had long lived ; and without the stern manner of Chamorro, he had won more the affection of his party. Father Vigil, after ministering to the spiritual wants of the unhappy man, asked that the rigor of the sentence might be relaxed in his behalf ; but he soon saw that the mind of the general-in-chief was fixed, and desisted from efforts clearly useless. Then the night before the fatal day the daughters of Corral, accompanied by many of the women of the city, came with sobs and anguish and tears to attempt what the priest had failed to accomplish. But he who looks only at present grief, nor sees in the distance the thousand-fold sorrow a misplaced mercy may create, is little suited for the duties of public office ; and hard as it was to resist such entreaties as the daughters of the prisoner pressed, Walker promised them to consider the pleas they had urged, and closed the painful interview as soon as kind feeling permitted.

The next day the hour of execution was postponed from 12 m. to 2 p. m., and at the appointed hour the sentence was executed under the direction of Colonel Gilman, the officer of the day.

The remaining Legitimists who had been placed under guard for a short time were released, with the exception of D. Narciso Espinosa. There was some vague and uncertain evidence as to his complicity in the plot to introduce foreign troops into the State for the subversion of the government; but it was not sufficient to justify serious proceedings against him. In the then condition of affairs, however, it was judged well for him to leave the Republic, and he was accordingly sent to New-York by one of the steamers of the Accessory Transit Company. His conduct in the United States was such as might be expected of a man without principle and without shame.

The Ministry of War made vacant by the arrest of Corral' was filled by D. Buenaventura Selva, who had held the same office under the government of Castellon. Although a native of Granada, and having numerous connections there, he was among the most decided of the democrats. The family of which he was a member was large, and much divided in its political affinities. Don Hilario was a moderate Legitimist; and one of the sisters married to Narciso Espinosa, was among the bitterest and most violent of the same party. Several of the other sons, Pedro Ygenio, Domingo, Raymundo, and Gregorio, were Democrats; and the mother of them all, while not very decided between the native parties, was firm in her friendship for the Americans, and devoted in her attentions to the sick or such as needed her assistance. The divisions of this family are but one instance out of the many produced by the unhappy wars of Nicaragua; and too often political parties were used for the purpose of gratifying family feuds and domestic hatreds.

On the 10th of November the government of Rivas was recognized by the American Minister. The Minister was escorted from the Legation to the Executive Chamber, and as he passed the President's guard, arms were presented, and the march beat. The chamber was filled with officers both native and American, and Mr. Wheeler, after being presented to the President, delivered an address congratulating the country on the peace just secured for it. D. Patricio Rivas made a suitable reply, saying that the relations between the United States and Nicaragua were now of more importance than ever, " since the Republic counts on new and powerful elements of liberty and order which cause us to conceive well-founded hopes that the country will march with a firm step in the path of progress toward the greatness offered it by its free institutions and natural advantages."

With the reception of Mr. Wheeler the administration of Rivas may be said to have fairly commenced ; and the course of events might have been very different if the federal administration at Washington had frankly approved the conduct of its representative. But let us not murmur at the Providence which works out its own ends by its own means.

Chapter Fifth.

THE ADMINISTRATION OF RIVAS.

In tracing the introduction of the American element into Nicaraguan society, it has hitherto been convenient to follow events in the order of time. As the facts become more complex it will be requisite to group them so that their relative relations may be distinctly seen, and thus the policy of the Rivas administration may appear with the unity it really possessed. The domestic policy of the government first claims our attention: for its foreign relations were the consequences of the internal changes it aimed to effect. Thus, too, we may clearly perceive the cause of the war which afterward raged in Nicaragua.

From the outset the Provisional President aimed to heal the civil discords, which had heretofore divided not only districts but even families. With this view appointments to the principal offices were made indifferently from both of the old parties, and the Legitimists were, in spite of the Corral conspiracy, invited to share with the Democrats in the duties of government. Rivas was himself moderate in his political opinions and was much disposed to place in office men of the same stamp. He was also honest and, therefore, desired the co-operation of all " hombres de bien," good men, in the Republic. Hence his gratification when he was able to secure for the service of the State such men as D. José, Maria Hurtado, who occupied the place of prefect of the Meridional Department. His aversion to the dishonest Democrats, such as Trinidad Salazar, forced on him by the Leonese element in his cabinet, was strong, and it was with reluctance that he consented to appoint such men to responsible offices.

The authorities of the Church zealously co-operated with the civil power to allay the passions which had so long divided the State, and the servants of Christ did not fail in their public as in their private ministrations, to inculcate the doctrines of peace and good-will characteristic of their faith. Soon after the inauguration of the new government, the vicar-general, Father José Hilario Herdocia, wrote from Leon, the seat of the See of Nicaragua, congratulating Walker on the success of his efforts to secure peace ; and the general-in-chief, in his reply, was careful to deny the charge of irreligion the enemies of the Americans had brought against them. " It is very acceptable," so the general wrote, " for me to hear that the authority of the Church will be used in favor of the existing government. Without the aid of religious sentiments and religious teachers there can be no good government ; for the fear of God is the foundation of all social and political organization....... In God I put my trust for the success of the cause in which I am embarked and for the maintenance of the principles I advocate. Without his aid all human efforts are unavailing, but with his divine assistance a few may triumph over a legion." The bishopric of the diocese being vacant, the vicar-general was the highest ecclesiastical authority of the State, and during all the trials through which the Republic passed, Father Herdocia worthily and faithfully performed the duties of his holy office. Had the good father been able to influence by his conduct all the priests within his diocese, the dissensions of the country would have been speedily cured. But, unfortunately in Nicaragua as elsewhere the tonsure does not always destroy the earthly passions of the mortal; and the emblematic crown of thorns may be worn by those possessed of little of the spirit of humility which adorned the Holy Redeemer.

To secure internal order, however, Rivas did not rely so much on the efforts of the civil and ecclesiastical authorities to extinguish the party passions of the past, as on the speedy increase of the American element in the government of the Republic. Therefore one of his earliest decrees was that of colonization. By this decree each adult immigrating to the State was entitled to two hundred and fifty acres from the public lands, and after six months' residence on it might secure a title for the same. A family was entitled to a hundred additional acres, and all personal effects, furniture, agricultural implements, 'seeds, plants, and domestic animals, were permitted to pass in free of duty. A director of colonization, Mr. Joseph W. Fabens, was appointed to carry out the objects of the decree, and to collect seeds and plants for the use of immigrants. The decree was published the 23d of November, 1855.

As a means of diffusing information concerning the natural resources and advantages of Nicaragua, no less than as a chronicle of current events, the newspaper called " El Nicaraguense " had been established at Granada soon after the signature of the treaty of peace. It was printed with types found in the town at the time of its capture, and one half of the paper was published in English, the other half in Spanish. To collect such knowledge of the country as might be useful to immigrants, commissioners were sent into different parts of the Republic, and their reports were duly published. First, George H. Campbell, formerly of Calaveras county, California, explored a portion of Chontales. Then a Saxon, Max Sonnenstern, visited not only Chontales, but other districts, and his reports were full of useful facts. These surveys were made under the direction of the general-in-chief, and the expenses of them were paid almost entirely from the chest of the commissary of war. In fact, for some time, there was no other fund from which to defray the civil no less than the military expenses of the State.

But in addition to these acts, by which it was expected to introduce American colonists into Nicaragua, a decree was also published authorizing the general-in-chief to increase the American element of the army. Under the contract of Castellon, dated in the July previous, Walker was empowered to raise three hundred men for the military service of the State ; and early in December Jerez drew up the decree fixing the pay and emoluments of those enlisted by the general. Before this the question has probably suggested itself as to the

7

means by which Americans had been already brought to Granada; and the answer to this involves the policy which was pursued in reference to the Accessory Transit Company. As the course the Rivas government pursued toward this corporation has been much misrepresented and censured, it is necessary to narrate fully the facts as they occurred, and to explain clearly the causes for the revocation of the company's charter. It will then be seen that this important act of the Rivas administration was vital to its safety and welfare, no less than just toward a corporation which had abused the privileges granted to it.

Before leaving San Francisco Walker had tried to ascertain the wishes of the Transit Company concerning the introduction of Americans into Nicaragua. It was generally said that the company was indebted to the Republic in a large amount, and Walker hoped to secure its co-operation by proposing an advantageous mode of settling this debt. But the agent of the company in California stated that his principals had instructed him to have nothing to do with such enterprises as he supposed Walker to contemplate. The company, however, did not practise that neutrality between the contending parties in Nicaragua, its instructions to the California agent seemed to inculcate. In July, 1855, they sent from New-York to Castillo a company of armed men, organized militarily for the purpose, as was alleged, of protecting their property on the Isthmus. These men were mostly Europeans—Poles, French, Germans, and Italians. A brother of Walker happened to be aboard of the steamer which carried these men from New-York to San

Juan del Norte, and saw them, a few days after leaving the former display, the uniform provided for their use in Nicaragua. After remaining several weeks at Castillo, most of these men were engaged by D. Patricio Rivas at San Carlos for the service of the Legitimist government, and were a part of the force under Corral during the months of September and October.

These men, gathered from all nations and professing to be nothing but pure mercenaries, using their arms for no higher purpose than the pay they got, were intended for the special object of protecting the property of the company from one H. L. Kinney, who, it was said, aimed at punishing the corporation for the wrongs he fancied he had received at its hands. Kinney had been engaged in trade on the frontier between Texas and Mexico, and had been suspected by many Texans, during the days of independence, of giving information to their enemies for the privilege of trading beyond the Rio Grande. He had acquired that sort of knowledge and experience of human nature derived from the exercise of the mule-trade, and having succeeded in making money, by bargaining for horses and cattle, he fancied himself capable of establishing an American colony on the Musquito shore. Alleging that he had an interest in the Shepard and Haley grant from the Musquito chief, he went to Washington for the purpose of interesting influential persons in his colonization schemes. Through the instrumentality of one Phillips, a Washington correspondent for newspapers, he made the acquaintance of Sidney Webster, the private secretary of the President ; and Webster becoming interested in

Kinney's projects, it was surmised that Mr. Pierce and the government would be favorable to them. It was also reported—but with how much truth it is almost impossible from the character of the witnesses to determine —that the Accessory Transit Company engaged to cooperate with Kinney. But the United States Government, willingly or unwillingly, was led by the remonstrances of Marcoleta, the representative of Nicaragua at Washington, to take steps against the Kinney movement. Then, too, the Accessory Transit Company pronounced against the colonial projector, and Kinney, breathing fire against the traitors, as he called them, escaped to San Juan del Norte with an inconsiderable body of followers. Hence the pretext for the mercenaries who finally fell into the ranks of the Legitimists.

In the month of June, Estrada had appointed D. Gabriel Lacayo and D. Rafael Tejada commissioners, to proceed to New-York, and to treat with the company concerning its liabilities to the State, and Castellon soon afterward notified the corporation that he would consider null and void any settlement made with these commissioners. In July, Castellon appointed Colonel Walker commissioner to negotiate and arrange with the company, and that officer showed his credentials to the agent, Mr. Cushing, a few hours after the action at Virgin Bay on the 3d of September. Mr. Cushing, as he said, notified the company of Walker's powers, but nothing was ever attempted to be arranged under this authority. During September and October, while the democratic forces occupied the Transit, their relations with the agents and servants of the company were of the most friendly character.

When Colonel Gilman arrived at San Juan del Sur he gave Walker to understand that there was a struggle in the company itself, between rivals parties aiming to get the control of it. The impression made on Walker was that the agents in New-York and San Francisco were acting together to depress the market price of the stock, so as to buy in and get the majority of the shares. The advance by Macdonald, however, indicated another plan on the part of Garrison and Morgan. With the conviction that Garrison might be brought to co-operate largely in the policy of introducing the American element into Nicaragua, Walker wrote to an intimate friend, A. P. Crittenden, of San Franscisco, saying that any arrangements he might make to get five hundred men into the country would be fully approved. This letter was written immediately after the signature of the treaty of peace ; the necessity for more Americans in Nicaragua was urgent, and Walker had entire faith in Crittenden's honor and discretion.

Meanwhile the president of the company in New-York was, early in the month of November, peremptorily notified, under a clause of the charter, to appoint commissioners to settle the matters in controversy with the government. To the notification given by the Minister of Hacienda the company replied, enclosing an opinion of the counsel of the corporation, Joseph L. White. The opinion maintained that the matter had passed from the hands of the company, by the appointment of two commissioners to treat with Tejada and Lacayo, although the powers of these latter had been formally revoked, and the four, even if properly appointed, had not, as the charter required, appointed a fifth to complete the commission. The answer of the president of the company was a mere evasion ; and while this official correspondence went on, White, who was the leading mind of the corporation, was writing letters to the agent, Mr. Cushing, threatening the authorities unless they settled with the company on its own terms.

On the 17th of December, 1855, Edmund Randolph, accompanied by W. R. Garrison, a son of C. K. Garrison, and by Macdonald, arrived at San Juan del Sur, and soon afterward reached the headquarters of the army at Granada. The friendship between Randolph, Crittenden, and Walker, was of a character not to be expressed by words ; but the existence of such a sentiment between these three is essential for an understanding of the perfect confidence which marked their acts in reference to the Transit. And to the noblest qualities of the heart, Randolph and Crittenden added the loftiest attributes of the intellect. To those who have heard the former at the bar, it will not be deemed the voice of friendship alone speaking, when it is said that his legal talents are such as would adorn courts when learning, and logic, and eloquence, were more appropriate to the profession than they appear to be in these latter days. And they who have studied the legislation of California —not the evanescent laws born of party passion or impure interest, but those which mould society, and form its habits—can best appreciate the capacity, and the patient labor of Parker Crittenden.

After reaching Granada, Randolph informed Walker that he and Crittenden had carefully examined the charter of the Accessory Transit Company, and were both clear and decided in the opinion that it had been forfeited. Then he stated what the lawyers would call the points of the case ; and they were almost too clear for argument. As they are fully stated in the decree whereby the charter of the Transit Company, and of the Atlantic and Pacific Ship Canal Company were revoked, they will properly appear when the publication of that decree is narrated. Suffice it to say, at present, that after due reflection Walker was entirely satisfied as to the views of Randolph and Crittenden. At the same time Walker was informed that under his letter Crittenden had agreed with Garrison to obtain a new transit charter from the government of Nicaragua, and with this view Randolph had come to Granada. In virtue of this agreement of Crittenden with Garrison, more than a hundred Americans for the service of the Republic came down with Randolph on the steamer Sierra Nevada ; and it was promised that as many as possible should be hereafter brought from California ; Garrison advancing to the State the price of their passages.

Up to that time nearly all the Americans in Nicaragua had come from California, and a very large proportion of them had been brought thither at the expense of Garrison. The immigration into the country by persons paying their own passage was small ; for at that time little was known in the United States of the natural advantages of Nicaragua. It was necessary to get at once a number of persons capable of bearing arms into the State ; and none were more urgent in this policy, or more anxious when the steamer arrived to hear how many passengers were for Nicaragua, than the Provisional President and the members of his cabinet. Internal order as well as freedom from foreign invasion depended, in their eyes, entirely on the rapid arrival of some hundreds of Americans.

It will thus appear that the agreement of Crittenden with Garrison was the means, and at that time, the only means, for carrying out the policy vital to the Rivas administration.   True, neither the President nor the cabinet knew of the means whereby their objects were accomplished ; and it was in fact highly necessary to the success of the measures that they should be known by as few persons as possible.   After Randolph and Walker had agreed on the terms of a new transit grant, a copy was sent up to Garrison at San Francisco, Macdonald being the bearer of it.   W. R. Garrison went to New-York for the purpose of informing Charles Morgan of the arrangements which had been, and were about to be made ; while Randolph remained in Granada to await the return of these parties.   Nothing was said to Rivas of the new transit contract, Walker and Randolph had drawn up and agreed to.

At length Macdonald arrived again from San Francisco, and W. R. Garrison from New-York, and it was decided that the blow should be struck.   Randolph had been living at the house of Niña Yrena, and was in bad health ; therefore Walker went to his room in order that they might draw up the decree of revocation.   It was necessary, in an act of such importance, to state clearly and fully the causes for it, so that it might appear properly before the world.   Hence the considerations of the decree were drawn with no common care.   As the Acces-

sory Transit Company held its charter for the sole purpose of facilitating the building of a ship canal, the destruction of the Canal Company implied the destruction
of the Accessory Transit. Hence the decree recites the
failure of the Ship Canal Company to perform its agreements. The company had agreed to contract a ship
canal across Nicaragua, and it had not only failed to
commence the work but had declared it impracticable ;
it had agreed to construct a railroad, or a rail and carriage road, in case the completion of the canal was not
possible, and it had done neither one nor the other ; it
had agreed to pay the Republic annually ten thousand
dollars, together with ten per cent. of the net profits on
any route it might establish between the two oceans,
and it had failed to pay these amounts, falsely and frau-
dulently alleging that no profits were made and no commissions due ; and finally, it had been notified to appoint
commissioners to settle the matter in dispute between the State and the company, and had expressly refused to comply with the demand. If failure to perform its obligations, coupled with falsehood and fraud in
its dealings with the government, and accompanied by
marked contempt of the sovereignty from which it derived its existence, were insufficient to warrant the revocation of the charter, there is small merit in law
or its remedies.

At the same time the charters of the companies were
revoked, three commissioners, D. Cleto Mayorga, E. J.
C. Kewen, and George F. Alden, were appointed to ascertain the amount due from the Canal Company to the
State ; and for this purpose they were ordered by the

7*

decree to notify the agents of the companies to appear before them forthwith. They were also commanded to cause all the property of the companies to be seized and held by responsible persons, subject to the order of the Board. Ignorant and prejudiced people have said the property of the companies was confiscated ; but this is untrue. The seizure was in the language of the civil law prevailing in Nicaragua, a provisional one for the purpose of securing the payment of the debt due from the company to the government. And, in order to preserve the property, it was in the meantime placed in the hands of persons giving the necessary bonds. Nor was the condition that the property be forthcoming when called for by the Board of Commissioners the sole agreement of the undertakers on the bond. In order that the transit of passengers might not be interrupted, they were required to transport the passengers who might arrive on the sides of the Atlantic and Pacific oceans, the expenses of such transportation to be charged against the companies.

After the decree of revocation was drawn up in English, Walker broached the subject to the Provisional President, and to D. Fermin Ferrer, then acting as Minister General ; and neither of them made any objections to the measure. In fact, there was a general prejudice on the part of the Nicaraguans against the Accessory Transit Company, because of the arrogant tone it had used on all occasions toward the authorities of the Republic. As collector of customs at San Carlos, D. Patricio Rivas had frequent opportunities to observe the haughty and overbearing character of the company, and he was gratified at the proposal to take away its privileges. Accordingly, the decree was translated from English into Spanish by Walker, the minister correcting the language of the rough translation. The President signed the decree, not only without hesitation but with undisguised pleasure.

After the decree of revocation was signed, the decree for a new charter to Randolph and his associates was submitted to the President; but there was much difficulty in obtaining his approval of this act. Even at this time the mind of Rivas had been poisoned by evil-disposed persons; and in discussing with D. Fermin Ferrer the new contract, he said it was " a sale of the country," meaning thereby that it placed the government entirely in the hands of the American element. In consequence of Don Patricio's feelings, the translation of the decree for the new charter was so made as to deprive the grantees of many privileges they required; and it became necessary to have the first draught of the Spanish decree materially modified. With much difficulty the signature of Rivas was finally obtained to the decree for the new charter, and it bore date the 19th of February, 1856, the day after the date of the decree of revocation.

Although copies of the decrees had been signed and delivered to Randolph and his associates on the 18th, the publication was delayed until the day after the passengers from California crossed the Lake for San Juan del Norte. Thus Morgan and Garrison had news of the acts before they were known to the companies; and it was an object to give the former as much time as possible, to get ready for running their steamer before the old grantees stopped their line. The advantage of this course was shown some days afterward ; for, on the steamer of the Accessory Transit Company which left New-Orleans on the 27th of February, more than two hundred and fifty passengers for the service of Nicarágua were carried to San Juan del Norte, their passages being paid with drafts of D. Domingo de Goicouria on Cornelius Vanderbilt, the president of the company. Had the decree of the 18th gone to New-Orleans before these passengers left—as it might have done if published a day earlier—they would certainly not have been carried to Nicaragua at the expense of Mr. Vanderbilt or of the company. As it was, the price of these passages was so much secured by the State on the indebtedness due from the corporation.

The necessity for the American element to predominate in the government of Nicaragua sprang from the clauses in the treaty of peace. In order to carry out the spirit of that treaty—to secure to the Americans in the service of the Republic the rights gauranteed to them by the full sovereign power of the State—it was requisite to get into the country a force capable of protecting it, not only from domestic but from foreign enemies. Hence the " sale of the country," in Rivas' use of the term, was a foregone conclusion after the 23d of October. Walker had sworn to have the treaty observed in all respects. He was responsible before Nicaragua and before the world for the faithful execution of it, and above all he was bound to the Americans on the Isthmus to gain for them the strength requisite for the maintenance of their privileges. And for this object it was of the first importance to place the Transit in the hands of those pledged by every consideration of interest to secure the permanence of the new order of things. The old Transit Company aimed at being master of the government; the new charter made the owners of the grant the servants of the State and the agents of its policy. The control of the Transit is, to Americans, the control of Nicaragua: for the lake, not the river as many think, furnishes the key to the occupation of the whole State. Therefore, whoever desires to hold Nicaragua securely, must be careful that the navigation of the lake is controlled by those who are his stanchest and most reliable friends.

The commissioners proceeded, under the decree, to seize the property of the companies, and place it in the keeping of Joseph N. Scott, after he had given a full and satisfactory bond. The subsequent proceedings of the commissioners, and the conduct of the grantees under the new charter, will be hereafter related. In this connection the main object is to show how the policy of Rivas toward the Accessory Transit Company was, as it were, the keystone of the arch supporting his administration. With a different policy the Provisional President would have found himself with a very small force to oppose the combination which threatened him almost from the day he was inaugurated.

Under the influence of these measures of the government, the number of Americans had been rapidly increasing since the first of November, 1855. Mr. Fabens, who was in Granada at the time Walker entered the city, went, soon after the treaty was signed, to San

Juan del Norte, and induced many of the Americans with Kinney to join the army of Nicaragua. On the 7th of November Capt. R. W. Armstrong, with a com-. pany from San Francisco, arrived at Granada, and thus the American force was swelled to upward of two hundred men. After this, until the arrival of Capt. Anderson on the 17th of December, the increase was by small numbers at a time, and in the meanwhile the cholera had appeared at Granada. The disease seemed to select those officers who were most capable and useful, and there were suspicions that the people of the town, mostly Legitimists, were not entirely ignorant of the cause which produced the deaths of leading Americans. Among the first victims of the disease were Capt. Davidson and Col. Gilman; and the death of the latter was a severe loss. Then Capt. Armstrong and Major Jesse Hambleton passed away. The deaths finally became daily, and the frequent sound of the dead march, as the funeral escorts passed through the streets, began to exercise a depressing effect on the troops. The surgical staff was inexperienced, and the services of some volunteers were valuable. Dr. James Nott was the most efficient of these, and many a Nicaraguan, who owed his life to this surgeon's kind and skilful attention, regretted his departure and mourned his death, which occurred on the passage from San Juan del Norte to New-Orleans. It was only after the arrival of Dr. Israel Moses, early in February, 1856, that the surgical staff was well organized and its duties well performed. He gave such order and system to this department of the army that the good effects of his administration were felt long after he ceased to act as surgeon-general. Indeed, it is safe to say that after the appointment of Dr. Moses few military hospitals were better administered than the hospitals at Granada and Rivas.

In spite, however, of the fearful ravages of disease, the number of Americans continued to increase, most of the immigrants coming from California until the month of March, 1856. A few, during January and February, had come from New-York and New-Orleans, but it was not until Goicouria arrived, early in March, that any numbers were received from the Atlantic side. So successful had been the policy of the Rivas administration for the introduction of the new element, that on the 1st of March, 1856, there were upward of twelve hundred Americans, soldiers and citizens, in the Republic, capable of bearing arms. It remains, now, for us to see what effect this domestic policy of the Provisional Government had produced in its foreign relations.

Immediately on the organization of the Rivas Government, the Minister of Relations, Jerez, sent circulars to the several States of Central America, announcing the terms of the treaty of the 23d of October, and expressing friendly feeling for the respective governments to which the circulars were addressed. The State of San Salvador gave an early reply, declaring the gratification of that cabinet in the peace secured to Nicaragua. No replies were received from the other States, and the silence was expressive. It was clear that the clauses in the treaty which secured and encouraged the presence of the Americans in Nicaragua were not acceptable to the neighboring Republics, and the journals of Costa Rica were particularly virulent in their remarks on the course of events in Granada. Guatemala, Honduras, and Costa Rica, were at that time governed by the adherents of the old servile or aristocratic party, while San Salvador was under liberal influences. Gen. Cabañas, driven from Comayagua by the assistance of Guatemala, had found refuge at the mines of Los Encuentros, near the borders of Honduras and San Salvador, and Guardiola was canvassing for the Presidency of the former State, in place of his exiled rival, whose legal term was to expire on the 31st of January, 1856.

General Trinidad Cabañas was the oldest and most respected among the Liberals of Central America. He had been the faithful companion of Morazan in his efforts to preserve the Confederacy, and although generally unfortunate as a soldier, none doubted his courage or his devotion to the principles he professed. Americans who had met him pronounced him the most honest public man within the limits of the five Republics, and his conduct toward the Nicaraguan Democrats had certainly been that of a self-sacrificing man. The aid he gave to Castellon was undoubtedly the cause of his losing power in Honduras, and Walker was easily induced, after the news of the retirement of Cabañas to San Salvador arrived at Granada, to invite the ex-President to visit the capital of Nicaragua.

Cabañas arrived at Leon in the latter part of November, and when it was known that he was on his way to Granada, Col. Hornsby was ordered to Managua to conduct the ex-President to the capital. On the 3d of December he was received by Walker with every mark of respect, and he was entertained as the guest of the State. A guard of honor was placed at his orders, and the attention due a good man in fallen fortunes was scrupulously bestowed. But the Honduranian desired assistance to regain his power in his own State; he asked that a body of Americans might be given him to re-enter the capital from which he had not long been expelled. Jerez urged that the request of Cabañas be granted; he recalled the signal services the ex-President had rendered Castellon and the democratic army. Rivas, however, was not disposed to hearken to the prayers of Cabañas. He saw clearly that if assistance were given to the exiled General-President and an American force entered Honduras, it would be the signal for a coalition of the other four States against Nicaragua.

Walker regarded the plans of Cabañas with the same eye as Rivas. It was easy to perceive that sooner or later there was to be a struggle of force between the American policy of the Nicaraguan cabinet and the other governments by which it was surrounded. But it was expedient and proper to make the enemies of the Americans strike the first blow. To have sent troops to Honduras, even with the design of reëstablishing Cabañas, would have afforded a pretext for the declaration that the Americans of Nicaragua were aggressive in their nature. It was only necessary for the Americans to wait in order to have their enemies move, and it would have been unwise to hasten the struggle by seeking to restore a man, however worthy, who had just been driven from his own State.

Jerez admitted the reasonableness of the views of

Rivas, yet he continued to insist on the aid Cabañas sought. The ex-President was a man of narrow mind, strong prejudices, and bitter animosities, and seemed to have his heart set on getting back to Honduras before the 31st of January. The very obstinacy with which he asked to be restored before the expiration of his time, was a proof of the tendency of his mind to dwell on unimportant points. Incapable of looking at the affairs of Central America with general views, he seemed a Morazan federalist dwindled by age to a Honduras official. But as his opinions had been contracted with time they had hardened also, and with the dull perceptions of age he had its obstinacy and its hatred of new things. Not understanding the American movement, he was disposed to regard it as an evil unless it could be converted to an agency for driving Guardiola and Lopez out of Honduras. The past reputation of Cabañas, however, his long service in the ranks of the Liberal party, together with the feeling of gratitude for the treatment the Nicaraguan Democrats received in Honduras, wrought on the mind of Jerez. The Minister of Relations was readily moved by generous sentiments, and it was not difficult to lead him on a false course through his emotions. His head, too, as one of his friends often said, was filled with the legends Plutarch has palmed off on the world as the lives of his Greek and Roman heroes ; and Jerez was constantly imagining somebody was plotting against the Republic, and that it was his function to save the State. Vega, one of the leading Legitimists, soon after the organization of the Rivas cabinet, sent to Walker a printed paper, on the margin of which there was a sketch of all the ministers, and the shrewd old Granadino described Jerez as a conspirator by nature. It may be readily imagined how Cabañas would act on Jerez after he saw that Walker was determined not to send any of the Americans to Honduras.

After a sojourn of some twenty days at Granada, the ex-President went to Leon accompanied by the minister, Jerez. He would wait at Leon, he said, the final decision of the government in regard to his requests. When Jerez returned, the mind of Rivas was fixed in opposition to the propositions of Cabañas, and then Jerez resigned his place in the ministry. About the same time, D. Buenaventura Selva resigned the ministry of war, because a Legitimist, Arguëllo, was put in office. Jerez retired to Leon ; Selva went first to Rivas and San Juan del Sur, whence he sailed for San Salvador to remain, as he said, until " hombres de bien" were restored to power in Nicaragua. As many Legitimists had been put in office by Rivas before the appointment of Arguëllo, it was probably the private enmity of Selva toward the latter which led to his resignation ; and thus, by the friendship of one Minister for Cabañas, and the hatred of another toward Arguëllo, Ferrer was, for a time, sole minister.

It was not enough, however, that Nicaragua showed, by her course toward Honduras, the policy she sought to follow in relation to Central America. On the 12th of January, 1856, a circular was addressed to the several Republics, declaring the peaceful intentions of Nicaragua, and requesting the appointment of commissioners to discuss and arrange the terms of a union of the separate States. The latter proposition was made because the old serviles, who had always been against Federalism, were now zealously discussing a union, for the purpose of affording pretexts to interfere against the Americans of Nicaragua. It was thus made manifest that the Rivas government, satisfied of the honor and straightforwardness of its intentions, was not afraid of placing itself in closer relations with the other States of the old confederation.

The only response given to this circular was that of the Honduras commissioner, D. Manuel Colindres, who did not get beyond Leon. He had been sent by the government of Honduras to assure Nicaragua of its peaceful purposes; though it is possible his secret design may have been to watch the movements of Cabañas. On the 24th of January, however, Señor Colindres, in acknowledging the receipt of a printed copy of the circular, said he had no doubt his government would reply favorably to that of Nicaragua. But no such answer as the commissioner anticipated was ever received. After Guardiola, however, was elected President of Honduras, he showed little disposition to interfere with the domestic policy of Nicaragua; and the thirst for war his enemies attributed to him was not manifested in his course toward the Central American coalition.

The most violent invectives against the domestic policy of Nicaragua had been published in the official journal of Costa Rica. Besides this, a large number of the Legitimists had fled to Guanacaste, and were thence threatening the tranquillity of the Meridional Department. To remonstrate against the presence of the Legitimists on the frontier, and at the same time to endeavor to correct some of the errors which had spread in Costa Rica, it was decided to send a commissioner to that Republic. Accordingly, on the 4th of February, Louis Schlessinger and Manual Arguëllo, accompanied by Captain W. A. Sutter, left Granada for Virgin Bay, with instructions to proceed to San José. Schlessinger had been selected because he was one of the few among those attached to the American force possessed of any knowledge of Spanish; nor were his previous career and character as well known then as afterward. In fact, he had come to Nicaragua with excellent recommendations from people of repute; and as he had some tact and address, it was thought he might accomplish some of the objects of the commission. D. Manuel Arguëllo was joined with Schlessinger because, being a Legitimist, he might remove prejudices, and probably induce many of his old party to leave Guanacaste and return to their homes and estates near Rivas.

D. Rafael Mora, however, had made up his mind to act at once against Nicaragua. Schlessinger and Sutter were, therefore, ordered out of the Republic; and Arguëllo remained in Costa Rica only to join its army. On the 1st of March, 1856, President Mora formally declared war against the "filibusters," as he styled the Americans of Nicaragua. And in order to trace some of the causes which led to this step, it is necessary to examine events outside of Central America. This brings us to the course the United States and Great Britain pursued in reference to Nicaragua.

Not long after the recognition of the Rivas government by the American Minister at Granada, French was sent as minister from Nicaragua to the United States. He was appointed to that office with a view of getting him out of the Hacienda Department and out of the country. He was utterly unfitted for the administration of the hacienda, having little knowledge of either the principles or details of public business, and not having either the modesty to be sensible of his defects or the patience to overcome them. Moreover, his rapacity made him dreaded by the people of the country, and, as a measure of policy, it was necessary for the Americans to get rid of him. He was, however, of not less character than Marcoleta, a Spaniard, who at the time represented Nicaragua at Washington ; for French had not been ordered out of the State Department for pilfering papers from its archives. On his arrival in the United States it was generally reported that the federal government would not receive the new minister because of his previous history. After waiting for some time French presented his credentials and was refused recognition because it was impossible for the American Secretary of State, Mr. Marcy, to determine whether or not the government he represented was the government of the people of Nicaragua. When it is remembered that Mr. Marcy, in a conversation with Mr. J. W. Fabens, placed Nicaragua among the South American Republics, his inability to decide whether the government of Rivas was in existence or not, need create little surprise. His entire ignorance or wilful misrepresentation of Nicaraguan affairs appears to much advantage in his correspondence with Mr. Wheeler.

From the beginning of the movement Mr. Marcy had set his face against the introduction of Americans into Nicaragua. In one of his first despatches on the subject he spoke of the entrance of Americans into the country as an invasion, and with him the establishment of peace and the provisional government of Rivas was " a successful foray of arms." He censured Mr. Wheeler for his visit to Rivas at the instance of the people of Granada, and intimated that the danger he incurred was the due reward of the minister's efforts to act as mediator between the parties. Hence, it is an error to suppose that the refusal to receive French was owing in any manner to the character of that person. Nor is it more correct to assign the interest certain parties near the President had in the Shepard and Haley grant and in Kinney's schemes, as the reason for the action of the Secretary of State. At that time it was scarcely known what policy the Rivas administration would pursue in reference to the claims on the Mosquito shore. The causes for Mr. Marcy's conduct were far deeper than such as were suggested at the time, and they will prob. ably be seen more clearly in the sequel.

The refusal of the United States government to recognize the Rivas administration created great surprise in Nicaragua, and encouraged the enemies of the Americans in Costa Rica. The public men of Nicaragua, ignorant of the internal machinery of the federal government at Washington, and of the secret springs controlling the actions of parties in the United States, were unable to divine the motives of the cabinet of Mr. Pierce. It was an enigma they could not solve; and while some of the native Nicaraguans attributed the course of the Republic of the north to fear of England, others resorted to the common ground on which political action is always put when it cannot be otherwise reasonably explained, and traced the conduct of the federal cabinet, and more particularly of the Secretary of State, to personal prejudices and passions. All the Nicaraguans saw, however, the effect of the Marcy policy on the neighboring States ; for while it furnished them with an excuse for withholding diplomatic intercourse it also encouraged them to take active and decided measures against the Rivas government.

But while the policy of the United States appeared inexplicable to the people of Central America, that of the British government excited no surprise. From long familiarity with British diplomacy the Spanish-American States are generally able to divine what its course will be, though they scarcely take the trouble to analyze its motives or to arrive at the objects of its policy. Before examining, however, the course of the British cabinet toward the Rivas administration, it may aid us to ascertain, if we can, the motives of English policy in reference to all the Spanish American States. There is a unity in this policy which must spring from a simple motive.

The English policy is as old as the time of Elizabeth, and sprang immediately from the contests of that sovereign with Philip the Second. The privateers, in the habit of plundering the towns of the Spanish main, were the first fruits of the policy. England, shut out from a large portion of America by the jealous colonial regula tions of Spain, sought to make profit out of these countries by the double means of buccaneering and of contraband trade. This system continued during the whole time of the Spanish dominion on the continent; and traces of it yet remain in the settlements at Balize—named after the freebooter and smuggler Wallis—and in the relations of England to the Indians on the Mosquito shore. The object of the policy was not to acquire colonies, but to acquire trade; hence the wood-cutters at Balize were not colonists, but mere floating settlers, with a right to cut mahogany and dye-woods, yet without the right to organize for themselves a society or a government. And in the same manner it was sought to raise the roving tribes of the Mosquito shore into a community claiming, as did the wood-choppers at Balize, the protection of the British crown. The settlers at Balize, and the Indians and Zambos of the Mosquito shore, might be called, in one of the elegant cant phrases of the day, "squatter sovereigns."

When the Spanish colonies declared their independence, the relations between Spain and England were vastly different from what they had been in the time of Elizabeth; and the Peninsula, just emerging from the struggle with Napoleon, supposed her alliance with Great Britain would secure the neutrality of her old rival in the contest between herself and her rebellious subjects. But England, true to her traditional policy, favored by all possible means the independence of the colonies. British arms, British soldiers, and British counsels, were freely furnished to several Spanish-American States, and their independence was speedily acknowledged

8

by the British crown. Then British merchants flocked to the new fields opened to their enterprise, and organized everywhere the old system of the buccaneers and smugglers. They found the new governments fit tools of their system. Open and general bribery of customhouse officers supplanted, it is true, the plain and less corrupt smuggling of former times, and British men-of-war, sent to collect British claims for advances made to revolutionary governments at most usurious rates, took the place of the old buccaneers; but in reality the substance of things was the same as before.

By this system England derives from the Spanish-American States all the advantages of trade she receives from her colonies; and yet she has not the expense or the trouble of governing them. And it is her interest to keep them in this condition. Now they furnish her with an excellent market for her fabrics; and, through her merchants, scattered over the central and southern portions of the continent, she manages to control the distribution of the products of these countries. Thus her shipping is swelled, her sailors educated, and an opportunity is offered for scattering her men-of-war like sentries along the coasts of both oceans, from Mexico to Patagonia. Her aim is to maintain the *status quô*, for she could scarcely hope to better herself by any change that might be attempted.

The British consul at Realejo, Thomas Manning, was a type of the class of English merchants in the Spanish-American States. Arriving in Nicaragua without means —a sailor, it is said, on a merchant vessel—he had married a woman of the country, and soon built the foundations of a fortune. Without any education, or any habit of regarding political events in the light of principle or of fixed policy, he yet had that keen instinct for property and his own interests which enabled him to use British power to aid his trading adventures. He sometimes lent money to the Republic, only, however, when it was in great straits and promised extravagant interest ; and when the principal and interest had accumulated to a suitable sum, he would call on the British fleet to blockade the ports of the States until the debt was paid. As early as 1849, Manning had foreseen the danger of Americans passing in numbers through Nicaragua ; and while the Californians were crossing the Isthmus, on their way to and from the land of gold, he had written to Lord Palmerston that unless England averted the calamity, in ten years the country would be " overrun by North American adventurers." It is wise for England to make her merchants consuls, and to intrust them somewhat with diplomatic business ; the sting of self-interest keeps the sentry from sleeping on his post.

Manning had houses both at Leon and at Chinandega, and his commercial and social relations were mainly with the residents of the Occidental Department. Hence, in the revolution of 1854, he naturally favored Castellon and his adherents, though his notions about government, if he could be said to have any, inclined him more toward the Legitimists. Besides, however, his personal relations with some of the leading Democrats, the all-subduing sense of interest led him with the Leoneses. The rivalry between the towns of Leon and Granada was a rivalry of trade and of interests as well as of social and political power. True, the political principles prevalent at Granada naturally led to high tariffs, while those of Leon tended to free trade ; but the geographical position of the two towns did most to beget the commercial contest between them. Granada received its goods from the Atlantic, by the way of the lake and San Juan river, while Leon was supplied from vessels obliged to pass Cape Horn. It was difficult, however, to carry on smuggling by the river, while the facilities for contraband on the Pacific side were great. Thus Leon was able to compete with Granada by making up in smuggling what she lost by the voyage round the Horn. It may thus be readily conceived how the British consul's interests induced him to wish for the success of the Leoneses, not only in the Occidental Department but throughout the State. Their success would necessarily aggrandize Leon and depress the trade of Granada.

Of course Manning's relations with the Castellon government were intimate, and especially with the Minister of Hacienda, D. Pablo Caravajal. It was through the officers of the hacienda that all arrangements had to be made for landing goods at Realejo ; and the interests of the minister might sometimes be opposed to the interests of the government he served. So, too, it was with the hacienda Don Tomas—as the people called Manning— treated, when he was so kind as to advance a little money at the rate of one and a half or two per cent. a month. And as Caravajal was the minister who countersigned the first contract of Castellon with Cole, and none besides himself and the director knew its character, he was probably obliging enough to drop a copy of it where Don Tomas might find it. At any rate Manning heard of the Cole contract soon after it was made, and he immediately remonstrated with Castellon as to the policy he was pursuing. The director, however, had been in England to negotiate on the part of Nicaragua concerning the Mosquito coast, and was sagacious enough to perceive the drift of British policy and the subjection in which it sought to retain his country. The remonstrances of Manning were, therefore, of little avail.

It is then probable that the British cabinet was, from the beginning, well informed as to the American movement in Nicaragua. While the government of the United States had merely newspaper reports of events in Nicaragua, previous to the surprise of Granada, Lord Clarendon was undoubtedly receiving minute and detailed statements from official sources. Hence, when we can get at the facts, it is not strange to see that Lord Clarendon is deeply interested in the events of Central America, and that, by act as well as words, he is urging Costa Rica to make war on the Americans in Nicaragua.

The sources of information on this subject are exclusively Costa Rican, and the only published facts are those contained in certain letters taken from the English mail for San José, in the month of March, 1856. Among this intercepted correspondence was the copy of a note from the Under-Secretary of State for Foreign Affairs, Mr. E. Hammond, to E. Wallerstein, consul-general for Costa Rica at London. The note is dated from the

Foreign Office, February 9th, 1856, and acquaints the consul-general that Lord Clarendon has been informed by the War Department " two thousand smooth bore muskets (Witton's), which are not so highly finished as the Line pattern muskets of 1842, can be supplied" to the government of Costa Rica, " at £1, 3s. each ; or, if it should be preferred, two thousand of the Line pattern muskets of 1842 can be furnished at 56s. 8d. each." Then a letter from Wallerstein to D. Bernardo Calvo, Minister of Relations for Costa Rica, advising him of the offer of Lord Clarendon, says : " I have written a private letter to the secretary, entreating him to send me an order to examine the two kinds. After seeing them I will still consider if it is proper to take the muskets without positive instructions from his Excellency, the President ; but, in the meantime, I am persuaded his Excellency will see, in the promptness with which H. B. M.'s government has complied with my request, a strong proof of its sympathy and good will toward the Republic. Nothing is said, it is true, about the time the money should be paid ; this shows it is for your government to decide that point." And while writing officially to his chief in the cabinet, Mr. Wallerstein does not forget to send a private letter for his esteemed friend, D. Juan Rafael Mora. After telling the President, " The pleasure I felt was such, on receipt of Mr. Hammond's letters, I could not sleep at all that night ;" the complacent consul-general goes on : " I have letters from Guatemala and San Salvador, requiring me to request from this government help and succor ; but what can be done for republics or people who cannot help themselves ? When I was telling Lord Clarendon Costa Rica had already an army of eight hundred men on the frontiers, he was much pleased, and said that was a right step ; and I am persuaded my having made that intimation is the reason for their giving us the muskets."

Through these letters we can perceive the prudence and yet the decision with which the British cabinet acted in reference to the Rivas administration. There is no doubt or hesitation in its conduct, because it acts in accordance with a traditional policy. England does not desire firm and steady government in Central America, because her merchants would thus be restricted to the common profits of legitimate trade ; and she is, above all, opposed to the establishment of such governments there by American influences, for fear other goods than her own would be thrown into the markets of those countries.

Urged on, therefore, by Great Britain, tacitly encouraged by the United States, Costa Rica declared war against the Americans in the service of Nicaragua. Mora is careful to make the issue clearly and distinctly. He does not declare war against the Republic of Nicaragua, but against certain persons in her service. And as the manner in which the war is declared defies the restraints of public law, so the way in which it is to be waged points not to the rules adopted by Christian nations. The same day war was declared, a decree was published ordering all prisoners taken with arms in their hands to be shot. Yet there have been found Christian people unblushing enough to praise the conduct and the policy of Juan Rafael Mora. And in the blindness of party passion Americans have not been ashamed to support the man who distinctly enounced the principle that they were to be excluded from Central America, and if venturing there against his will, they should be shot.

On whom, then, rests the responsibility of the war which for more than a year drained the resources of Nicaragua and made her fields the scenes of deadly conflict rather than of abundant harvests? Not surely on those who exhausted every effort in order to maintain peace and bring about a diplomatic discussion rather than armed arbitrament of the questions at issue. Costa Rica scorned to discuss the right of Nicaragua to employ Americans in her military service. Mora refused to listen to the voice of reason, and defiantly seizing the clarion, blew the note of war. If it is permitted, however, to anticipate events not yet narrated—if we may "see the future in the instant," in order to gather therefrom a lesson of justice and of right—it may not be inappropriate to say that Costa Rica has derived nothing from the war except a scarcity of labor for her fields, a heavy debt to embarrass her treasury, and the prospect of civil commotions to disturb her industry. Mora, too, reaps in exile the fruits of his policy; but let us pass Mora in exile, as Ugolino in hell, afar off and with silence.

Chapter Sixth.

On the first of March, 1856, the regular American force in the service of Nicaragua was about six hundred men. It was organized in two battalions, one denominated the Rifle and the other the Light Infantry Battalion. The first was commanded by Colonel M. B. Skerrett, with E. J. Saunders as lieutenant-colonel and A. S. Brewster as major. The light infantry was commanded by Colonel B. D. Fry, with J. B. Markham as major. Nearly all the rifle companies were then stationed at Leon, a single company under Captain Rudler being at Rivas, where Major Brewster acted as commandant. The light infantry was at Granada. Since the appointment of Colonel P. R. Thompson as adjutant-general early in February, more system and order had been given to the army organization. The medical staff was well directed by the surgeon-general, Dr. Moses ; and Colonel Thomas F. Fisher had charge of the quarter master's department. W. K. Rogers had been recently appointed assistant commissary-general with the rank of major, and was then at the head of the commissariat. Colonel Bruno Von Natzmer was inspector-general ; but

8*

was, at that time, stationed at Leon, having general and indefinite powers to regulate the civil administration there and to see that the wants of the American force were properly provided for. His knowledge of the people in the Occidental Department made his services valuable, inasmuch as there were constant rumors of trouble and difficulties on the part of the natives at Leon.

During the four months which had elapsed since the establishment of the provisional government, the Americans had been, for the most part, stationed in Granada. But the sickness prevailing there, as well as the partial necessity for a force elsewhere, had caused small bodies to be sent in several directions through the Republic, thus familiarizing the people of the remote districts with the appearance of the Americans, and furnishing the latter with a knowledge of the roads and local prejudices of the inhabitants. Thus Colonel Fry, with a party of voltigeurs, had spent several weeks in the neighborhood of Matagalpa, proceeding even as far as Juigalpa in order to quell certain disturbances the Legitimists were creating among the Indians. It would have been better for the discipline and spirit of the troops if they had remained less and in smaller bodies at Granada; but this being the depot of arms and the seat of government by the terms of the treaty, the disposition of the Legitimists of the town made it necessary to keep a strong force in the place. The quantity of liquor there, and the fondness of many officers for drink, not only injured the health of the troops, but tended materially to prevent its growth in military virtue.

In addition to the regular force of the Americans there were more than five hundred men capable of bearing arms engaged in civil business either at Granada or along the line of the Transit. At the capital there were numbers of Americans employed in the civil offices, besides the laborers engaged in building a wharf at the old fort; and at Virgin Bay and San Juan del Sur, the Transit Company had scores of persons engaged in the construction of their works at these two places. Some of these were organized as volunteer companies, and at Virgin Bay a company of this description, with a good uniform, and commanded by George McMurray, had nearly fifty members. Many persons supposed these men could be relied on, in case of disturbance, with as much certainty as the regular force, and hence it was estimated that in the event of invasion nearly twelve hundred Americans could be brought into action for the defence of Nicaragua.

A few days afterward, on the 9th of March, the regular force was largely increased by the arrival at Granada of more than two hundred and fifty men, under the direction of D. Domingo de Goicouria. The night before these recruits arrived a bearer of despatches from San Salvador, Col. Padilla, had reached Granada; and on the morning of the 9th, dressed in a ludicrous uniform, and wearing a cocked hat he had brought all the way over the mountains from Cojutepeque, he sallied forth on a visit to the general-in-chief. The new men had just reached the Plaza, and were drawn up so as to show their numbers to the best advantage, when Padilla entered the general's quarters. The surprise of the San

Salvadorian, at the sight of so many strange-looking men, was equal to the amazement the Americans found in his long, lank person, run into trowsers too short for his legs, and with the chest and arms tightly encased in a small military coat, buttoned up to the throat, and obstinate in the habit of slipping its lower edges above the pit of the stomach. As Padilla had brought despatches from the Minister of Relations at Cojutepeque, Señor Hoyos, asking why Americans were being introduced into Nicaragua, the arrival of Goicouria and his recruits was not inopportune.

Schlessinger had, in the meanwhile, returned from Costa Rica with an account of his treatment there. Manuel Arguëllo, for whose sake Selva left the cabinet, remained with his Legitimist friends near Mora, and his conduct was a sample of the actions of the old Granada faction. On the 11th, therefore, the new recruits were organized in a battalion of five companies, under the command of Schlessinger, and Capt. J. C. O'Neal was raised to the rank of Major, and attached to the corps. The same day a proclamation was issued by the general-in-chief, closing with the order to the troops to assume and wear the red ribbon. The object of the proclamation was to secure the zealous co-operation of the Nicaragua Democrats as well as of the liberals of the other States in the war immediately impending, and the cause assigned for resuming the red ribbon was the course of the Nicaragua Legitimists. " The self-styled Legitimist party of Nicaragua," so the proclamation ran, " has repelled our efforts at conciliation. They have maintained communication with their fellow serviles in the other

States. They have, by all means in their power, attempted to weaken the present provisional government, and have given aid and encouragement to the enemies of Nicaragua outside of the Republic........ They owe us for the protection they have had for their lives and property—they have paid us with ingratitude and treachery."

A few hours after Walker wrote this proclamation he received the Mora decree of the 1st of March, declaring war against the Americans in Nicaragua. As soon as this decree was read, the Provisional President published a proclamation of war against Costa Rica, and on the 13th the general order was issued : " The Supreme Provisional Government of the Republic of Nicaragua having formally declared war, by decree of March 11th, 1856, against the State of Costa Rica, the army will be held in readiness to commence active operations."

Col. Schlessinger, after organizing his battalion and receiving muskets for the several companies, was ordered to prepare for marching. He proceeded with his command to Virgin Bay, and, according to instructions, sent the weakest of his companies, under Lieut. Colman, to Rivas, while Capt. Rudler, with Co. F of the Rifles, was ordered to report to Schlessinger. The four full companies of the new battalion were commanded respectively by Capt. Thorpe, Capt. Creighton, Capt. Prange, and Capt. Legeay. The companies of these two latter officers consisted entirely the one of German and the other of French, and Schlessinger's familiarity with the languages of these companies, no less than his acquaintance with Spanish and with the Department of Guanacaste, was the cause of his selection for the service on which he was about to be sent. After Rudler's company reported, Schlessinger's command numbered about two hundred and forty men.

Walker ordered Schlessinger to march with this force into the Department of Guanacaste. His object was to strike the first blow of the war on the territory held by the enemy, and also to have a strong outpost at some distance south of the Transit, to guard against any surprise on the line of American travel across the Isthmus. With the same view companies were occupying Castillo and Hipp's Point, at the mouth of the Serapaqui. It was necessary to hold the Transit with more tenacity than any other part of the State, not only because the property there had more need of protection than any other in the Republic from the foreign enemy, but also because of the new arrangements made it was from the Transit the Nicaragua force was to be fed and supplied with new troops. As there are very few people between the Transit road and the line of Guanacaste, the necessity for a corps of observation toward the south was the more urgent. The greatest difficulty in war, that of knowing accurately your enemy's movements, is increased in Central America by the want of facilities for communication, and by the habit frequent revolutions have begot of spreading the most exaggerated reports about most trifling facts. You can always get some facts, however, from any report ; so that, all things considered, it requires more labor to get facts from thinly settled than from populous districts.

On the 16th, Schlessinger marched from San Juan del

Sur toward the La Flor, a small stream which separates Guanacaste from the Meridional Department. Before leaving he had much irritated Major Brewster, who was commanding at Rivas, by the numerous irregularities he practised, but with natural reluctance that officer was slow in reporting such facts at headquarters. The march to the La Flor and beyond it to Salinas was characterized by the same irregularity which marked the command while on the Transit ; and so great was the disorder that the surgeon of the command, a new-comer, and ignorant of the grave fault he was committing, left the force and returned to Granada with letters from Schlessinger. This fact, all too late, revealed the weakness of the commander who had permitted his only surgeon to leave at a time when he might any day engage the enemy. With such ignorance of duty, on the part of both commander and surgeon, it was necessary to carry on the war in the best manner possible. This instance of Schlessinger and his surgeon, one out of many, illustrates a difficulty which beset the Americans during the whole war.

It was not until late at night on the 20th that Schlessinger arrived at the country-house of Santa Rosa, the men hungry and exhausted by the long and weary march. The guard seems to have been properly posted during the night, and the next morning mounted men were sent to get news and, if possible, guides. An inspection of arms had been ordered first for two and afterward for three o'clock in the afternoon ; and the men were lounging in all directions in and around the camp, when, shortly before the inspection was to take place, the alarm was

given and the cry of " Here they come," was uttered by
a mounted rifleman as he rode up to the main building
where the colonel was quartered. Schlessinger was taken
entirely by surprise, and, in the confusion, could not be
found by the adjutant. Capt. Rudler with his rifles
seized a corral near the main house with a view of protecting the American flank ; but the fire of the advancing enemy soon forced him to leave it. In the meanwhile
Capt. Creighton, aided by Major O'Neal, had formed his
company, its right resting on the house, and fired a few
volleys at the Costa Ricans ; but the German company
had broke and left the field, while the French under Legeay retired from the hilly, broken ground, they had attempted to occupy. In five minutes, the whole command,
led by its colonel, was in full and most disorderly retreat. Major O'Neal, with several other officers, strove
in vain to turn the men and carry them back toward the
enemy ; but the panic was such that they found few willing to listen or to follow.

The Costa Rican force attacking at Santa Rosa was the
advance guard of the whole army, then on its march
toward the northern frontier. It consisted of about five
hundred men, and among its officers was Manuel Arguëllo, the Legitimist. They wore the red ribbon, with the
view both of deceiving the Americans and of conciliating
the Nicaraguan Democrats. After the main body of the
army, with the President, Rafael Mora, at its head, reached Santa Rosa, the Nicaraguan prisoners, many of them
wounded, were tried by court martial and ordered to be.
shot. The cruel sentence was too faithfully executed.

After wandering for some time between Santa Rosa and

the lake of Nicaragua, the disorganized remains of Schlessinger's force arrived at a point near Tortugas, whence they found their way to Virgin Bay. They came to the latter place by squads rather than by companies, some without hats and shoes, and some even without arms. In their flight many had been torn by the thorns through which they had been forced, and it was days and even weeks before straggling men of the expedition ceased to arrive. The depression of spirits was great, and some of the soldiers, in order to diminish the shame of their retreat, were but too ready to exaggerate among their comrades the disciplined air, fine military conduct, and excellent arms and equipment of the enemy they so hastily saw at Santa Rosa.

Meanwhile Walker was concentrating the American force at Granada, and preparing for the war in which, it was probable, the other three Central American States would join Costa Rica. The Rifles were ordered from Leon; and about the time they entered Granada, a company of recruits arrived from San Juan del Norte under the command of Capt. Mason. With this company came Turnbull and French; but both those persons, finding their services were not required, soon left the Republic. While the Rifles were marching into the capital, the general-in-chief was in bed with a violent attack of fever; but thanks to good medical attendance and a strong constitution, he was able, on the next day, Sunday the 23d, to go to the dinner-table. Scarcely able to sit up, he had a note from Major Brewster put in his hands, bearing the first hasty news of the reverse at Santa Rosa. The same evening he managed to get aboard the steamer, and was, on the morning of the 24th, at Virgin Bay. The news of the stragglers from Santa Rosa was a better tonic than a cold bath. The necessity for mental and moral action has a wonderful effect in driving the reluctant body to perform the tasks the will imposes.

The disaster in Guanacaste made Walker determine to move the main strength of the Americans to Rivas. He did not know what effect the rout at Santa Rosa might have on the native Nicaraguans, or how far it might shake their confidence in the ability of the Americans to protect the State from its enemies. Orders were given accordingly ; and in the meanwhile arrangements had been made for removing the government to Leon. Rivas was anxious to fill the vacancies in his cabinet ; and Jerez had intimated that if the President would go to Leon he might resume his place in the government. Before leaving Granada, however, the President issued a decree whereby the Oriental and Meridional Departments were put under martial law, and the general-in-chief was invested with absolute power over these portions of the Republic. The Minister of Public Credit, Ferrer, remained at Granada as commissioner, to cooperate with the general, as far as the latter might require, in supplying means for carrying on the war, and for ministering to the wants of the army.

The day Walker established his headquarters at Rivas, Schlessinger arrived to report in person the incidents of his march and retreat. He urged the inexperience of the men, and their want of disciplined courage as the cause of his misfortune ; and he forthwith proposed to organize a new force for the occupation of

Guanacaste. But the officers of the expedition who began to arrive all agreed as to the incapacity and cowardice shown by their late commander. Some, indeed, hinted that he had sold his command ; but such conduct was not suited to his timid nature. Had he sold his men, he would never have returned to Nicaragua. The charges, however, made against him required a court of inquiry ; and the report of the court of inquiry led to his arrest and trial before a court martial on the charges of neglect of duty, of ignorance of his duties of commanding officer, and of cowardice in the presence of the enemy. To these was afterward added the charge of desertion.

The movement of the army from Granada to Rivas by Virgin Bay had developed the necessity for more vigor in its means of transportation. Therefore C. J. Macdonald was appointed quartermaster-general with the rank of colonel ; but this office he held only a few days for causes which will soon appear. Up to the 30th, the re-organization of the men who had retnrned from Costa Rica was going on, and efforts were being made to increase in several respects the efficiency of the army. But a general depression seemed to pervade officers as well as men. Applications were constantly made for furloughs to return to the United States ; and the spirit of the troops was yet more depressed by the Americans outside of the army thronging to headquarters in order to get passports to leave the country. Two or three ladies—Mrs. Thompson, the wife of the adjutant-general, and Mrs. Kewen, the wife of Mr. E. J. C. Kewen, a civil officer of the State—aided to keep up the courage of the men by the cheerfulness with which they met all forms of fatigue and danger. But the sphere of such influences was necessarily narrow, and it was requisite to infuse some enthusiasm into the army or let it dissolve from the effects of one shameful panic.

Accordingly, on the afternoon of the 30th, the force in Rivas was paraded on the main Plaza, and the general-in-chief addressed them a few minutes in such words as he could find for the occasion. He endeavored to place before them the moral grandeur of the position they occupied. Alone in the world, without a friendly government to give even its sympathy, much less its aid, they had nothing to support them in the struggle with the neighboring States save the consciousness of the justice of their cause. Maligned by those who should have befriended them, and betrayed by those they had benefited, they had to choose between basely yielding their rights and nobly dying for them. Nor did their general seek to hide from them the peril in which they stood; but from the urgency of the danger arose the greater necessity for becoming conduct. The words were few and simple, and drew little force from the manner of him who uttered them; but they had the desired effect and created a new spirit among the men. It is only by constant appeals to the loftier qualities of man that you can make him a good soldier; and all military discipline is a mere effort to make virtue constant and reliable by making it habitual.

On the 1st of April the arrival of the steamer Cortes from San Francisco at San Juan del Sur was announced. W. R. Garrison had come as passenger with a view of making arrangements for the new transit; but no men had come for the service of Nicaragua. Soon after news reached Rivas of the arrival of the steamer, Walker received intelligence that she had again put to sea, towing out the coal-ship then in the harbor. The up-going steamer of the Pacific Mail Steamship Company had spoken the Cortes before she entered the port of San Juan, and had borne to her commander the orders of his principals in New-York. Captain Collens, of the Cortes, had, however, left Mr. Garrison ashore; and the latter, when he got to Rivas, informed Walker that this sudden movement of the old company had not been provided for, and that it might be several weeks, at least six, before another steamer would come from California. Thus one motive for holding fast to the Transit was, for the moment, taken away. Thus, at the very outset, the new contractors, Morgan and Garrison, by their timidity —to use no harsher word—jeoparded the welfare of those who had acted on the faith of their capacity and willingness to fulfil their agreements.

At the same time that Garrison and Morgan were embarassing Walker's communications with the United States by the hesitation and weakness of their conduct, Rivas was writing that news every day reached Leon of an intention on the part of Guatemala and San Salvador to join in the war against Nicaragua. It was clear that the people in the Occidental Department began to shake at the idea of an invasion from the northern States. As the Transit was, for the time being, made useless by the action of persons having an interest in the property on the line of travel, the general-in-chief

decided to move northward so as to restore confidence
to the Leoneses. He was not then aware of the large
force Mora had on the frontier. Scouting parties of the
enemy had come as far as Peña Blanca, a point on the
southern boundary of the Meridional Department; but
these were not of such force as to indicate the presence
of the numbers Mora was leading through Guanacaste.

Just as orders were being issued to prepare the army
for its movement to Virgin Bay, Col. Macdonald resigned
the office of quartermaster-general. At the time,
Walker attributed this act to the projected departure of
the troops from the Transit, Macdonald then being on
the Isthmus to watch the interests of Garrison and
Morgan. But after events showed that his conduct was
more the result of mortification at the apparent bad
faith of his principal at San Francisco, than of any disaffection toward the cause of the Americans in Nicaragua. His resignation was, however, a loss at the time;
for his clear head and energetic action were much needed
in the coming crisis. At that time the general-in-chief
knew something of the value of Macdonald's head; but
it was only at a later period that he had the opportunity
of discovering other admirable qualities the sturdy
Scotchman possessed. With the Highland blood, he
had the Highland loyalty; but his dogged tenacity of
purpose was that of the Lowland borderer.

After Macdonald's resignation, D. Domingo de Goicouria was appointed intendente-general with the rank
of brigadier-general. He was a Cuban, and had been
engaged with the patriots of that island in some efforts
to gain its independence. Before going to Nicaragua,

Goicouria had sent a pure-hearted and devoted son of the island, Lainé, to negotiate with Walker for future assistance against the Spanish dominion. And the latter, while pledging his personal efforts to the Cuban cause, had been careful not to involve the relations of Nicaragua by such promises. On his part, Goicouria had promised much help in the way of money, arms, and clothing; and his manner and conversation, more mercantile than military, were calculated to make you imagine him capable of inspiring capitalists with confidence in his commercial ability. As many persons concurred in representing Goicouria's credit to be good, his desire for rank was gratified by the appointment, and it was hoped thus to secure some recompense in the shape of shoes, jackets and equipments for the soldiers. The duties of the quartermaster's department were devolved on the intendencia; and the chief, Goicouria, recommended for first and second assistants Fisher and Byron Cole—who had lately returned to Nicaragua—with the ranks respectively of colonel and lieutenant-colonel. These appointments were accordingly made.

The intendencia, thus hastily organized, received immediate orders to prepare transportation for the whole force then in Rivas, with all the property of the army there, to Virgin Bay. Walker himself repaired to the latter point to see that everything was ready to embark the troops on one of the lake steamers. After reaching Virgin Bay he was called up about midnight by the new intendente-general, who had rode all the way from Rivas to propose that he should be left with a few Americans and some native troops in charge of the

Meridional Department. The conceit of Goicouria, excited by his new rank and title, had turned his head;
and although he had scarcely been a month in the country, he foolishly presumed to thrust his opinion unasked
on his general-in-chief. Of course he got a short answer;
and Walker began to think the shoes and shirts might
be too dearly purchased by the appointment of Don
Domingo.

By the evening of the 5th of April, all were at Virgin Bay, and the embarkation was commenced. Most
of the American residents about the Transit road, thinking from the preparations that the Meridional Department was to be abandoned, flocked with the troops aboard
the San Carlos. When all were on the steamer she
was ordered to the San Juan river, and the morning of
the 6th found her off San Carlos Fort. Captain Linton's company stationed at that point was embarked, and
the steamer proceeded down the river to Toro Rapids.
A company intended to garrison Castillo Viejo was sent
down to relieve the force previously there; and when the
returning company had reached the San Carlos, she was
ordered to Granada. On the morning of the 8th, the steamer anchored off Granada, and the troops were rapidly dis-
embarked. Thus the movement northward was, for a
time, concealed from the people of the Meridional Department, among whom the enemy had numerous spies,
and the impression was temporarily created, that the
Americans intended to move either out of the country
or toward San Josè. The enemy seems to have adopted
the former opinion.

It seems that Mora, after his success at Santa Rosa,
was pressing on toward the frontier; but hearing Walker

had occupied Rivas in force, he stopped to watch his adversary. Then seeing the preparations for abandoning the department, he allowed the embarkation of the Americans almost in his very presence. Of course, with the Legitimists in and about Rivas, it was far easier for Mora to get reliable news than for the Nicaraguan general. As no villages or even country-houses were to be passed, it was not difficult to bring a force of three thousand men to the neighborhood of the Transit road, without its being at all known in the department. Walker had no sooner left Virgin Bay, than Mora moved forward with a view of occupying Rivas and the Transit road.

Early on the morning of the 7th, according to the testimony of sworn witnesses, examined by the American minister, Mr. Wheeler, the Costa Rican troops entered Virgin Bay and surrounded the office of the Transit Company. The officer in command gave the order to fire, and nine American citizens, mostly laborers in the service of the company, and all of them entirely unarmed, were killed or wounded by the first volley. The wounded were immediately run through with the bayonets of the soldiers and swords of the officers. Then the doors of the building were broken open, the trunks stored in it were rifled, and the persons of the murdered Americans were robbed of the money, watches, and jewelry, found on them. Nor were the brutal passions of the invaders satisfied with these acts. They afterward set fire to the wharf the Transit Company was just completing, and declared their intention to exterminate every American on the Isthmus. They commenced the work of destruction by burning to the water's edge

9

the wharf which American capital had constructeɑ for the use and advantage of Nicaraguan labor and Nicaraguan products.

To San Juan del Sur and to Rivas, the entrance of the Costa Ricans was more orderly. At Rivas, particularly, Mora made every effort to conciliate the people of the country. A prefect was appointed, and D. Evaristo Carazo, who for several years had been accumulating a fortune from the transit of Americans across the Isthmus, accepted the office. Orders were also issued prohibiting the impressment of men for military service ; but urgent invitations were made to the people to join those who professed to have come for their liberation from the yoke of the Americans. Few, however, if any, accepted the invitation ; and the President of Costa Rica did not fail to express his disappointment at the backwardness of the people to join his ranks. He had trusted too much to the partial representations of the Legitimists, and he afterward complained bitterly of the deception practised on him.

An hour or two after Walker landed at Granada, on the morning of the 8th, an American from the Transit came to inform him of the events occurring there. At the same time the letters from Leon indicated that the alarm there had subsided. Hence orders were at once issued to have the whole marching force then in Granada, with the exception of two companies to garrison that place, ready to move the next morning by daylight.

The American force had been sensibly diminished by the expedition to Santa Rosa, and after the return from that disastrous field the French and German companies were disbanded and all who could not speak English were discharged from the army. Thus, on the morning of the 9th, not more than five hundred and fifty men marched out of Granada toward Rivas. The men were, however, in good spirits and went at a brisk pace, so that early in the afternoon they were halted for dinner a league to the southward of Nandaime. Here they met Col. Machado, a Cuban, who had been left at Rivas with a few native troops when Walker marched the American force thence. The officer commanding at Rivas was Jose Bermudez, who remained and took service under Mora, but the rank and file of the native Nicaraguans forsaking Bermudez had followed Machado, and left Rivas some hours before the Costa Ricans entered. Thus was it generally in Nicaragua ; the people adhered to the Americans ; the *calzados*, those wearing shoes, deserted to the enemies of the Republic.

After rest and dinner, the command strengthened by Machado's men, marched to the Ochomogo, where it encamped for the night. Then it was ascertained that Mora had entered Rivas the day before with a large army, the woman, who brought the story, saying at last three thousand. But as the ideas of the people of the country about numbers are rather vague, not much confidence was put in the report. On the 10th, the march was slow and toilsome, owing to the heat of the day and to the long stretches of dry and dusty road without any shade to protect the men from the fierce tropical sun. During the morning a native from Rivas was taken, carrying proclamations from Mora to his Legitimist friends about Masaya, and, after some threats, much information was educed from the messenger concerning the position and strength of the enemy. As the force approached the Gil Gonzales, a body of rangers, under command of Capt. Waters, was sent on to the point where the main road to Rivas crosses the river, and there exchanged shots with an outpost of the enemy placed near Obraje. The main body of the Americans, however, left the high road half a league from the river, and taking a trail to the left struck the Gil Gonzales some distance below the point where Waters had encountered the enemy. About sunset Walker camped for the night on the south bank of the Gil Gonzales, and due silence was kept in order to prevent the enemy from perceiving his presence there.

Just before reaching camp a herdsman, hunting cattle for the Costa Ricans, had been made prisoner, and the soldiers had scarcely reached the several points in the camp assigned to them, before a man, found skulking near the river, was brought to the general-in-chief. At first he denied all knowledge of the enemy at Rivas, but a rope thrown around his neck and cast over a limb of the nearest tree brought him the use of his memory, and he gave an accurate and detailed account of the several points at which the Costa Ricans were posted. He stated the houses in which Mora and the principal officers quartered, the place where the ammunition was stored together the quantity of it, not forgetting two pretty little pieces of artillery commanding some of the streets. Unfortunately for himself, he let out the fact that he had been sent to gather news of the Americans, and hence was punished as a spy. But his information was so full, and, after severe cross-examination there was so little contradiction in his story, that Walker formed his plan of attack on the facts thus obtained. The result showed that the statements of the spy were entirely accurate. The fear of death had so discomposed his mind that he could not invent a lie.

Before retiring for the night, Walker sent for the principal officers, and explaining the plan of attack for the next day, assigned to each his separate duty. Lieut.-Col. Sanders, with four companies of Rifles, was to enter by the streets running along the north side of the Plaza, and was to keep his men in full charge, if possible, until they reached the house where Mora was quartered, about eighty yards from the main square. Major Brewster, with three companies of Rifles, was to enter by the street on the south side of the Plaza and was, also, to attempt to reach the headquarters of the enemy. As Walker expected to surprise Mora, he hoped to get possession of his person before he could escape; and at any rate as his headquarters were opposite the magazine, the occupation of the former would command the latter. Hence the object in ordering the Rifles to strike for the house Mora was known to occupy. Col. Natzmer, with Major O'Neal and the Second Rifles—as his command was called—although then armed with muskets, was to pass to the extreme left of the town thus threatening the right of the enemy and yet being within easy distance of Brewster. Machado with the natives was to pass by a road which enters the Plaza from the north, and would thus find himself on Sanders' right. Col. Fry was to hold his companies of light infantry as a reserve.

Between two and three o'clock in the morning, the several companies were formed and the march toward Rivas began, Dr. J. L. Cole acting as guide. Owing to the darkness of the night and the obscurity of the trail, the march was for a time slow and interrupted by frequent halts; but when day broke, and the command fell into the road through Potosi, the pace of the men became brisk and lively. The quick yet firm step of the soldiers showed that their spirit was good, and the dust of the road, though thick and heavy, affected them little. The deep silence of the expectant ranks was only broken by the low voice of one asking his comrade for a drop of water from his gourd; and the bark of the watch-dogs, common in the huts along the roadside, was passed unheeded, save with the half-uttered hope that the noise of the brute might not give the enemy notice of their approach. Soon after they passed Potosi the sun rose in all the splendor of his southern skies, and when the Americans, making a detour toward the lake, fell into the road from San Jorge to Rivas, about a mile from the latter place, it was near eight o'clock.

Not more than half a mile from the edge of the town Walker met some market-women, who told him the enemy were not aware of his approach; they had left the Plaza only a few minutes previously, and the Costa Ricans—*hermaniticos*, as the San Jorge women called them—were as careless and indifferent as if they were in their own country. A short halt was made at the Cuatro Esquinas to give the rear time to close up; and when the rear-guard appeared the order was given for the several divisions of the force to advance in the manner indicated the night before.

Sanders, being in the advance, drove in a small picket near the edge of the town, and ·proceeding at a double quick step, entered the Plaza and rushed up the street toward Mora's quarters. The enemy, taken by surprise, had scarcely commenced to return the fire of the Rifles when the latter reached a small brass gun standing in the street, about half way between the Plaza and the magazine of the Costa Ricans. Sanders' men, shouting over the gun they had taken, carried it to the Plaza ; but in the meantime they had given the enemy time to recover from the first shock and the Costa Ricans' fire now became galling. Brewster had succeeded also in clearing his side of the Plaza of the enemy, and, with Captain Anderson's company in front, was urging his command on toward the houses occupied by the Costa Ricans. A few sharp-shooters, however, of the enemy, French and Germans, got possession of a tower in front of the Rifles, and so annoyed them that they were finally forced to seek cover. Natzmer and O'Neal got possession of the houses on Brewster's left and were doing good execution, keeping their men well protected and pouring a sharp fire into the enemy's ranks. While Machado, leading on his natives in the most gallant manner, had himself fallen ; and his soldiers, after his death, took small part in the engagement.

Thus, in a few moments, the Americans had possession of the Plaza and all the houses around it, while the enemy shutting themselves up in the buildings in the western part of the town, kept up an irregular fire from the doors and windows, as well as from the loop-holes they soon began to cut through the adobe walls. As for the Americans, after the first enthusiasm of the attack had died away, it was impossible to get them to storm the houses where the Costa Ricans were hiding from the deadly aim of the riflemen.   Many of the men, exhausted by the first charge, actually set their muskets against the walls, and throwing themselves on the ground, could scarcely be driven to any active exertion.   When Col. Fry came up with his reserve an effort was made to get them to charge down the street to Mora's house ; but Fry and then Kewen—who as volunteer aid acted gallantly during the day—urged the men in vain to the attack.   The depression of the companies, blown by the first onset, had its effect on the fresh men ; and it was impossible to get any portion of the force to renew the attack with the vigor which marked its commencement.

The few Rangers, under Captain Waters, had dismounted early in the action and had taken part in the conflict.   Young Gillis, an impetuous lieutenant under Waters, had already fallen ; while the captain taking possession of the tower of the church, on the east side of the Plaza, was able to observe to advantage the movements of the enemy and to annoy them with his rifles. Some of Sanders' men were also placed on the roofs of the houses to the west of the square, and were able to do execution from this position.   It soon became evident,. however, that it might require days to drive the Costa Ricans from the houses they occupied after their first surprise was over, especially as the Nicaraguan force had no artillery, and would have to depend on the pick and crow-bar for working through the thick adobe walls of the town.   Mora, it was clear, was closely pressed, for at different times during the day the Costa Rican troops from San Juan and Virgin Bay were observed entering Rivas. The president had concentrated all the strength he had in the department to repel the attack of the Americans.

But when the enemy saw the Nicaraguans made no advance, they assumed the offensive and undertook to get into a house to the north of the Plaza, whence they might pour a destructive fire into the American flank. This movement was defeated by Lieutenant Gay with a number of others, officers principally, who volunteered for the service. The gallantry of those who went with Gay was, in its spirit, more like that of the knights of feudal times than of the officers and soldiers of regular armies. Among those with the young lieutenant were Rogers of the commissary department, bearing the rank of major, Captain N. C. Breckenridge and Captain Huston. There was no thought of rank, but each one went forth with his revolver, ready to do the part of a true man in the fray. Not more than a dozen went out to drive away upward of a hundred, and their charge swept the enemy completely away. Gay and Huston fell, and Breckenridge received a slight wound in the head ; but the remainder of the party came off unhurt.

During the afternoon the enemy set fire to some of the houses held by the Americans, and the fire of their rifles from a tower, in front of Brewster's command, interfered somewhat with free communication between the east and west sides of the Plaza. As night, too, approached, the fire from both sides slackened, each apparently exhausted by the excitement and strife of the

day. In the meanwhile, Walker was preparing to withdraw, and after dark the wounded and disabled were
moved over to the church on the east side of the square.
Then the several companies were gradually gathered toward the same point, a few men being still left in the
burning houses to keep the enemy from embarrassing
the American movement. The surgeons examined the
wounded, and those declared mortally hurt were left in
the church near the altar, while the others were provided with horses for the march. It was past midnight
when all arrangements were completed, and the command slowly and silently defiled from the town, the
wounded in the centre, and Major Brewster commanding the rear-guard.

Soon after daylight, the little force, weary and foot-
sore, ragged, but resolute, crossed the Gil Gonzales near
Obraje, and halted for a short rest. Their guide, Dr.
Cole, and Macdonald, who had gone to Rivas as a volunteer, were missing, although they had left the town
with the command. Nor was Captain Norvell Walker
anywhere to be found. The rear guard had been well
commanded by Brewster, and his coolness and firmness
conduced much to the orderly character of the march.
It was not until the Americans were some miles beyond
the Gil Gonzales that Captain Walker, marching by
himself, overtook the rear-guard, and showed by his story
that his absence was not due to any laxity of the guard
in keeping up stragglers. He had fallen asleep in the
tower of the church on the Plaza at Rivas, and not
waking until daylight, was surprised to find himself
alone in a town occupied by the enemy. But the Costa

Ricans had not, up to the time he left, discovered that the Americans had retired : hence he was able to escape with safety. Cole and Macdonald, overcome by fatigue, wandered into a bye-path near Rivas to take rest. Finding themselves separated from the Nicaraguan force they sought and obtained refuge from a poor native, who kept them hid near San Jorge for a week. They did not re-appear in Granada until ten days after the action.

On the night of the 12th the camp was again on the banks of the Ochomogo. Col. Natzmer was sent forward to Granada with orders to have all the disposable horses and mules, together with some provisions, brought to Nandaime ; and about noon of the 13th the force had reached the latter village. Here the first report of the losses at Rivas was made by the adjutant-general. The official report showed 58 killed, 62 wounded, and 13 missing. Most of the latter afterward came in ; so that the whole loss may be put at 120. A very large proportion of both the killed and wounded were officers. Among the former were Captains Huston, Clinton, Horrell and Linton, Lieutenants Morgan, Stoll, Gay, Doyle, Gillis and Winters ; of the latter were Captains Cook, Caycee and Anderson, Lieutenants Gist, Jones, Jamieson, Leonard, Potter, Ayers, Latimer, Dolan and Anderson. The loss of the enemy is difficult to determine : for the Central Americans never, even to their own officers, state their losses accurately. But there were probably near six hundred of the Costa Ricans put hors de combat ; two hundred killed and four hundred wounded. Their force at the beginning of the action was upward of three thousand; and their losses may be estimated by the wounded they afterward took away from Nicaragua.

From Nandaime to Granada the march was long and wearisome, in spite of the additional facilities of transportation. Hence, it was near midnight when the shattered forces of the Republic entered the capital. The friends of the government in Granada were, however, awake, in order to receive the force with every demonstration of respect and confidence. The bells rang forth a joyful peal, rockets were sent up into the air, and all appeared thankful for the services the army had rendered the State. Although the Americans had not succeeded in driving the Costa Ricans from Rivas, they had struck a blow which paralyzed the enemy. Mora was surprised by the suddenness and the force of the attack made on him; and the sight of the crowded hospitals at Rivas depressed the spirits of his soldiers, new to the trials and sufferings of war. The people, too, of the Meridional Department, as well as those of the Oriental and Occidental, seeing the Americans were not intimidated by the numbers brought against them, regained their confidence, somewhat lost by the disgrace of Santa Rosa.

While Mora had marched into the Meridional Department, a body of 250 Costa Ricans had been sent to the Serapaqui in order to cut off Walker's communications by the San Juan river. Capt. Baldwin, a vigilant and intelligent officer, was at Hipp's Point when he ascertained the enemy were cutting a road toward the river. He did not wait for the enemy to reach him; but, ascending the Serapaqui, he vigorously assailed the

Costa Ricans while they were cutting the road, and drove them back with large loss and in extreme confusion. He himself lost one killed, Lieut. Rakestraw, and two wounded; while the enemy left more than twenty dead on the field. This affair of the Serapaqui took place on the 10th of April; and the routed Costa Ricans did not stop in their flight until they had fallen back to San José.

Immediately on reaching Granada the general-in-chief wrote to the President at Leon a detailed statement of the action at Rivas; and a day or two afterward he sent Mr. Fabens with letters to Don Patricio, suggesting the appointment of Father Vigil as Minister to the United States. The President replied to the letter concerning the engagement with the Costa Ricans, thanking the army, in the name of the Republic, for the courage and the conduct it had shown in the attack on the invaders of Nicaragua; and Mr. Fabens brought back with him the credentials and instructions of Vigil as Minister. The latter forthwith got ready to leave for San Juan del Norte in company with Mr. John P. Heiss. The priest agreed to leave his easy home in the tropics for the purpose of explaining properly to the cabinet at Washington the nature of the events occurring in Central America.

During the absence of the main body of the army on the expedition to Rivas, Schlessinger had been left at Granada on parole. He had an opportunity to regain, to some extent, his lost character, by volunteering to march with the Americans against the enemy. But he did not take advantage of the occasion; on the contrary, he remained to acquire, if possible, new infamy by adding desertion to his former crimes. The court martial which was ordered to try him, found him guilty of all the charges brought against him; and he was sentenced to be shot, and to be published throughout the civilized world. He afterward joined a body of the Legitimists acting against the Americans, and in such society he sank, by the way he permitted himself to be treated, beneath the contempt of the lowest soldier in even a Central American army. He is now fallen so far that it would be an unworthy act to execute on him the sentence of an honorable court.

After the return of the Americans to Granada an enemy fiercer and more malignant than the Costa Ricans began to ravage their thinned ranks. The fever which had before carried off many, re-appeared in an even aggravated form. Major Brewster was one of its first victims; and few could have been more missed than he. He had the calmness of spirit no danger disturbed; and it was only in the hour of trial and misfortune his full value could be known. It was the loss of officers—dying just as they began to be formed, and as their character and value began to be known—which prevented the American force from acquiring the discipline and steady virtue it might otherwise have attained. During the earlier as well as the later stages of the war in Nicaragua, it was the officer, ambitious of gaining a knowledge of his profession, and zealous in the pursuit of duty, who was most apt to seek the post of danger, and was therefore most likely to fall by the bullets of the enemy; and at times, too, it seemed as if disease also seized on such with more avidity than it did on others who might have been better spared.

New-comers, however, began to arrive to take the place of those cut off by battle and disease. On the morning of the 21st of April the steamer arrived at Granada with about two hundred men in charge of General Hornsby, who had been absent on business in the United States. As the Americans had been re-organized after the 13th in two battalions, one rifle, the other light infantry, the new recruits were formed into a second infantry battalion, with Leonidas McIntosh as major, and James Walker and James Mullen as captains. Upward of twenty men had come at their own expense to Granada, and they were enlisted for four months, and put into the rangers under Captain Davenport. This addition to the numbers of the army of course re-animated the old troops—for some of them, considering the services they had seen, might with propriety be called old troops; and after the arrival of the new men all were as eager as ever to march against the enemy at Rivas.

And while the Nicaraguan force was increasing, that of Costa Rica was rapidly sinking from the double cancers of cholera and desertion.

When the Americans retired from Rivas, the Costa Ricans were encumbered with so many dead that instead of regularly burying the bodies they threw them into the wells of the town. Their surgical staff, too, was weak; and the hospitals being crowded and ill-regulated, the festering sores of the wounded soldiers tended to produce disease even if the cholera had not appeared. The epidemic which began to prey on their camp soon after the 11th of April, was probably the same *colerin* that attacked the Democrats at San Juan del Sur the year before, and afterward troubled the Americans at Virgin Bay. The spasms of this form of disease are not so violent as those of the Asiatic cholera, nor does the patient sink so rapidly. Its fatal effects were increased in the Costa Rican camp by the general depression of spirits which pervaded the officers as well as the men after they saw the results of the first conflict with the enemy they had come to drive, as they imagined, by easy marches, and by the mere force of their numbers, out of Central America.

Walker soon heard, through the people of San Jorge, the condition of the Costa Rican camp. Far from receiving recruits from the Nicaraguans, all fled the infected town. Mora began to build barricades as soon as the Americans retired ; and this of itself showed fear of another attack. But when cholera and desertion supervened, the invader lost the hope of holding his ground even behind the adobes of Rivas. Nor was it possible for the Costa Rican officers to conceal from the soldiers the fact that the Americans were receiving reinforcements. Increased depression followed the growing apprehension of attack ; and the pestilence found its victims each day yielding more readily to his deadly grasp. Then, too, there were vague rumors of movements in Costa Rica against the rule of the Moras. The people, beginning to feel the burden of the war, were asking why it was made ; and the party which had for years been banished from the business of the State, was heard to raise its voice against the unjust war an ambitious executive was waging for the increase of his own personal power. D. Rafael Mora saw he must leave Rivas and return to San José; so, placing his brother-in-law, General José Maria Cañas, in charge of the army, with orders to lead it back to Costa Rica, the troubled President mounted his horse, and almost alone took the road to Guanacaste.

It was no part of the Nicaraguan general's plan to waste his strength on an army which was being effectually destroyed by other causes; so he did not move from Granada until he heard the Costa Ricans were preparing to abandon Rivas. Then putting the rifle and light infantry battalions on the lake steamer, he proceeded with them to Virgin Bay. The battalions were landed as quickly as the charred and ruined state of the wharf admitted; and the order was given to advance along the familiar Transit road toward San Juan del Sur. But the force had gone not quite a league when a breathless messenger rode up to inform the general that Cañas was already marching with rapid and disorderly steps toward the La Flor. At the same time the messenger bore a letter addressed to "Wm. Walker, General-in-chief of the Nicaraguan Army," signed "José Maria Cañas, General-in-chief of the Costa Rican Army," and couched in the following terms: "Obliged to abandon the Plaza of Rivas, on account of the appearance of the cholera in a most alarming form, I am forced to leave here a certain number of sick it is impossible to carry away without danger to their lives; but I expect your generosity will treat them with all the attention and care their situation requires. I invoke the laws of humanity in favor of these unfortunate victims of an awful calamity, and I have the honor of proposing to you to exchange them when they get well, for more than twenty prisoners who are now in our power, and whose names I will send you in a detailed list for making the exchange. Believing that this, my proposal, will be admitted, according to the laws of war, I have the honor of subscribing myself, with feelings of the highest consideration, your obedient servant." It is needless to. add, that the surgeons immediately received orders to take charge of the sick of the enemy wherever found.

Such, then, was the conclusion of the first act in the war of extermination. Had the Nicaraguan chief been a proud man, or one capable of rejoicing in the humiliation of a foe, he might have been excused for some elation of spirit at receiving the letter of Cañas. The enemy which, not two months before, had declared war against the "filibusters," and ordered all taken with arms in their hands to be shot, now supplicated the commander-in-chief of the Nicaraguan army to spare the lives of the suffering soldiers left behind at Rivas. The victims of the murderous court-martial at Santa Rosa, the bayonet stabs inflicted on the wounded prisoners found near the altar of the church at Rivas, the insults to the bodies of the brave dead who gave up their lives on the 11th of April, for a country theirs only by adoption, were to be avenged by mercy, and care, and attention, bestowed on the sick and wounded of those who had done the wrongs. It was a revenge such as the Americans might well be proud of—not unworthy either of the cause they advocated, or of the race from which they sprang.

It is scarcely necessary to follow the Costa Ricans in their sad and dreary march from San Juan to San José. The path to the La Flor was blocked with the bodies of stragglers who had fallen behind when the fatal spasms seized them, and prevented them from returning with their comrades. Nor did the scourge cease to pursue them when they entered the territory of Guanacaste. It tracked them to San José, and so well was its work of destruction done, that not more than five hundred of the brave array which had gone forth to exterminate the "filibusters," returned to the capital of the Republic. Then the pestilence turning from the army it had almost wholly devoured, sought its prey among the peaceful families of the land. Young and old, women and children, succumbed to the disease, and some estimate that as many as fourteen thousand died from its effects. Probably, however, the more moderate estimate of ten thousand might cover all the loss to the population of the State.

While the Costa Ricans were occupying Rivas, it was reported that the Legitimists were attempting to raise men in the District of Chontales, and in the departments of Matagalpa and Segovia. Goicouria was sent with Captain Raymond's company to scour the hills of Chontales ; and meeting a small collection of the old Granadinos at Acoyapa, he scattered them in the course of a few moments. Then traversing the greater part of the district, he returned to Granada, and reported all quiet on the other side of the lake. Valle, who was military governor of Segovia, readily dispersed the Legitimists who made some show of a movement near Somoto Grande ;

while Mariano Salazar, sent by the government as commissioner to Matagalpa, pacified the Indians of that region, and returned with his command to Leon. Thus,
in a few weeks, order and quiet were restored to the
whole Republic, and the commands of the provisional
government were respected in all parts of the State.

In the Meridional Department it was necessary to make
examples of some Legitimists who had marched with
the Costa Ricans from Guanacaste to invade the Republic. A principal one of these was Francisco Ugarte,
who had been married to a sister of Dr. Cole's wife. The
general-in-chief heard that Ugarte remained in the department after the departure of the enemy ; and a detachment sent in search of the traitor, found him and
brought him to headquarters. He was tried by a military commission, and ordered to be hung. This mode of
punishment for such offenders being unusual in the country—shooting being resorted to rather than hanging—the
execution of Ugarte made a strong impression on the people, and infused a salutary dread of American justice
among the plotting Legitimists. As there had been some
questions concerning the guardianship of Ugarte's
children, and the administration of their mother's estate
between him and his connections, the natives generally. attributed the arrest of the criminal to information derived from his wife's brother-in-law, Dr. Cole ;
and the prevalence of the suspicion indicates that the
people were not unaccustomed to see adherence to a
party, or proposed devotion to the public interests, made
the stalking-horse for the gratification of family feuds
and personal passions.

For two or three weeks after the departure of Cañas from Rivas, the main body of the Americans were kept at Virgin Bay, detachments being constantly sent to different points of the department, with a view of restoring confidence in the strength of the Rivas administration. The fever was fierce at Granada, carrying off many of those who had lately reached the country. After some days, too, the cholera or colerin appeared at Virgin Bay, and numbers died from it there. Nor were the resident Americans or the soldiers the only victims of fever and cholera at this time. The owners of the Transit not having made proper arrangements for their line, the passengers for California who had come to San Juan del Norte, in April, were obliged to remain in Nicaragua a whole month. Many of these passengers being destitute of means, and irregular in their course of life, readily yielded to the fever then prevailing at Granada ; and the reports they gave of the country, thrown into it as they were without any of the common comforts of civilization, prevented many from going thither. It was not until the 19th of May, that the steamer arrived at San Juan del Sur, and gave these suffering passengers a chance to go to San Francisco.

In spite, however, of the sickness which prevailed among the Americans, their spirits were good and their hopes high. To the casual observer the political elements appeared at rest, and all seemed more tranquil than at any time since the treaty of the 23d of October. The common people, with their strong religious instinct, thought that Providence had sent the cholera in order to drive the Costa Ricans from the soil. The Americans with that faith in themselves which has carried them in a wonderfully short period from one ocean to another, regarded their establishment in Nicaragua as fixed beyond the control of casualties. But to him who knows that great changes in states and societies are not wrought without long and severe labor, the difficulties of the Americans in Nicaragua might appear to be only beginning. To destroy an old political organization is a comparatively easy task, and little besides force is requisite for its accomplishment; but to build up and re-constitute society—to gather the materials from the four quarters, and construct them into an harmonious whole, fitted for the uses of a new civilization—requires more than force, more even than genius for the work, and agents with which to complete it. Time and patience, as well as skill and labor, are needed for success; and they who undertake it, must be willing to devote a lifetime to the work.

At that time there was one man at least in Nicaragua who saw that the path of the Americans was even then beset with thorns. Edmund Randolph, who since the beginning of April, had been in the Occidental Department, came down to Virgin Bay to take passage for New-York. During his stay at Leon and Realejo he had been very ill, almost dead at one time, from an affection of the liver; but in the intervals of his painful sickness, his quick eye had seen an under-current in the affairs of the provisional government. On the 20th of May, just before leaving for San Juan del Norte, he told Walker there was something wrong at Leon; but that confined as he was to his bed he had not the means of ascertaining precisely what was the nature of the evil.

Nor was the information given by Randolph unsupported by other facts. A day or two before the Costa Ricans evacuated Rivas, a courier from Leon had been brought to Granada, and on him were found letters directed to His Excellency, D. Juan Rafael Mora. Walker, on opening these letters, was surprised to find them signed by Patricio Rivas; and one was an official communication from the government stating that it desired to send a commissioner to treat for peace. Of course the general-in-chief detained the courier and the letters, he well knowing that Mora was about to abandon the town of Rivas. The Provisional President in his letters to Walker from Leon, said nothing about these communications with the enemy for some days; and the fact that he had sent such letters to Mora without advising with the general-in-chief was suspicious.

It became, therefore, highly important for the Americans to ascertain the state of affairs at Leon. Hence as soon as the mails for California and the Atlantic States had been despatched, Walker determined to repair to the Occidental Department. The events which transpired at Leon in consequence of that visit present another and a new phase of the war in Nicaragua

Chapter Seventh.

THE DEFECTION OF RIVAS.

ONE of the avowed objects of Jerez in desiring the Provisional President to remove to Leon was to establish friendly relations with the states to the north and particularly with San Salvador. Accordingly, even before the departure of Rivas from Granada, commissioners were sent to Cojutepeque for the purpose of explaining to the cabinet of San Salvador the actual condition of affairs in Nicaragua. But the commissioners met with a cold reception; and on the 7th of May the government of San Salvador sent a communication to the Provisional President declaring that the presence of the Americans in Nicaragua threatened the independence of Central America. The tone of the communication was so insulting that D. Patricio Rivas refused to make any reply. After, however, the retreat of the Costa Ricans from Rivas was known at Cojutepeque the news from San Salvador became more pacific; but soon came news that Guatemala was preparing troops to march against Nicaragua. So frequent and so circumstantial did these reports become, that on the 3d of June Rivas published a proclamation to the people declaring that the troops of

Carrera were marching against the State, and calling on all to take up arms for the Republic.

On the 31st of May, Walker, accompanied by Lieutenant-Colonel Anderson in command of two hundred Rifles, and by Captain Waters with two companies of Rangers, left Granada for Leon; and Gen. Goicouria, who fancied he understood native character because he spoke Spanish, joined the general-in-chief in the excursion to the north. Not far from Masaya the party was met by D. Mariano Salazar, who came to inform Walker of the authenticity of the reports from Guatemala and of the necessity for a portion of the American force to protect the northern frontier. Salazar represented that the people of the Occidental Department were bitter in their hostility to the troops of Carrera and might be depended on for resisting their entrance into the State; but as the Guatemalan force was said to be large and well organized, it was necessary to have some of the Rifles at Leon ready to meet it.

Walker arrived at Leon on the 4th of June, and was received in the most enthusiastic manner. At the entrance to the town, he was met by all the dignitaries of the government and of the department. The streets through which he passed were filled with crowds of the people, shouting a welcome to their deliverers, as they styled the Americans; and the doors and windows of the houses were thronged with women dressed in all the colors of the rainbow. A feast had been prepared for the occasion; but before taking his seat at table the general-in-chief was called to the court-yard of the house where he was quartered, and there had gathered the

10

women of every age and every condition to thank him
for the protection the Americans had given to their
homes.   In the evening the musicians came to sing
songs in praise of American valor, and the local rhym-
sters of the place—of whom there were not a few—
poured forth the sonorous sounds of Castilian verse in
glory of the strangers who had delivered Nicaragua
from the oppressions of her enemies.   All seemed to vie
with each other in their demonstrations of respect and
good-will toward the Rifles and Rangers.

But in the midst of the general joy, it was easy to see
that some of those connected with the government were
not well pleased at the enthusiasm shown by the people.
The face of Jerez had a cloud over it, and he appeared
anxious and nervous ; nor did Rivas seem as much at
ease in the presence of Walker as he had formerly been.
The threatening attitude of San Salvador and the rumor-
ed march of the troops of Carrera alarmed the Provisional
President, and it was evident that Jerez did not strive to
diminish the apprehensions of Rivas.   Soon after Walker
reached Leon the President told him the cabinet of Cojutepeque had proposed the reduction of the American
force in the service of Nicaragua to two hundred men,
and had intimated that if the proposal were accepted
relations would be established with the provisional government.   The manner in which Rivas spoke of the proposal indicated that he was not averse to the plan, but
the reply of Walker that such a proposition could be
entertained only when the State was ready to pay the
men it discharged, showed the President he need not
expect the general-in-chief to co-operate in the policy
suggested by San Salvador.

During the month of April an election had been called for president as well as for senators and representatives. An election had taken place at different times during the month of May, in several of the districts of the State, but the irregularity in the voting had been such and the condition of the Republic was so disturbed that all parties considered the election as invalid. Little or no attention was paid to it, and as quiet now prevailed throughout the State, the propriety of a decree for a new election was being discussed at the time Walker left Granada for Leon. The votes polled in May were mostly in the Occidental Department, and were divided between Jerez, Rivas, and Salazar. The Granadinos, alarmed at this and fearful that the seat of government might be permanently fixed at Leon, were speaking of Walker as the fit person for the presidency, while the Republic was threatened with invasion by the adjacent States. When the general-in-chief reached Leon the question of calling an election was also discussed there, and he was surprised to find the President and Jerez, who had a few weeks before insisted on an election, now hostile to the measure. The only minister who seemed at all friendly to the proposition for a new election was D. Sebastian Salinas, then holding the portfolio of Relations. Walker urged the President to call the election, for he saw that Don Patricio was frightened by appearances in the north, and could not be relied on to face the coalition preparing against Nicaragua, and he thought it prudent to have the election called while the State was comparatively quiet and before it was more seriously menaced.

While this decree was being discussed news reached

Leon of the reception of Father Vigil by the United States government as Minister from Nicaragua. At the same time the arrival of Col. Jaquess at Granada with about one hundred and eighty men, was announced. Hereafter it may be necessary to examine the manner of Vigil's reception and the causes which led to it; at present the fact is merely stated in order to show the effect it had on the deliberations at Leon. Of course it strengthened the American influence in Nicaragua, and while it tended to make the prospect of hostilities from San Salvador more remote, it gave an additional reason for fixing the government on a firm basis by an appeal to the popular will; attended, too, by an addition to the numbers of the Americans, it made the friends of the election stronger than before.

Several circumstances, in the meanwhile, occurred to show the disaffection of many of the principal men toward the Americans. D. Mariano Salazar, as Walker ascertained after reaching Leon, had made a sale of some brazil-wood he owned to the government, on terms advantageous to himself, and tending to diminish the receipts of the customs at Realejo. In the actual condition of affairs it was necessary for the State to get every cent of revenue possible; and hence it was reprehensible for a friend of the government, and especially for a military officer, to speculate on the necessities of the Republic. Under the army regulations derived from the old Spanish service, it was not permitted for an officer to contract with the State, unless with the permission of the general-in-chief. Hence Walker, to rebuke the act of Salazar, put him under arrest, and kept him in his house for some hours. Several of the leading persons of the city came to intercede for Salazar during his short arrest, and endeavored to excuse his act as not unusual in the country ; and it was easy to see that they were not at all favorable to an authority which aimed to protect the State from contractors and speculators.

The Sunday after reaching Leon, Goicouria proposed to call together the chief persons of the city and converse freely with them about the state of affairs. He constantly labored under the delusion that he knew the natives, whereas he always under-estimated the capacity of the leaders and the virtues of the people. But he got a number of the prominent politicians together, and gave them a rambling discourse on his ideas—most crude they were—of re-organizing the country. He touched on the ecclesiastical authority, and suggested an application to the Pope for the appointment of a Bishop who might be free from the metropolitan of Guatemala. The suggestion was innocent enough in itself, but D. José Guerrero, a wily intriguer who once, while Director, had got up a revolution against his own government as an excuse for prolonging his authority, distorted Goicouria's suggestion into such a shape that it was soon reported through the city the Americans aimed to draw Nicaragua from the jurisdiction of the Roman See. Goicouria expected to influence the ambition of the higher clergy, by placing before them visions of the mitre and the crosier, but a more dexterous politician than himself managed to turn his suggestion to his own disadvantage. The fact is, the natives disliked Goicouria because they took him for a Spaniard, and the Nicaraguans hate the

Spaniards more than they do any other foreigners. Of course the general-in-chief knew nothing of Goicouria's suggestion until after it was made; his policy had always been to leave the church entirely to the management of its own affairs. But it was easy for the disaffected to make Goicouria's speech appear the inspiration of his commanding officer; and the reports circulated about this silly meeting showed Walker that there were many in Leon desirous of exciting popular passions and prejudices against the Americans. Those, too, whose loyalty to the Americans was beyond doubt, were every day telling the general-in-chief that certain agencies were at work to destroy the confidence of the people in the naturalized Nicaraguans. Valle, who was rather superciliously treated by the educated leaders, because he could not read or write, insisted that no faith was to be put in the friendly professions of many who owed power to the will of the general-in-chief. D. Nasario Escoto, also, who had succeeded Castellon in the provisional government, previous to the treaty of peace, said no reliance should be placed on the firmness of the persons then directing the government. In fact, all things tended to show that, in case Nicaragua were invaded by San Salvador and Guatemala, the Americans might find the machinery of the government they had created and sustained turned against themselves. Hence, unless disposed to carry off Rivas as a prisoner—and thereby the whole moral force of his government would have been lost—it was necessary for the welfare of the Americans that a new election should be called.

Finally, after much deliberation, the decree calling an

immediate election was drawn up in full cabinet session, and was signed on Tuesday the 10th of June. Walker proposed to leave for Granada early on the morning of the 11th. The evening before his departure he was visited several times by Jerez, who had an anxious and nervous manner not unusual with him. Three or four times he called in the course of as many hours; and there was much conversation between him and the general-in-chief relative to another minister to the United States, as it was thought Father Vigil would prefer returning to Nicaragua. Jerez himself had been spoken of for the place, and Walker mentioned to him that if he desired it the appointment might be urged on Don Patricio. Afterward the minister remarked, " My visit to the United States is then decided on ;" but in such a tone as intimated it might be an excuse to get rid of him. The immediate reply was, his appointment should be pressed only in case he desired it. This incident serves to show the temper of Jerez, and points out the influences which wrought on the pliable mind of Rivas.

Early on the morning of the 11th Walker left Leon escorted by the Rangers and leaving Anderson's Rifles with Col. Natzmer in the city. The President and many others of the chief citizens of the department accompanied him several miles on his journey ; and at parting Don Patricio affectionately embraced the general-in-chief, remarking with moist eyes that he might be depended on in every emergency. Salazar, in spite of the arrest, was also of the party ; but Jerez was absent. All cordially saluted the general ; and the latter proceeded to Managua where he remained over night, and the next day arrived at Masaya early in the afternoon.

Walker had not been many hours at Masaya before he received letters from Col. Natzmer relating strange events at Leon. On the morning of the 12th the military governor of the department, Escobar, had asked a detail of Americans to guard the *Principal*—a strong building on the Plaza where the arms and ammunition were stored—and no sooner was the sentry from the Rifles posted than a singular movement was perceptible in the town. The President and the Ministers hastily left the government house near the Principal, and Mariano Salazar on horseback rode through the streets, proclaiming that the Americans were about to make Rivas prisoner and to assassinate the Ministers and chief men of the city. The excitement soon became intense; the barriers of San Felipe, one of the most turbulent quarters of the town, began to send forth its unquiet residents, some of them armed and all endeavoring to increase the popular ferment. Then it was reported Rivas had left the city; and the women, regarding the movement as a revolution and the signal of war, commenced packing their trunks and closing their doors and windows. Natzmer, seeing the threatening aspect of the men at the barriers, called the Americans to the Plaza and placing them under arms, prepared for defence.

At once a courier was despatched to Chinandega with orders for Lieut. Dolan—who was there with a company of Rifles—to march immediately for Leon. Dolan was but a short distance on his march, when he met Rivas and Jerez riding toward Chinandega. The singularity of the fact made him suspect something was wrong, and he thought of arresting them on their way; but the surgeon with him, Dr. Dawson, who had lived for many years in Nicaragua, suggested that it would not be proper for a simple lieutenant to arrest the President and one of his Ministers. Dolan, therefore, marched on without molesting them, and soon joined Anderson in the Plaza.

As soon as these tidings reached Walker, he ordered Col. Jaquess, then in Masaya with his command, to prepare for a march; and Jaquess with the Rangers was in a short time on the road to Managua. Couriers met Walker every few hours on his way toward Leon; and when near Nagarote he was met by Ferdinand Schlessinger—a man to whom Rivas had given a commission to fortify the harbor of Realejo. Schlessinger told the general-in-chief, that Rivas and Jerez were at Chinandega, barricading the town, and pressing natives into military service; also, that they had given him orders to stop the works at Point Ycaco, and in consequence of his suspicions he had made good his escape. At the same time, letters from Natzmer informed Walker that Jerez, as Minister of War, had issued orders to him to disoccupy the towers of the cathedral, where riflemen had been placed, in order that troops of the country might be stationed there. Natzmer forwarded the order to Walker, awaiting his instructions on the subject.

As soon as Natzmer's letter reached Walker, he sent the order to obey the command of Jerez, and to withdraw the whole American force from Leon to Nagarote. The designs of Rivas and Jerez were now apparent to everybody; and they had, on their arrival at Chinandega, gone so far as to send a commissioner to invite the

10*

troops of Carrera into the State, and to urge their immediate approach to Leon. Jerez had given the order to Natzmer, supposing it would not be obeyed, thereby hoping to make the movement against the Americans turn on their disobedience to a lawful authority. But Walker was not disposed to have the coming struggle occur on any such issue. He determined to have the contest made on more formal grounds. Not knowing, either, how far the defection of the native leaders had spread, he was anxious to concentrate his force scattered on a long line from Leon to Castillo ; therefore military no less than political reasons led him to await with Jaquess at Nagarote the arrival of Natzmer and Anderson, and then to march with the united force toward Granada.

A number of the native residents about Leon and some families accompanied the Rifles to Nagarote, and among them were D. José Maria Valle and D. Mateo Pineda. The latter was a man of rare truth and fidelity for a Central American—in fact, his virtues would make him remarkable in any country. With a name so pure that it has escaped the malice of his enemies during all the civil disturbances of Nicaragua, he stands almost a solitary example, in that distracted land, of spotless faith and unshaken loyalty. He has required no defence save his high honor and stainless character to protect him from the persecutions of political enemies ; and if other proofs were lacking of the devotion the Americans in Nicaragua yielded to right and justice, they might find ample evidence in the single fact that Mateo Pineda adhered to their fortunes in each extremity of good and evil.

When the Rifles reached Nagarote they, with the Rangers and the new infantry battalion, took up the line of march for Masaya. At Managua they found the commandant of the post, José Herrera, firm in his faith to the Americans, and he remained true until death, in spite of a brother's efforts to seduce him from the path of military duty, being executed by the allies, under the sentence of a court-martial some time afterward, for his adhesion to the Americans.

On arriving at Granada, the general-in-chief published the decree re-constructing the provisional government by virtue of the treaty of the twenty-third of October. That treaty guaranteed the naturalized Nicaraguans equality of privileges with the native born; but the President and his ministers had violated it by attempting to create distinctions to the prejudice of the naturalized citizens. Walker had sworn, not only to observe the treaty himself, but to cause it to be observed. He remained the sole sponsor for Rivas before Nicaragua and before the world; and he would have deserved to be branded as a perjured man had he permitted Rivas with impunity not merely to excite the passions of the people against the Americans, but to invite the foreign foe into the State with a view of expelling the naturalized soldiers. In addition to the duties devolved on Walker by his oath to cause the treaty to be observed, he had been invested with unlimited authority to protect the Oriental and Meridional Departments from the foreign enemies of the Republic; but how could such protection be afforded if the orders of the political power, giving the enemy free entry into the State, were to be respected ? Therefore, the commissioner for the Oriental and Meridional Departments, D. Fermin Ferrer, was named Provisional President until the people might select their own ruler, under the decree issued by Rivas on the 10th of June. The same day the decree was published Walker issued an address to the people of Nicaragua, and after reciting the acts of the Rivas government, he concluded: " With such accumulated crimes—conspiring against the very people it was bound to protect—the late provisional government was no longer worthy of existence. In the name of the people I have, therefore, declared its dissolution, and have organized a provisional government, until the nation exercises its natural right óf electing its own rulers."

Under the decree of the 10th of June the election for President took place on the fourth Sunday of the month and the two succeeding days. The voting was general in the Oriental and Meridional Departments ; but as D. Patricio Rivas rescinded his own decree after reaching Chinandega, and as the Guatemalans had already passed the northern frontier of the State there were no ballots cast in the Occidental Department. A large majority of the votes polled were for the general-in-chief; and the Provisional President, Ferrer, declaring the result of the election by decree, fixed on the 12th of July for the inauguration of the President elect. Accordingly, on the appointed day, with due observances, both civil and religious, Walker took the oath of office on the Plaza of Granada, and was installed as Chief Executive of the Republic of Nicaragua.

A few days after the decree of the 20th of June was

published, the Costa Rican schooner, San José, commanded by Gilbert Morton, entered the port of San Juan
del Sur. She had been purchased from her former
owner, Alvarado, by Mariano Salazar, and he had made
Morton nominal half-owner of the schooner, supposing
she might thereby get the right to carry American colors.
The American vice-consul at Realejo, one Giauffreau,
gave the schooner what Morton called a sailing letter; and
the vice-consul, according to all accounts, was either so
ignorant or so neglectful of his duties as to permit the vessel to fly the American flag and to be cleared from the
port of Realejo under this pretended sailing letter. The
commandant at Chinandega, a Cuban, by the name of
Golibard, had been ordered away by Rivas because he
refused to forsake the Americans; and Golibard was
aboard the San José when she arrived at San Juan del
Sur. Morton, thinking he could impose on the port
authorities with his sailing letter from Giauffreau, had
not hesitated to enter the harbor; and he, as well as
Salazar, supposed they might, under the American flag,
drive a profitable trade with the schooner during hostilities between Nicaragua and the other States.

But the San José had not been many hours in the
port of San Juan before she was seized, the charge
against her being that she was without a flag and without lawful papers. The schooner was American-built
and had passed from the flag of the United States to
that of Costa Rica. Even if she had then been re-sold
to an American citizen she could not have recovered her
original character without an act of Congress. Morton,
after the seizure, appealed for relief to the U. S. States

Minister at Granada : but on a careful examination of the subject Mr. Wheeler was satisfied that the schooner, far from being entitled to protection by American authority, was really amenable for an abuse of the American flag. The San José was, therefore, condemned by a court of admiralty jurisdiction at the port of San Juan ; and being forfeited to the government of Nicaragua, she was converted into a schooner-of-war, bearing the flag of the Isthmian Republic.

The Granada was armed with two six-pound carronades and was placed in charge of Lieutenant Callender Irvine Fayssoux. This officer was a native of Missouri, and had served for a time in the Texan navy under the orders of Commodore Moore. He had also accompanied Gen. Lopez in his expedition to the Island of Cuba in May, 1850 ; and at Cardenas he had contributed essentially to the successful landing of the force from the steamer Creole, by swimming ashore with a rope in his mouth when there was much embarrassment as to the means of getting the boat up to the wharf. His high qualities will hereafter appear when we come to relate the history of the schooner ; and it is only necessary here to say, that his system and order were such, the Granada was ready for service in a very short time. The men detailed from different companies of the army for service on the schooner were soon brought under good discipline by their efficient commander ; and all of them felt they were subject to the orders of one capable of command, and determined to have each man do his duty on all occasions.

On the 29th of June, Col. John Allen of Kentucky

arrived at Granada with one hundred and four men for the service of the State; and on the 6th of July about the same number were landed coming from New-York, from New-Orleans and from California. A day or two after the latter arrival, Major Waters, with about a hundred Rangers, marched to Leon and reconnoitred the town. He found it barricaded in every quarter, and the Guatemalans under General Paredes were occupying the main Plaza. On the approach of Waters all the pickets of the enemy were drawn in, and their whole force was put under arms for action. But no portion of the enemy ventured to leave the barricades. After passing through the suburbs of the city and examining the preparations of the enemy for defence, Waters returned to Granada with a report showing the inability of the Allies—as they called themselves—to move until they had received large additions of force.

After the inauguration of Walker on the 12th of July, his cabinet was formed by the appointment of D. Fermin Ferrer as Minister of Relations, D. Mateo Pineda as Minister of War, and D. Manuel Carrascosa as Minister of Hacienda and Public Credit. The organization of the new government was duly communicated to the American Minister; and on the 19th of July Mr. Wheeler was received by the President at the government house in Granada. The Minister opened his address to the Executive of Nicaragua, saying: "I am directed by the President of the United States to notify you that I am instructed to establish relations with this State." Mr. Wheeler thus showed himself far bolder and more decided than Mr. Pierce had been at Washington. It is

true the government at Washington had instructed its
minister " to establish relations" with the government
of Nicaragua ; but at the time the order was given
it was thought Rivas would be in power at Granada.
Mr. Marcy had also instructed Mr. Wheeler to ask
explanations concerning the revocation of the charter
of the Accessory Transit Company, and to request the
discharge from the Nicaraguan army of two or three
boys—among them a son and nephew, I think, of Senator Bayard of Delaware—who had run off from school
and gone to Central America in search of novelty and
adventure.   Of course the explanations of the decree of
revocation and the discharges of the boys could be obtained only from Walker ; and hence the minister had
either to disregard the orders of Mr. Marcy or to recognize the government of the lately-elected President.

The message Mr. Pierce sent to Congress, touching the
reception of Father Vigil, was strongly marked with the
weakness and hesitation of American diplomacy.   The
whole tone of the message was apologetic ; and the
American President was throughout overcome by the
false idea many people in the United States had formed as
to the Nicaraguan movement being one of annexation to
the Republic of the North.   The representatives of
France, Spain, Brazil, and the Spanish American States,
at Washington, seeing the weakness of the United States,
combined for the purpose of driving Father Vigil from
the country.   So well did they succeed, that the Minister
of Nicaragua withdrew from the Federal Capital not
many days after his reception, and thus Mr. Marcy, aided by the intrigues of the foreign representatives, might

be able to take advantage of any opportunity circumstances afforded to relieve the American cabinet from the
awkward position in which he fancied it had been placed.
Hence the vexation of the Secretary of State may be
imagined when he heard Mr. Wheeler had, in literally
carrying out his instructions, recognized the government
which displaced that of Rivas.

Mr. Wheeler, being on the ground, and seeing the
actual condition of affairs, was never in doubt as to the
policy his country ought to pursue toward the parties
contending in Nicaragua ; but the Secretary of State at
Washington, remote from the scene of trouble, constantly
wrought on by the ministers of foreign countries, and
dreading the effect the new Nicaraguan movement would
have on old political organizations in the United States,
was always averse to any action which might favor the
Americans in Nicaragua. Not many days, however,
after Mr. Wheeler recognized the Walker government,
facts occurred showing in a strong light the good policy
of the American minister.

Lieut. Fayssoux, as soon as he was ready for sea, received orders to sail northward from San Juan and
cruise about the Gulf of Fonseca. It was well known
that the enemy were communicating with San Salvador
and Guatemala by bungos from Tempisque to La
Union, and it was hoped the Granada might intercept
letters showing the state of affairs at Leon and the relations of Rivas with the other States. The presence,
too, of the schooner in those waters could not fail to
alarm the enemy and embarrass the reinforcements going
toward Leon. It was also reported that the enemy were

preparing vessels to send after the Granada in order to capture her, and that these vessels were being fitted out at La Union, in the State of San Salvador.

On the evening of the 21st of July, the schooner hove anchor and put to sea, and on the afternoon of the 23d she was cruising off the entrance of the Gulf of Fonseca. "At 3h. 30m.," so the log runs, "saw a sail standing out of the gulf: made chase. At 5h. 30m. brought her to with a shot from the port gun. Capt. De Brissot (a passenger on the schooner) boarded her. She proved to be the Italian brig Rostan, from La Union, bound to San Juan del Sur. She reported two Chilian brigs and one Sardinian schooner lying at La Union, and the French frigate Embuscade at Tiger Island. At 7, took in flying-jib and foresail, and stood off and on, on the lookout for a schooner that the Rostan reported due from the northward and westward." Then, on the 24th: "At 9h. 15m. A. M., saw a sail standing out from La Union. At 2 P. M. light breezes from S. and W. At 4, standing to the E., passed, on opposite tracks, the French frigate Embuscade. At 4h. 30m., saw a number of small craft to the E.: called all hands to quarters. At 5, boarded the launch Maria, Capt. Braganda. She proving to be French, and her papers all right, she was allowed to proceed on her course to Tempisque. Capt. Braganda reported the same as the brig Rostan, therefore, as there were none of the enemy's vessels in the gulf, we concluded to go out to look for the schooner from the N. and W."

Nothing, however, was seen of the vessel expected from the northward and westward, and on the 26th, the

Granada again stood up the gulf. On the 27th, a bungo, with several passengers, was captured, and on the 28th, a large boat from Tempisque was taken, and one of the passengers proved to be Mariano Salazar. When Salazar was brought aboard the Granada he gave his name as Francisco Salazar, but De Brissot had seen him at Realejo, and, although not certain of the fact, told Fayssoux he thought the prisoner was Don Mariano. In the same bungo with Salazar were several letters for persons in San Salvador. The day after Salazar was taken, the Granada sailed for San Juan del Sur, whence the prisoner and the letters were immediately, on the schooner's arrival, despatched for Granada.

Salazar was executed as a traitor on the Plaza of Granada late in the afternoon of the 3d of August. It was Sunday, and the people of the town gathered in numbers to witness the execution. They regarded Salazar as the author of most of the misfortunes they had undergone during the civil war. It was his money had fitted out the democratic bands which had burnt the Jalteva, and robbed the shop-keepers of the suburbs; and they regarded it as a special providence that he should be taken by a schooner he had himself owned, and be executed by the Americans he had first used and then attempted to betray. There was the same joyful feeling shown by the old Legitimists at the death of Salazar as had been shown by the Democrats at the execution of Corral.

Among the letters taken in the gulf was one from Manning, the British vice-consul at Realejo, to his correspondent at San Miguel, D. Florencio Souza. It was

dated at Leon, on the 24th of July, and is so characteristic that the most of it deserves insertion as an instance
of British conduct and British policy. He pathetically
begins: " Dear Friend ; I am here without knowing
where to go, since Walker will not give us a passport
to pass through Granada. I understand the man is
furious against me, attributing to me the change. It is
certain that all his acts are rapid : and we have not
passed here without great apprehensions that he will
make an attack on Leon. He came as far as Managua,
and all we know is that he returned to Granada. If
this man receives forces and money, I assure you it will
not be so easy to drive him out of the State ; for as the
forces come from the other States in handfuls of men
nothing is accomplished, and the expenses and sacrifices
are made in vain. I am much afflicted to think that
under these circumstances no more activity is used in
so serious an affair. At the present there are 500 men
from San Salvador, 500 from Guatemala, and 800 belonging to this place, and according to my judgment
double that number is required." Then from public
affairs the wily trader comes to business. " Altogether
affairs are wretched in Nicaragua and very distressing,
and if I remain here much longer I shall not have a
shirt I can put on. Already you can suppose how much
I have suffered by these convulsions." He prepares to
make Souza useful to himself by seeming to have a care
for the interests of the Salvadorian : " It is known," he
writes, " that a certain Fabens has sailed to Boston with
the gold quartz, and that with one Heiss he has bought
the mine from Padre Sosa. You need not be afraid but

I will do all I can for your interest in this affair with all earnestness ; and you should write to Davis in Boston via Omoa, inquiring whether the ore Fabens and Heiss took was from the mines of Bestaniere." At last, and like a lady's postscript, comes the gist of the letter: " The troops here are altogether naked. If you have any drilling you can sell at 12½ cents per yard, I will take ten bales. Don't forget my request in favor of my adopted son, Mr. George Brower, to have him appointed to represent San Salvador in Liverpool." Much as the vice-consul sympathized with the cause of the allies, he could not let the chance slip of making some money from the drilling the soldiers required.

When the friends of Salazar at Leon heard of his capture in the gulf, they immediately arrested Dr. Joseph W. Livingston, an American long resident in Nicaragua, and sent a courier to Granada saying they would hold him as a hostage for Salazar's safety. The British vice-consul did not disdain to write a letter to the American Minister entreating him to save the life of Salazar in order that Livingston might go unharmed. But the courier arrived several days after the execution of the Leonese traitor ; and Mr. Wheeler was not a man to be startled from his propriety by the cunning devices of Mr. Manning. In his reply to the British vice-consul the American Minister draws the distinction between Salazar and Livingston in such words as probably little suited his correspondent. " Salazar," he writes, " was one—and a most prominent one—of a faction revolting against the lawful government of the Republic, and a general in their forces. He knew that he was liable to the penalty of treason. Dr. Livingston is an American citizen, much loved and respected, and owes no allegiance to the authorities of Nicaragua, much less to a disappointed faction; nor has he ever been mixed up with the parties by any overt or belligerent act." At the same time he answered Mr. Manning's letter, Mr. Wheeler wrote to General Ramon Belloso, commanding-in-chief the Allied forces, informing the latter that if any harm befell Dr. Livingston, the government of the United States would promptly hold the governments of San Salvador and Guatemala to a strict accountability. He concluded by saying, that "if one hair of Dr. Livingston's head is injured, or his life taken, or that of another American citizen, your government and that of Guatemala will feel the force of a power which, while it respects the rights of other nations, will be ready and is able to vindicate its own honor and the lives and property of its citizens." Brave words these; and they might have resulted in worthy deeds if Mr. Wheeler had controlled the necessary force; but when read with the gloss of after events, they are turned into a biting sarcasm on the government he represented. The life of Livingston was, however, probably saved by the energetic words of the Minister; though he was ordered from the State in which he had been living for ten years.

Some days after these events occurred, Hon. Pierre Soulé arrived at Granada. He went thither with the object of securing some modifications in a decree which had been published by Rivas a few days before his flight from Leon to Chinandega. The decree authorized commissioners to negotiate a loan of five hundred thousand dollars, to be secured by a million of acres of the public lands. The modifications suggested by Mr. Soulé were soon made, and S. F. Slatter and Mason Pilcher became the commissioners to act under the decree. The bonds issued under this decree are the only legal bonds of the Republic ever sold in the United States, and the common impression that large quantities of Nicaraguan obligations are afloat is altogether erroneous.

But, although the decree for the loan was the immediate object of Mr. Soulé's visit, his presence in Nicaragua had other beneficial results. His fine head and noble air made a deep impression on the people of the country, peculiarly sensitive as they are to the charms of feature and of manner; and then he spoke the Castilian with such lofty elegance, and addressed the common people with so much kindness and insight into their wants and feelings that all listened to him with mingled delight and reverence. The docility of the native Nicaraguans, especially of the Indians, is great, and when approached with gentleness and persuasion they may be led in almost any direction. The influence of such words as Mr. Soulé spoke to them remained for a long time, and often after he left they used to ask when His Excellency, a title they give to persons they consider of rank, would return to Nicaragua.

During the month of August not many persons arrived in the country, either for military service or for civil pursuits. A new and more dangerous disease, also, began to make its appearance in the army; desertion, more fatal than cholera, commenced its ravages in the ranks. The first notable desertion was that of one Turley with a whole company of Rangers. They were sent from Managua by the commandant, Capt. Dolan, with orders to examine the road along the southwestern shore of the lake, as far as Tipitapa. For several days Dolan anxiously awaited their return ; but news reached Granada of their being seen on the Malacatoya river. It was not until many days, however, that their purposes and fate were known. They appear to have deserted with the intention of proceeding through Chontales, robbing and plundering as they went, and of finally reaching the sea by the Blewfields river. Some circumstances indicate that the plan was formed before Turley and his men reached Nicaragua; for on their arrival they were very urgent in the request to remain a company by themselves, and they had been in the service only a few weeks when they deserted. Their plan, however, whether long meditated or the result of sudden resolution, met with the punishment it deserved.

Many days after Turley's disappearance a French trader, from the mining town of Libertad, came to Granada to inform Walker of the fate of the deserters. When they first appeared in Chontales the people supposed they were on duty, but their violent and rapacious acts soon betrayed their true character. They passed into the mining district, and near Libertad they tied up and flogged a Frenchman, in order to make him disclose the place where he kept his gold. Then the French of the district, composed mostly of those discharged from the army at Rivas in the March previous, acting together, raised a number of the people of the country and attacked the robbers. Turley's party was, it seems, short of ammunition, and they finally agreed to give up their arms if they were furnished with a guide to conduct them to the Blewfields. Their arms were given up, and soon thereafter, while they were being marched, by their captors, toward the town, fire was opened on them, and they were all, except two, slaughtered on the spot.

With the exception, however, of Turley's company, desertion among the Americans was, at that time, rare. The desertions, though not many, were principally confined to the Europeans in the ranks. Many of these Europeans had gone to Nicaragua with the idea of enlisting for the mere pay they were to get; and without the foresight or patience which might enable them to wait for time to enhance the value of the lands they were to receive, they became dissatisfied with the scarcity of money, and sought means of leaving the army and the country. New-comers, also, were frightened by the reports constantly circulated as to the number and strength of the enemy; and it was among those who knew least of the land that the disposition to despond was greatest. In addition to these causes, tending to diminish the strength of the army, a large proportion of the men going to Nicaragua at the expense of the State, were found unfit for military service. As they could not be examined surgically in the United States, their defects were not known until they came under the eye of the surgical staff at Granada. Those familiar with medical statistics, may readily imagine how many of the men were rejected for the single disease of hernia.

The enemy, however, were not without causes of weakness and dissension. Some of the faults of their

11

force arose from its allied nature. The soldiers in Leon were drawn from Guatemala and San Salvador; and besides these, Rivas had pressed numbers of laborers about Leon and Chinandega into the ranks. The Guatemalan contingent was made up entirely of Indians, and fierce was the feud between them and the Leoneses. Not unfrequently collisions would occur between the Guatemalans and the people of the town, at the numerous liquor shops scattered through the suburbs of Subtiaba; and in the quarrels knives would be drawn, and blood spilled. So pressing was the evil that the Guatemalan soldiers were finally ordered to remain in their quarters, and it was necessary to keep them out of the streets, in order that the insults of the people might be avoided. The Salvadorians were tolerated by the Leoneses; but the local authorities could not prevail on the latter to regard the former as their deliverers from tyranny and oppression.

The allied troops had not been many days at Leon, before fever and cholera attacked them. The Guatemalans especially suffered from this disease; and so great was their loss, that many among the soldiers, and some even of the officers, attributed the malady to poisonous substances mixed in their food. But it was easy for a medical eye to perceive sufficient causes for the mortality of the troops in their sudden removal from the highlands of Guatemala to the plains of Nicaragua, and in the total want of comfort and cleanliness about the quarters and persons of the soldiers. As Manning wrote, the troops were almost without clothing; and this was a severe deprivation to the Guatemala Indian, accustomed to the use of the thick woollen jacket, which protects him from the cold of his native hills. And woollen covering at night is indispensable to the health of the soldier in Nicaragua. The warm days, followed by the clear cold nights, render blankets necessary at all seasons of the year ; and it was the want of care in sleeping which produced much of the disease, not only among the Guatemalans at Leon, but also among the Americans at Granada. When you add to these causes, the little attention Central American officers pay to the health of their soldiers, and the small skill of their surgeons and physicians, it is not difficult to understand the mortality among the Allies.

While disease was destroying the soldiers and dissensions were spreading between the people and the troops, the leaders were not more friendly in their feelings toward each other than were their followers : the consequences were divided counsels and conflicting conduct. The chief command of the allied force had been given by the provisional government of Rivas to General Ramon Belloso, the commander of the San Salvador contingent. But Paredes, who commanded the Guatemalans, was little disposed to obey the orders of a man he regarded as altogether his inferior in knowledge and capacity, and he also thought it unworthy of his Republic to yield the control of her forces to the general of a much feebler State. The Guatemalans consider theirs the best organized and the leading State of Central America ; and the pure Spanish race, which maintains its supremacy at the seat of the old captain-generalcy by the aid of Carrera and his Indians, regards, with some disdain, the irregular governments the mixed races attempt to establish. On the contrary, the self-styled liberals throughout Central America have a bitter hatred toward Carrera and his minions, as they call the Aycinenas and the Pavones, who really direct the affairs of the Republic, under the nominal presidency of the illiterate Indian. And it was jealousy of Guatemala which induced Rivas and Jerez to place the command in the hands of the Salvadorian general. Paredes, however, seems to have retained the privilege of refusing to obey Belloso whenever he thought proper, and the latter was not in the position to enforce obedience or to dispense with the services of the Guatemalans.

Besides the dissensions in the allied camp, there were two authorities in the upper part of Nicaragua claiming the supreme executive power. At Leon, D. Patricio Rivas and his cabinet asserted their right to be esteemed by the Allies the sovereign authority of the Republic ; while at Somoto Grande, in Segovia, D. José Maria Estrada had set up his government, and issued orders in the name of the people of Nicaragua. Each of these cabals ridiculed the claims of the other, and their contentions were like to involve the allied States in new difficulties. Estrada had sought refuge in Honduras after the treaty of the twenty-third of October, and had published a pamphlet, claiming a right to be chief executive of Nicaragua, because he had written a private decree, declaring null and void the treaty made by Corral under the absolute power he had conferred. Everybody laughed at the idea of giving force to a decree which was unheard of until published in Honduras ;

but when the defection of Rivas took place, Estrada entered Segovia under the protection of a few Legitimists, commanded by Martinez. The latter proceeded toward Matagalpa, in order to press the Indians of that region into his service, while the Senator-president, as Estrada called himself, remained at Somoto Grande.

The Legitimist pretender was now in the way of his own party. He had not the discretion to perceive that by thus placing himself as an obstacle to the union of the two factions against the Americans, he made his removal from Nicaragua an object with his friends as well as his enemies. The idea of his being purposely left at Somoto Grande without any adequate guard, seems not to have entered his mind. But the fact of Estrada's defenceless condition was soon known at Leon —known in so short a time as almost to preclude any explanation, save that the information was sent by some of his own adherents. Immediately, a violent Democrat, who had been imprisoned at Granada during the civil war and was released by Walker on the thirteenth of October, 1855, collected a band of some forty-five or fifty armed men and hurried on toward Somoto Grande. This man, by name Antonio Chavis, could scarcely have acted as he did without the knowledge and assistance of the Rivas administration. Chavis reached Somoto Grande without Estrada hearing of his approach, and while the Granadino was indulging his dream of regaining power in the Republic, the Democrats from Leon surprised and murdered him in the streets of the mountain village.

The murder of Estrada reminds us of the dark craft

which marks the history of the Italian Republics during the thirteenth, fourteenth, and fifteenth centuries. The same causes which in Italy produced the Carraras of Padua, the Viscontis of Milan, and finally the master-piece of the school, Cæsar Borgia, Duke of Urbino, have brought forth the same type of character in the politicians and soldiers of the Spanish American Republics. It is true, there is wanting in the latter the exalted intellect and refined taste of the former, and the mixed race of Central and South America could never produce a Machiavelli capable of depicting with terrible truth the principles, if such they may be called, controlling the political action of his countrymen. But the Spanish American is as dark, though not as deep and wise, in his craft as the Italian. And long civil war seems to have the power of creating this type of politicians, even among races least affected toward it ; for the English wars of the Roses produced the subtle genius of the third Richard, who vied with the best Italian of them all in his adherence to the maxims of the illustrious author of The Prince.

Thus, by the death of Estrada, the old Legitimists who had emigrated after the treaty of the twenty-third of October, were led to acknowledge the authority of D. Patricio Rivas. Thenceforth Martinez who had, with a few men and some arms, penetrated as far as Matagalpa acted unders the orders of the provisional government at Leon. It was easier, however, for the leaders to settle their differences and to agree on a common plan of action than for them to extinguish the hatreds and animosities they had kindled and fed among their respective followers. They did not venture for some time to place Legitimists in the same camp with the Democrats they had either inveigled or forced into their service, and it was necessary, during the war, for them to keep the soldiers of the two factions as widely apart as possible.

Toward the close of the month of August the arrangements of the Walker administration with Garrison and Morgan, for bringing Americans to Nicaragua, were completed. The commissioners appointed to investigate the indebtedness of the old Canal Company to the government had reported in July; and the dues from the company, according to the report, amounted to more than four hundred thousand dollars. Some payments, had, however, been made, but the report did not estimate them, because the company had failed to appear, and the judgment against them was by default. After deducting all payments, still the indebtedness was upward of three hundred and fifty thousand dollars, and this was much more than the value ot all the property on the Isthmus. The property was, therefore, sold to Garrison and Morgan, they paying therefor in the bonds they had received for advances made to the Rivas government. In the meantime the American minister, obeying the instructions of his chief, examined the facts which led to the revocation of the charters of the Canal and Accessory Transit Companies. Besides the explanations given by the Nicaraguan government, and the facts brought out in the report of the commissioners, Mr. Wheeler examined a number of witnesses, whose depositions he forwarded to the State Department at Washington. The facts reported by the minister were so conclusive as to the legality and justice of the proceedings against the companies, that Mr. Marcy never wrote another word on the subject.

In fact the Accessory Transit Company had itself furnished the American government with the most satisfactory evidence of its own unscrupulous and criminal character. On the 8th of April, while Mora was yet in Nicaragua, Thomas Lord, the vice-president of the company, wrote to Hosea Birdsall, authorizing him " to ask for the assistance of the commander of any man-of-war of Her Britannic Majesty's navy in the port of San Juan." " The object of the Transit Company," so its vice-president wrote, " is to prevent accessions of filibusters to Walker's force, pending his hostilities with Costa Rica, and to effect this purpose, no pains must be spared or effort left untried." In conclusion he adds: " Unless our boats are seized by the filibusters on the Orizaba and Charles Morgan they cannot get into the interior, and without large accessions Walker must fail and Costa Rica be saved. To this result Her Majesty's officers in San Juan can materially contribute, by protecting American property in the manner indicated." It was made clear, by such acts, that the company was afraid to trust the justice of its own government.

It was the necessity for completing the arrangements about the Transit, no less than the rainy season, which kept Walker from moving against the Allies. It would have been folly to advance against Leon without having the Transit secure and communication with the United States certain. Leon was well barricaded, and the Amer-

icans had not numbers to spare for an assault; neither
had they artillery to aid their attack, even if the roads
had admitted of its easy transportation. Besides, disease and dissension were weakening the Allies; and it
was only after the death of Estrada that they got even
an appearance of unity. It was early in the month of
September that events occurred to encourage the Allies
in an advance toward Granada. But before narrating
these events, it may be well to mention the celebration
of the 1st of September, at the capital, as it displays an
element which entered into the war in Nicaragua.

At different times a number of Cubans had found
their way to Nicaragua; and after Lt. Col. F. A. Lainé
was appointed aide-de-camp to the general-in-chief, they
were formed into a body-guard for the President. The
Cuban company consisted of about fifty members, and
their familiarity with the two languages—Spanish and
English—made their services valuable. Early in the
year the Cuban element in Nicaragua had attracted the
attention of the Spanish authorities in the island; and
in June, 1856, General Morales de Rada, who naturally
disliked those called " filibusters," because his running
away from them had made him the laughing-stock of all
the Havana wits, was sent to San José for the purpose
of advising with President Mora in reference to the war
against the Americans of Nicaragua. The Cubans with
Walker were well known for their devotion to the cause
of independence. Two of the aides of the general-in-
chief, Lainé and Pineda, had been engaged in revolutionary schemes on the island, and the prefect of the
the Oriental Department, D. Francisco Aguëro, was a

11*

native of the disaffected district of Puerto Principe. Hence the interest with which Spain watched affairs in Nicaragua.

On the 1st of September, a mass for the repose of the soul of Lopez was celebrated in the parish church at Granada, and the day was in other respects observed by the Cubans in the service. The ardent minds of these southern youths dreamed, however, more of the future than they meditated the past; they thought more of the time when they should sail for the island to avenge the death of Lopez and his followers, than of the dark and painful scenes which attended their execution. And it is this reluctance of the southern imagination to dwell on the gloomy side of affairs which fits its possessors less for the real work of revolution, than the robust children of the North, whose fancies do not fly from the grave and its surroundings.

Chapter Eighth.

THE policy of the Walker government was, of course, the same as that of Rivas, so far as the introduction of the white race into Nicaragua was concerned. But the administration of Rivas was, from its nature, transitional. It sought to increase the American element without inquiring what place the new people were to occupy in the old society. Rivas and his cabinet felt that Nicaraguan society required reorganization, but they knew not how it was to be accomplished, nor would they have adopted the means necessary for the end even if the proper measures had been pointed out to them. Hence, when the reorganization, not merely of the State, but of the family and of labor, became necessary, another executive than Rivas was not a matter of choice. Not merely the secondary form of the crystal was to be modified, but the primary form was to be radically changed, and for this a new force was to be brought into play. It may be that the reorganization in Nicaragua was attempted too soon; but those who have read the foregoing pages may judge whether or not the Americans were driven forward by the force of events. Sooner or later the struggle between the old and the new forms of society must inevitably have occurred.

The difference of language between the members of the old society and that portion of the white race, necessarily dominant in the new, while it was a cause keeping the elements apart, afforded also a means of regulating the relations between the several races meeting on the same soil. In order that the laws of the Republic might be thoroughly published, it was decreed that they should be published in English as well as in Spanish. The reason of this was apparent to every one; but the object of another clause in the same decree, " That all documents connected with public affairs shall be of equal value whether written in English or Spanish," was not noticed except by the careful observer. By this clause the proceedings of all the courts, and the record of all the deeds in the State, might be made in English. It was not necessary to decree that all such records should be in English—the mere permission was sufficient to accomplish the object. Lawyers will readily see what an advantage such a clause gave to those speaking both English and Spanish, over those acquainted only with the latter language.

The decree concerning the use of the two languages tended to make the ownership of the lands of the State fall into the hands of those speaking English. But in addition to this, a decree was published declaring the property of all enemies of the State forfeited to the Republic, and a Board of Commissioners was named " to take possession of, direct, determine upon, and sell all such confiscated or forfeited properties." The Board was given the ordinary power of courts for citation, for examining witnesses, and for enforcing obedience to its orders. All property declared confiscated was to be sold soon after the rendition of the judgment, and military scrip was to be received in payment at the sale of such property, thus giving those who had been in the military service of the State an opportunity to secure their pay out of the estates of the persons engaged in the war against them.

The land titles in Nicaragua were in a very unsettled condition, and the same system prevailed there as in other Spanish American States. The limits of grants were indeterminate, and there was, of course, no registry law. Accordingly, in order to fix the number of outstanding grants from the Republic, a decree was published requiring all claims to land to be recorded within six months, and it was further decreed that after a certain date no conveyance or mortgage should be valid against third parties, unless duly recorded in the district where the land lay. This was a substitution of the English and American system for the rules of the Roman and Continental law. The recording of titles is undoubtedly for the public advantage, and those possessed of good titles to land in Nicaragua would in virtue of this decree have held their possessions by a tenure more certain than ever. But the system was fatal to the bad or uncertain titles. It also gave an advantage to those familiar with the habit of registry.

The general tendency of these several decrees was the same ; they were intended to place a large proportion of

the land of the country in the hands of the white race.
The military force of the State might, for a time, secure
the Americans in the government of the Republic, but in
order that their possession of government might be permanent, it was requisite for them to hold the land.   But the
natives who had held the lands for more than a generation
admitted that the cultivated fields had diminished in
number and extent every year since the independence,
for the want of a proper system of labor ; hence, according to the admission of all parties, the reorganization of
labor was necessary for the development of the resources
of the country.

In order to command the labor already in the country
a decree was issued for enforcing contracts for terms of
service.   A stringent decree against vagrants was also
published, and this was a measure of military caution
as well as of political economy.   When Martinez set
about recruiting in Matagalpa the men scattered on the
farms of Chontales and Los Llaños repaired to Granada in
order to escape the press-gang.   But these men had
nearly all been in the employ of Legitimist masters, and
when gathered in the city there was danger of their being used for bad purposes.   Few of them had any visible means of livelihood, and hence most would have come
under the provision of the decree concerning vagrants.
As they had little disposition for work they soon disappeared after the publication of the decree, and thus a
population which at the time might have proved dangerous around Granada was got rid of.

The decree of the 22d of September was, however, the
measure from which most was to be expected for organi-

zing the labor of the country. This was the act around which the whole policy of the administration revolved ; and as it has been much criticised it may be well to give the decree entire. It reads :

" Inasmuch as the Constituent Assembly of the Republic, on the 30th day of April, 1838, declared the State, free, sovereign, and independent, dissolving the compact which the Federal Constitution established between Nicaragua and the other States of Central America :

" Inasmuch as since that date, Nicaragua has been in fact free from the obligations the Federal Constitution imposed :

" Inasmuch as the Act of the Constituent Assembly, decreed on the 30th of April, 1838, provides, that the federal decrees given previous to that date shall remain in force unless contrary to the provisions of that act :

" Inasmuch as many of the decrees theretofore given are unsuited to the present condition of the Republic, and are repugnant to its welfare and prosperity as well as to its territorial integrity : Therefore it is

" DECREED :

" ARTICLE 1. All acts and decrees of the Federal Constituent Assembly, as well as of the Federal Congress, are declared null and void.

" ARTICLE 2. Nothing herein contained shall affect rights heretofore vested under the acts and decrees hereby repealed."

One of the earliest acts of the Federal Constituent Assembly was the abolition of slavery in Central America ; and as this, among other acts, was repealed by the decree of the 22d of September, it was generally supposed the latter re-established slavery in Nicaragua. Whether this be a strictly legal deduction may be doubted ; but the repeal of the prohibition clearly prepared the way for the introduction of slavery. The spirit and intention of the decree were apparent ; nor did its author affect to conceal his object in its publication. By this act must the Walker administration be judged ; for it is the key to its whole policy. In fact the wisdom or folly of this decree involves the wisdom or folly of the American movement in Nicaragua ; for on the re-establishment of African slavery there depended the permanent presence of the white race in that region. If the slavery decree, as it has been called, was unwise, Cabañas and Jerez were right when they sought to use the Americans for the mere purpose of raising one native faction and depressing another. Without such labor as the new decree gave the Americans could have played no other part in Central America than that of the pretorian guard at Rome or of the Janizaries of the East ; and for such degrading service as this they were ill suited by the habits and traditions of their race.

The difference between the colonial system of the English and Spanish Crowns explains the different results of the English and Spanish settlements in America. The colonies of Great Britain founded their own forms of society ; they made for themselves all the rules and regulations their new situation required, and hence they built firmly the foundation of a peculiar and original civilization. Their institutions sprang from their necessities, and were hence adapted to the climate and the soil they found on the new continent. But it was far otherwise with the Spanish possessions. The laws of the Indies were decreed by the Crown; and the regulations, sometimes for good but oftener for evil, were the result of monarchical will. In the case of Cuba the resolution of Isabella was swayed by the counsels of the benevolent Las Casas; and Spain owes her possession of the island at the present moment to the wise philanthropy of the simple-hearted priest. Negro-slavery is, without doubt, the cause of the present prosperity of the island as well as of its continued colonial government; and Cuba offers a fine contrast to Jamaica and St. Domingo, and displays to advantage the superior wisdom of Spain when compared with the false humanity of France and England. On the continent, however, Spain was not so fortunate as on the ever-faithful isle. Her conquest of force was there followed by no radical and permanent change in political organization. She carried thither the Roman law; but it did not inform the new society or breathe a fresh spirit into its institutions. The only real changes in Mexico and Peru, for example, were wrought by the church. The pagans of the continent were converted to Christianity and the mission fathers reclaimed the wild tribes from their savageism, teaching them agriculture and the ruder arts of life. Beyond the protection the Crown afforded the church in its labors for the re-construction of society, the Spanish government did little for its vast continental possessions. Slavery on the continent was not more than what the physiologists call a "trace;" and it soon yielded to the passions which followed the independence of the colonies.

The men who framed the Constitution of the United

States were not beyond the control of the influences which in France led to the horrors of Hayti and in England to the miseries of Jamaica. The wits and philosophers of the constitutional convention — the strong reason of Franklin and the brilliant genius of Hamilton, as well as the lofty soul of Washington—were not unaffected by the errors of the French reformers of the period. The mad rhapsodies of Rousseau, the sharp keen sarcasm of Voltaire, had infected the readers of that time with a sort of hydrophobia—a mortal aversion to the word *slavery.* Hamilton and Washington, though struggling against French notions, were still under the influence to some extent of the Genevese ravings about equality and fraternity. Mr. Jefferson not only yielded to the French fashions of thought and feeling, but actually cherished them as if they were the fruits of reason and philosophy. While such causes operated on the American leaders of the time, the people of the period were tainted with the notions of the English Buxton and Clarkson. The dissenters of Great Britain infused their opinions about the slave-trade into their religious brethren in America; and thus, by the union of French philosophy with English humanitarianism, the constitution of 1787 was burdened with clauses of which the evil effect is now constantly felt by the slaveholding communities of the United States.

If the strong, broad minds of the constitutional convention of 1787 were not able to resist entirely the opinions prevalent in France and England concerning slavery, how much less were the poor, imitative creatures Spanish policy left to her American colonies after their independence able to withstand the prejudices of the European world. Spain had, in fact, left them with too little slavery to preserve their social order. Instead of maintaining the purity of the races as did the English in their settlements, the Spaniards had cursed their continental possessions with a mixed race. Hence it would have been little less than a miracle if the Spanish American States had at the moment of independence decided to retain slavery in their midst. It is only of late years that the really beneficial and conservative character of negro-slavery has begun to be appreciated in the United States.

For a long time it was the fashion, and with many it still is, to regard the Northern States of the Federal Union as the conservative element of American society. It is true that the Northern States are the conservative element of the federal government ; because the Union is nearly altogether the creature of their will and of their interests. Therefore, on all occasions they have sought to strengthen the federal power through tariffs and banks and large schemes of internal improvement. But such conservatism as this does not touch the organic structure of society ; it merely determines its external form and appearance. The conservatism of slavery is deeper than this ; it goes to the vital relations of capital toward labor, and by the firm footing it gives the former it enables the intellect of society to push boldly forward in the pursuit of new forms of civilization. At present it is the struggle of free labor with slave labor which prevents the energies of the former from being directed against the capital of the North through the ingenious machinery of the ballot box and universal suffrage ; and it is difficult to conceive how capital can be secured from the attacks of the majority in a pure democracy unless with the aid of a force which gets its strength from slave labor.

The Spanish American States, after their independence, aimed to establish Republics without slavery ; and the history of forty years of disorder and public crime is fertile in lessons for him who hath eyes to see and ears to hear.   Carried away by his imagination, or rather by his sensibilities, Mr. Clay pleaded the cause of Spanish American independence, and anticipated good government as the result of the movement.   The policy he urged was undoubtedly wise both for the United States and for England, inasmuch as it opened the old Spanish colonies to other commercial nations.   But the effects of independence have not been beneficial on the people of the colonies themselves.   Spain gave order, at least, to the possessions she held in the New World ; and order, attended as it was by exaction, sometimes even by extortion, was better than the anarchy of so-called Republican rule.   In Nicaragua whole tracts which were cultivated under the Spanish dominion have gone to waste since the independence ; and the indigo of the Isthmus, which even ten years ago was a valuable article of export, has disappeared almost entirely from trade.

If Spain, then, failed to leave her colonies with the internal force or the system capable of re-organizing their independent society, the plan immediately suggests itself of applying to them the rules which have constructed a firm and harmonious civilization where the Anglo-American has found himself on the same soil with one of the colored races. The introduction of negro-slavery into Nicaragua would furnish a supply of constant and reliable labor requisite for the cultivation of tropical products. With the negro-slave as his companion, the white man would become fixed to the soil; and they together would destroy the power of the mixed race which is the bane of the country. The pure Indian would readily fall into the new social organization; for he does not aim at political power, and only asks to be protected in the fruits of his industry. The Indian of Nicaragua, in his fidelity and docility, as well as in his capacity for labor, approaches nearly the negroes of the United States; and he would readily assume the manners and habits of the latter. In fact the manners of the Indian toward the ruling race are now more submissive than those of the American negro toward his master.

Some, however, may urge that the climate of tropical America is unfavorable to the African negro. This idea has been set afloat by some statistics a British officer has published in reference to the comparative vitality of the European and negro regiments in Jamaica. The figures, as given, go to show, that the average mortality is greater among the negro than among the European regiments; and even Dr. Josiah C. Nott has been led to quote the statistics with approval, and to infer that tropical America is not suited to the African. But the figures of the British officer may be read in another sense, and probably with a nearer approach to natural laws. It is not the climate, but the profession of soldier, which destroys so rapidly the negro regiments of Jamaica. No avocation of life requires so much intelligence, so much knowledge of the laws of life, and so much resolution and self-denial in adhering to them, as that of the soldier. The great difference between a veteran and a raw recruit is, that one knows how to take care of himself, and the other does not. But you never can make a veteran of the negro; he remains always in the condition of recruit, and hence negro regiments will have the health and vitality of regiments of recruits. No one, who has seen the negro in tropical America, will, for a moment, allow the accuracy of the deduction, hastily drawn from the regimental returns of Jamaica.

In Nicaragua the negro seems to be in his natural climate. The blacks who have gone thither from Jamaica are healthy, strong and capable of severe labor. They were much employed by the Accessory Transit Company on the San Juan river and at Virgin Bay; and even on the bungos of the lake and river, they bore the toil and exposure to the sun as well as the natives of the country. In fact, the negro blood seems to assert its superiority over the indigenous Indian of Nicaragua. Some of the negro and mulatto officers in the Legitimist army were remarkable among their fellows for courage and energy, though with these qualities were generally joined cruelty and ferocity.

The advantage of negro slavery in Nicaragua would, therefore, be two-fold; while it would furnish certain labor for the use of agriculture, it would tend to separate the races and destroy the half-castes who cause the disorder, which has prevailed in the country since the inde-

pendence. But there are many who, while admitting
the advantage of slavery to Nicaragua, think it was im-
politic to have attempted its re-establishment at the time
the decree of the 22d of September was published. This
brings us to consider the decree in its relation with the
question of slavery in the United States.

At the time the decree was published it was clear that
the Americans in Nicaragua would be called on to defend themselves against the forces of four Allied States.
Their cause was right and just, but it then appeared to
touch themselves only. Up to that time there was no
American interest in the country, save that of the army
and of the Transit Company; hence it was expedient
by some positive act to bind to the cause for which the
naturalized Nicaraguans were contending some strong
and powerful interest in the United States. The decree,
re-establishing slavery while it declared the manner in
which the Americans proposed to regenerate Nicaraguan
society made them the champions of the Southern States
of the Union in the conflict truly styled " irrepressible "
between free and slave labor. The policy of the act consisted in pointing out to the Southern States the only
means, short of revolution, whereby they can preserve
their present social organization.

In 1856, the South began to perceive that all territory
hereafter acquired by the federal government, would
necessarily enure to the use and benefit of free labor.
The immigrant from the free labor States moves easily
and readily into the new territories; and the surplus of
population being greater at the North than at the South,
the majority in any new territory would certainly be

from the anti-slavery region. Besides this, the South has no surplus labor to send westward or southward. On the contrary the Gulf States are crying out for more negroes; and the uneasiness of Southern society results from the superabundance of its intellect and capital in proportion to its rude labor. It is impossible, in the present condition of affairs, for the South to get the labor kti lacs; and the only means of restoring the balance to its industry is to send its unemployed intellect to a field where no political obstacles prevent it from getting the labor it requires.

There are, however, some people in the Southern States who condemn every effort to extend slavery, because they say, it irritates the anti-slavery sentiment, and thus feeds and strengthens hostility to Southern society. With them, the great cure for abolitionism, is rest and inaction on the part of slaveholders. But such are the shallowest of thinkers. It is impossible to keep down the discussion of the slavery question in the United States. The question is one which touches the whole labor of the country, and involves the vital relations of capital with labor.* And this is the question which in all ages, and in all countries, has divided states and societies. Hence it is idle to speak of the question being settled; from the nature of things the contest be-

---

* It may be proper to say that these passages were written before Mr. Seward delivered in the Senate, his masterly speech of the 29th February, 1860. However much a person may differ from the Senator's views, it is impossible not to approve the force and vigor of his thoughts and language. The writer deems it a great error, on the part of Southern men, to attempt to belittle the intellect, or depreciate the motives of the leaders of the anti-slavery party. The higher their intellects, the purer their motives, the more dangerous are they to the South.

tween free and slave labor is " never ending, still beginning."

In September, 1856, the canvass for the presidency was developing the passions and the prejudices of the several sections of the Union ; and one of the great parties of the country, in convention assembled, had declared its sympathy and pledged its support to the efforts then being made to regenerate Central America. These promises and pledges were made by the party which relied on the slave States for its success, and it should have looked with favor on a measure which tended to strengthen slavery in the Southern States. But the manner in which the free labor democracy of the North received the decree re-establishing slavery in Nicaragua, is a proof of the hollowness of its professions of friendship for Southern interests. There was scarcely a voice raised in defence of the measure north of the Potomac ; though the free-labor States may find, when it is too late, that the only way to avoid revolution, and a conflict of force between the Northern and Southern States of the Union, is by the very policy Nicaragua proposed to establish.

It is true the author of the slavery decree was not aware, at the time it was published, of the strong and universal feeling which exists in the Northern States against Southern society. He did not know how thoroughly anti-slavery sentiments prevail in the free-labor States ; that they are taught in the schools, preached from the pulpit, and instilled by mothers into the minds of their children from infancy upward. But the knowledge of such a state of feeling would have made the publication of the decree a matter of sacred duty no

12

less than of policy. To avert the invasion which threatens the South, it is necessary for her to break through the barriers which now surround her on every side, and carry the war between the two forms of labor beyond her own limits. A beleagured force, with no ally outside, must yield to famine at last, unless it can make a sally and burst through the enemy which confines it.

While the slavery decree was calculated to bind the Southern States to Nicaragua, as if she were one of themselves, it was also a disavowal of any desire for annexation to the Federal Union. And it was important, in every respect, to make it appear thnt the American movement in Nicaragua did not contemplate annexation. This idea constantly haunted the minds of the public men of the Union, little accustomed to regard political questions except from party points of view. It disturbed the mind of Mr. Pierce, when he wrote his message at the reception of Father Vigil; it worried Mr. Marcy, when he contemplated the future fate of the democratic party. And it was, without doubt, the uncertainty the Secretary of State felt in regard to the effect the Nicaraguan movement might have on party action in the United States which prompted him to frown on the enterprise from the beginning. Mr. Marcy was an old man, ambitious of yet higher station than he had held under the federal government; and his long experience enabled him to calculate with nice accuracy the weight of old party issues in conventions and popular elections. But here was a new element about to be thrown into the politics of the Union; and to the distrust of new things common to age, was added the inability of the Secretary to estimate precisely the force and direction of the Nicaraguan movement. To show the spirit of Mr. Marcy, it is only necessary to state when the decree repealing the acts of the Federal Constituent Assembly and Federal Congress was published in Nicaragua, Mr. Wheeler advised his government of the fact, and merely remarked that he thought it a measure of advantage for the Isthmus. The despatch of Mr. Wheeler was, according to excellent authority, discussed in a full meeting of Mr. Pierce's cabinet. Mr. Marcy and Mr. Cushing insisted on the immediate recall of the minister; while Mr. Davis and Mr. Dobbin defended Mr. Wheeler, saying he had done nothing but his duty in advising his government of the decree published in Nicaragua, and of the effect it was likely to produce on the country. The Secretary of State insisted on the dismissal of Mr. Wheeler to the last; and only the day before he left office, he required of the President, as a personal favor, that he should procure the resignation of the minister.

The decree of the 22d of September was intended to destroy the delusion of the public men of the United States as to the desire of Nicaragua for annexation. To a thinking mind it was apparent that to enter the Federal Union would be to defeat the object of the decree ; for the federal law prohibits the introduction within the limits of its authority of any persons held to labor for a term of years. Nicaragua could not expect to draw her negro labor from States already complaining of the deficiency of their own supply ; and the Southern States would themselves have opposed the annexation of a territory which might drain from them the labor they so much need. In the heat of party passion, however, such views were not appreciated by the politicians, of whom Mr. Marcy was a type. They were too much absorbed in watching the currents of popular opinion and in distributing the spoils of party warfare, to devote any time to the consideration of the public weal or of a true and just public policy.

So far were the politicians of the Union from perceiving it was Walker's policy by the slavery decree to declare his hostility to annexation, that some of them supposed they had achieved a discovery by the publication of certain letters instructing Goicouria as to the course he should pursue in England. The intendente-general was authorized by Walker to proceed to London in order to impress on the English cabinet the fact that Nicaragua had no desire for admission into the American Union; and it was supposed that he, being a Cuban, might more readily get the ear of the British Ministry on the subject than a native of the United States. The letter of Walker to Goicouria instructed him to explain that the necessities of Nicaragua required "a republic based on military principles," such a republic being clearly unfit for admission into the northern Union. The English would readily perceive that the growth of such a republic toward the southern limits of the United States would tend to restrain the territorial extension of the latter power. Walker conceived that by such a policy he would promote the welfare of his native no less than of his adopted country; for the acquisition by the United States of any territory covered by a Spanish-

American population would be fertile of troubles and dangers to the confederacy, as well as of suffering and oppression to the inhabitants of the new territory. Above all, the acquisition of territory on the south would be fatal to the slaveholding States; for it would complete the circle of free-labor communities now girdling them on almost every side.

In France it would have been easier than in England to make the anti-annexation character of the slavery decree apparent. M. Ange de St. Priest, a savant who has published a large and valuable work on the antiquities of Mexico and Central America, accepted the office of consul-general for Nicaragua at Paris; and it was hoped through him to establish relations with the Imperial government. The steady policy of Napoleon the Third has been to increase the tonnage of France, and thereby to enlarge her facilities for educating sailors. It was hoped that such a treaty might have been made as would lead to the employment of French bottoms for bringing African apprentices to the ports of Nicaragua, thus furnishing labor to the latter republic, and increasing the trade of French ships. The Emperor has himself written a work on the subject of the inter-oceanic canal through Nicaragua; and his familiarity with the country would enable him to perceive the advantages of carrying negro labor thither. Next, too, to the possession of the isthmus by France, he would desire to have the canal route in the hands of a power bound to the empire by strong ties of interest and trade.

In fact it is the decided interest of all the continental powers of Europe, to favor the policy the Americans proposed to pursue in Nicaragua. By this policy they would secure tropical products at a much cheaper price than at present; and Russia, particularly, needs a supply of such articles from a country not under the control or influence of England. Even Great Britain, if she would look beyond the immediate gains of her grasping merchants, might perceive permanent advantages from the security and order negro labor would give to Nicaragua. Now that the Crown has taken the government of India from a trading corporation, it might disdain to be moved by the narrow commercial jealousy which sacrificed Jamaica to the East India Company.

But, it may be said, England will never permit anything which looks like the revival of the African slave-trade. They, however, who watch closely the phases of British politics, know that the influence of Exeter Hall is on the wane. The frenzy of the British public against the slave-trade has exhausted itself, and men have begun to perceive that they were led into error by the benevolent enthusiasm of parsons, who knew more about Greek and Hebrew than they did about physiology or political economy, and of middle-aged spinsters, smit with the love of general humanity, though disdaining to fix their affections firmly on any objects less remote than Africa. All the arguments used by the adversaries of the slave-trade were drawn from its abuses; and the true remedy was, not to abolish but regulate the trade. During the seventeenth and eighteenth centuries it was styled " a commerce for the redemption of African captives ;" and if the old name, descriptive as it is of the true character of the trade, were revived, many of the prejudices against the business would be removed.

It was the alliance of a skeptical philosophy with a purblind religious zeal which generated the opinion of Europe in regard to the African slave-trade. Confining their attention to the abuses of the system, the opponents of the trade failed to raise their eyes toward any large views of the subject. If we look at Africa in the light of universal history, we see her for more than five thousand years a mere waif on the waters of the world, fulfilling no part in its destinies, and aiding in no manner the progress of general civilization. Sunk in the depravities of fetichism, and reeking with the blood of human sacrifices, she seemed a satire on man, fit only to provoke the sneer of devils at the wisdom, and justice, and benevolence of the Creator. But America was discovered, and the European found the African a useful auxiliary in subduing the new continent to the uses and purposes of civilization. The white man took the negro from his native wastes, and teaching him the arts of life, bestowed on him the ineffable blessings of a true religion. Then only do the wisdom and excellence of the divine economy in the creation of the black race begin to appear with their full lustre. Africa is permitted to lie idle until America is discovered, in order that she may conduce to the formation of a new society in the New World. A strong, haughty race, bred to liberty in its northern island home, is sent forth with the mission to place America under the rule of free laws; but whence are these men, imbued with love of liberty and equality, to derive the counterpoise which shall prevent their liberty from degenerating into license, and their equality into anarchy or despotism? How are they,

when transplanted from the rugged climate where freedom thrives to retain their precious birthright in the soft,
tropical air which woos to luxury and repose ? Is it
not for this that the African was reserved ? And is it
not thus that one race secures for itself liberty with order, while it bestows on the other comfort and Christianity ?

But man, ever the dupe of his vain desires, always
oscillating between the extremes of opinion, and never
fixed in the possession of truth, was not content with the
place assigned the African in the plan of creation and of
Providence. The preachers of the new gospel of equality
and fraternity were not satisfied with descanting on the
horrors of the middle passage, or of weeping over the
miseries of men redeemed from the captivity of savage
masters. If the slave-trade be criminal, slavery, which
is the cause of it, should be extirpated. Therefore the
trial is made on St. Domingo, and the slave, suddenly
loosed from the restraints the law had put around him,
goes forth to murder and destroy. Then they determine
on another experiment more cautiously conducted and
more narrowly watched. Slavery is abolished in Jamaica, and forthwith the island goes to waste. The
time seems to be approaching when man, guided by a
less vain philosophy, will seek truth in some other direction than Haytian massacres or Jamaican impoverish-
ment.

If the views above expressed of the uses of the African in the economy of nature and Providence be correct,
slavery is not abnormal to American society. It must
be the rule, not the exception. But to keep it so re-

quires effort and labor. The enemies of the only original form of American civilization are many and powerful. They are resolute in their determination not merely to limit but to extirpate slavery. The man who leads the free-labor myriads of the United States—he, whose firm will and far-reaching mind do not quail either at the doctrines or the acts to which his political philosophy logically conducts him, has already declared that he hopes to see the time when the foot of not a slave shall press the continent. Yet the sluggards of slavery say, " a little more rest, a little more folding of the arms to slumber." Strafford sleeps though the axe of the headsman is whetted for his execution.

The contest between free and slave labor in the United States not only touches the interests and destiny of those immediately engaged in the struggle but it affects the fate of the whole continent. The question involved is whether the civilization of the western world shall be European or American. If free labor prevails in its effort to banish slave labor from the continent, the history of American society becomes a faint reflex of European systems and prejudices, without contributing any new ideas, any new sentiments, or any new institutions, to the mental and moral wealth of the world. The necessary consequence of the triumph of free labor will be the destruction, by a slow and cruel process, of the colored races which now inhabit the central and southern portions of the continent. The labor of the inferior races cannot compete with that of the white race unless you give it a white master to direct its energies ; and without such protection as slavery affords, the colored

12*

races must inevitably succumb in the struggle with white labor. Hence a Nicaraguan can not be an indifferent spectator of the contest between the two forms of labor in the United States ; and deeper yet must be his interest in the matter if born and educated in a slave State of the Union, he revolves in his mind the results which will ensue to the home of his childhood, and the firesides of the friends of his youth, in case victory smiles upon the soldiers of free labor. Do not, therefore, men of the South, deem it the voice of a stranger, or of one without a stake in your country's welfare, which urges you to strike a blow in defence of your honor, no less than of your hearths and your families, ere the blast of the enemy's bugle calls upon you to surrender your arms to an overwhelming force.

The tongue of truth and friendship is not that of undue praise or fawning flattery, and the soft songs of the suitor too often woo to danger and destruction. Therefore, be not displeased, sons of the South—for it is to you I now speak—if the criticism on your acts and policy appear harsh or severe ; but examine your conduct and that of your public servants for the last three years and see whither it has led you. It is now but little more than three years since you elected the President of your choice, and in your simplicity you thought this success a great victory. What fruits have you reaped from it ? Where are the rewards of your campaign ? In what triumphs of policy have all your toils and all your efforts ended ?

Your President—for he is the work of your hands— went into office pledged to your policy in Kansas and in

Central America. He attempted to deceive you in Kansas, and your leaders drove him to the course he was forced to pursue. Like sheep to the slaughter he and his Northern friends were led to the support of Southern policy in Kansas; but what has resulted from their sacrifice, or from all the efforts the Southern leaders made to drag them to the altar? Was Kansas admitted into the Union? Did you have even the empty pleasure of boasting over a barren victory? The Kansas contest was made, as all admitted, for an abstract right. Your leaders were true to you, because you were true to yourselves, when contending for an " abstract right"; let us see whether you and they were equally faithful to your honor and your interests when contending for a right not abstract.

The President was pledged to your policy in Central America even more explicitly than to your Kansas measures. The resolutions of the Cincinnati Convention on the Central American policy were drawn by no trembling or unsteady hand.* They were not couched in the Delphic sentences behind which timid politicians shrink when they seek the support of their constituents. Clear, distinct, and unmistakeable, they could not be read in a dozen senses by the jugglers, who fancy all political wisdom consists in deceiving the people with words which seem other than they are. Have the pledges given at Cincinnati been redeemed? Have those words, so full of meaning and of resolution, taken shape in acts; or have they died into the sobs and sighs

---

* The resolutions were written by Hon. P. Soulé.

and moans of a party which aspired to greatness yet dared not its accomplishment?

It needs no new word to tell you how basely the pledges made at Cincinnati have been violated. It was not enough to trample under foot the promises made, in the name of a party, to the country; it was necessary also to disregard all the principles of public law, and to proclaim before the world that the end justified the means. Violated faith excused violated law: and when the message of the President, excusing the acts of Commodore Paulding at Punta Arenas, in December, 1857, was sent to the senate, Mr. Seward might well say, in a double sense, that his Excellency had become a convert to the "higher law" doctrine.

And how did the leaders of the South act in the emergency? It was just at the time the news of Paulding's act at Punta Arenas reached Washington that the adoption of the Lecompton Constitution was ascertained. Then the President besought the men who were driving him on the Kansas question not to press him on the Central American policy, and the Southern leaders, giving up the substance, fled in pursuit of the shadow.* The Lecompton Constitution would not give another foot of soil to slavery, and the movement in Nicaragua might give it an empire; yet the latter was sacrificed to the former, and the insults of Paulding and the President have gone unrebuked by the South up to the present time.

---

* Hon. A. H. Stephens was among the few public men of the South who clearly perceived the full importance of the Nicaraguan movement.

Is it not time for the South to cease the contest for abstractions and to fight for realities? Of what avail is it to discuss the right to carry slaves into the territories of the Union, if there are none to go thither? These are questions for schoolmen—fit to sharpen the logical faculty and to make the mind quick and keen in the perception of analogies and distinctions; but surely they are not such questions as touch practical life and come home to men's interests and actions. The feelings and conscience of a people are not to be called forth by the subtleties of lawyers or the differences of metaphysicians; nor can their energies be roused into action for the defence of rights none of them care to exercise. The minds of full-grown men cannot be fed on mere discussions of territorial rights: they require some substantial policy which all can understand and appreciate.

Nor is it wise for the weaker party to waste its strength in fighting for shadows. It is only the stronger party which can afford to throw away its force on indecisive skirmishes. At present the South must husband her political power else she will soon lose all she possesses. The same influence she brought to bear in favor of the position she took in Kansas would have secured the establishment of the Americans in Nicaragua. And unless she assumes now an entirely defensive attitude, what else is left for the South except to carry out the policy proposed to her three years ago in Central America? How else can she strengthen slavery than by seeking its extension beyond the limits of the Union? The Republican party aims at destroying slavery by sap and not by assault. It declares now that the task

2*

of confining slavery is complete and the work of the miner has already commenced. Whither can the slave-holder fly when the enemy has completed his chambers and filled in the powder and prepared the train, and stands with lighted match ready to apply the fire ?

Time presses. If the South wishes to get her institutions into tropical America she must do so before treaties are made to embarrass her action and hamper her energies. Already there is a treaty between Mexico and Great Britain by which the former agrees to do all in her power for the suppression of the slave-trade, and in 1856 a clause was inserted in the Dallas-Clarendon Convention, stipulating for the perpetual exclusion of slavery from the Bay Islands of Honduras. This clause was suggested (as the writer was informed by the person himself who proposed it) by an American, for the purpose of securing the support of England to a projected railway across Honduras; and thus the rights of American civilization were to be bartered away for the paltry profits of a railroad company. And while Nicaragua was to be hemmed in by an anti-slavery treaty between England and Honduras on the north, Costa Rica made an agreement with New Granada that slavery should never be introduced within her limits. The enemies of American civilization—for such are the enemies of slavery—seem to be more on the alert than its friends.

The faith which Walker had in the intelligence of the Southern States to perceive their true policy and in their resolution to carry it out, was one of the causes which led to the publication of the decree of the 22d of September at the time it was given forth. Nor is his faith in the South shaken ; though who can fail to be amazed at the facility with which the South is carried off after chimeras ? Sooner or later, however, the slaveholding States are bound to come as one man to the support of the Nicaraguan policy. The decree of the 22d September, not the result of hasty passion or immature thought, fixed the fate of Nicaragua and bound the Republic to the car of American civilization. For more than two years the enemies of slavery have been contriving and plotting to exclude the naturalized Nicaraguans from their adopted country. But as yet not a single additional barrier has been interposed ; and the South has but to resolve upon the task of carrying slavery into Nicaragua in order that the work may be accomplished.

If other appeals than those of interest are required for stimulating the Southern States in the effort to re-establish slavery in Central America they are not lacking. The hearts of Southern youth answer to the call of honor, and strong arms and steady eyes are waiting to carry forward the policy which is now the dictate of duty as well as of interest. The issue between slavery and anti-slavery has been made in Nicaragua, and it is impossible for slavery to retire from the contest without losing some of its courage and character. Nor is the issue one of mere words. It is not a tilt of sport, a joust of reeds; but the knights have touched the shields of their adversaries with the points of their lances, and the tourney is one of mortal strife. And may fortune most favor them who best do their duty in the fray.

Something is due from the South to the memory of the brave dead who repose in the soil of Nicaragua. In defence of slavery these men left their homes, met with calmness and constancy the perils of a tropical climate, and finally yielded up their lives for the interests of the South. I have seen these men die in many ways. I have seen them gasping life away under the effects of typhus; I have seen them convulsed in the death agony from the fearful blows of cholera; I have seen them sink to glorious rest from mortal wounds received on honorable fields; but I never saw the first man who repented engaging in the cause for which he yielded his life. These martyrs and confessors in the cause of Southern civilization surely deserve recognition at its hands. And what can be done for their memories while the cause for which they suffered and died remains in peril and jeopardy?

If there, then, be yet vigor in the South—and who can doubt that there is—for further contest with the soldiers of anti-slavery, let her cast off the lethargy which enthrals her, and prepare anew for the conflict. But at the same time she throws aside her languor and indifference, let her, taught by the past, discard the delusions and abstractions with which politicians have agitated her passions without advancing her interests. It is time for slavery to spend its efforts on realities and not beat the air with wanton and ill-advised blows. The true field for the exertion of slavery is in tropical America; there it finds the natural seat of its empire and thither it can spread if it will but make the effort, regardless of conflicts with adverse interests. The way is open and it only requires courage and will to enter the path and reach the goal. Will the South be true to herself in this emergency?

Chapter Ninth.

In the beginning of September, 1856, the army of Nicaragua was organized in two battalions of Rifles, two of Light Infantry, one of Rangers, and a small company of Artillery. The First Rifles was the fullest as well as the best corps of the army, and it scarcely mustered two hundred effective men. The Second Rifles was a mere shadow of a battalion, and its discipline was almost entirely neglected. The Light Infantry battalions were larger than the Second Rifles, and some companies of these, as, for example, the company of Capt. Henry, of the Second Infantry, were in good order and condition. The Rangers consisted of three small companies, under the command of Major Waters, and were capable of effective service. Capt. Schwartz, with a few artillerymen, had shown capacity for organizing his corps, and possessed knowledge in his profession, he having served for some time as an artillery officer in Baden during the revolutionary troubles of 1848. The whole effective force scarcely amounted to eight hundred men.

Gen. Hornsby was in command of the Meridional Department, having his headquarters sometimes at San Jorge, sometimes at Rivas, and sometimes at San Juan del Sur. He had with him some companies of the First Infantry and the artillery squad—it could scarcely be called a company—of Capt. Schwartz. The First Rifles were at Granada, while the Second Rifles, under Lieut.-Col. McDonald, were at Tipitapa. The Second Infantry were at Masaya, and, in the absence of Col. Jaquess, it was commanded by Lieut.-Col. McIntosh. Capt. Dolan had been in command of a company of Rifles at Managua, but about the middle of September, Major Waters was sent thither with his Rangers. The principal depot of commissary, quartermaster, and ordnance stores, and all the workshops of the army, were at Granada. The San Juan river was guarded by two companies of infantry, and Lieut.-Col. Rudler was placed in charge of that frontier.

The main strength of the enemy was at Leon, under the orders of Gen. Belloso, and in the month of August Martinez began to collect men in Matagalpa, and even as far down as Chocoyas and Trinidad. The troops under Belloso were kept closely about Leon, and Rangers from Managua were in the habit of scouting beyond Pueblo Nuevo without meeting any signs of the enemy. Martinez, however, was collecting the herdsmen and servants attached to the Legitimist owners of cattle-estates in the upper part of Chontales and Los Llaños, and these being familiar with the country were easily able to provide their chief with any news in that region of country. A large proportion of the cattle used by the Americans was drawn from these districts, and they were generally driven to Granada by native officers, accompanied by small detachments of riflemen mounted for the occasion. One of the most efficient of these native officers was Ubaldo Herrera, whose services during the civil war have been heretofore related.

In the latter part of August, Herrera, with a few Americans, was sent to one of the cattle-estates of Los Llaños, and while carelessly driving cattle toward Tipitapa he was attacked and slain by a small band of Legitimists. This incident occurred not many miles from Tipitapa, and in consequence of it Lieut.-Col. McDonald received orders to cross the Tipitapa river, and marching toward Los Llaños, to ascertain whether any traces of the enemy were to be seen in that direction. The roads were, at the time, difficult, and all movements were necessarily slow and uncertain, owing to the heavy rains of the season. McDonald, however, with Capt. Jarvis, and about forty men, proceeded in the direction of San Jacinto, a large cattle-estate a few miles east and north of Tipitapa. It was reported that some of the enemy were quartered at the country-house belonging to the estate, and McDonald, arriving near the house before daybreak, postponed a nearer approach until he might be able to see the strength of the enemy. Soon after daylight he drew up his force for an attack, but while proceeding at a quick pace he was received by such a sharp, steady fire that he deemed it prudent to withdraw. Capt. Jarvis was brought off mortally wounded, and McDonald had ascertained that the enemy were in larger numbers than he expected, and strongly barricaded behind adobes.

The presence of the enemy at San Jacinto was a serious inconvenience to the commissariat, and when it was known at Granada there were numerous volunteers who proposed to drive the Legitimists from the house they occupied. The state of the roads made it almost impossible to send artillery against San Jacinto, even had there been the round shot or shell requisite for rendering a gun useful in an attack on adobes. There was a general impression at Granada that McDonald's Rifles had retired too soon, and the impression was due to the utter want of discipline in the corps. Seeing the enthusiasm of some officers and citizens, and desirous of ascertaining more exactly the strength of the enemy beyond Tipitapa, Walker consented that volunteers should be engaged for an attack on San Jacinto.

The volunteers were principally Americans who had been in the army, and who had been discharged or had resigned ; and these had their numbers swelled to about sixty-five or seventy by the officers at Granada and Masaya. Among the officers who joined the expedition were Major J. C. O'Neal, Captains Watkins, Lewis, and Morris, and Lieutenants Brady, Connor, Crowell, Hutchins, Kiel, Reader and Sherman. They left Granada on the afternoon of the 12th of September, and passing through Masaya reached Tipitapa on the morning of the 13th. At Tipitapa they offered the command of the party to Lieutenant-Colonel Byron Cole, who had been visiting several points in Chontales with a view of procuring cattle for the army, and Cole agreed to accept the offer. Wiley Marshall, a citizen of Granada, was named as second in command. The spirit of adventure which controlled not only these men but many others in Nicaragua can be judged of by the fact that under this improvised organization Major O'Neal consented to receive orders from a simple citizen, Marshall.

Cole and his command arrived before San Jacinto about 5 o'clock, on the morning of Sunday the 14th of September. They found the house well situated for defence on a gentle elevation commanding all the ground about it. Near the house was a corral, the sides of which afforded protection against rifle or musket balls. Cole halted a few minutes to arrange his plan of attack ; and dividing his small force into three bodies, placed the first in charge of Robert Milligan, an ex-lieutenant of the army, the second under Major O'Neal, and the third under Captain Watkins. The attack on the enemy was to be made at three several points, and the weapons to be used principally were revolvers. These arrangements being made, the order to charge simultaneously the points assigned to each division was given. The order was gallantly obeyed, and Cole with Marshall and Milligan had already gained the corral when they were struck down by the well-directed fire of the enemy. O'Neal was more fortunate, receiving only a wound in the arm, while Watkins was disabled by a shot in the hip. Thus, almost at the same instant, and when the men were within a few rods of the house, all of the leaders and nearly one third of the whole force were either killed or wounded. Then the others, seeing nothing was to be accomplished with their numbers, withdrew, carrying off their wounded ; and in a few minutes they were in full retreat toward Tipitapa.

Thus in the bold but fruitless charge he made on San Jacinto perished Byron Cole, whose energy and perseverance had done so much toward securing the presence of the Americans in Nicaragua. It was the first opportunity he had for being under fire ; and he had scarcely seen the flash of an enemy's musket before he met his fate. For months preceding the arrival of the Americans at Realejo, he had travelled and toiled in their behalf; and the only reward of all his labor and anxiety was death on the first field where he met the foe of the principles he had aided to advance. Nor was Cole the only loss of note on that fatal day. Marshall died of his wounds after reaching Tipitapa ; and among the missing was Charles Callahan, who had been appointed collector of customs at Granada. The latter was correspondent of the New-Orleans Picayune newspaper, and his genial nature secured for him a large circle of friends who regretted his untimely loss. The thirst for action led him to exchange his business in Granada for the excitement of the attack on San Jacinto ; and he never returned to fill the duties he had so well begun a few weeks previously.

The retreat of the volunteers from San Jacinto was irregular and disorderly ; and on such a command as that of McDonald at Tipitapa the arrival of the defeated party had an alarming effect. So great was the panic that the bridge across the river was torn up to prevent the expected enemy from using it. But no enemy appeared and the alarm gradually subsided. The news, however, of the defence at San Jacinto encouraged the Allies greatly ; and soon after the news of the affair reached Leon, Belloso, urged on by some of the more resolute of his officers, determined to advance toward Granada.

A few days after the affair at San Jacinto, about two hundred men arrived at Granada from New-York for the Nicaraguan service. They were soon organized into companies; but they showed from the beginning how worthless they were for military duty. A very large proportion of them were Europeans of the poorest class, mostly Germans who cared more for the contents of their haversacks than of their cartridge-boxes. With the exception of Captain Russell and Lieutenants Nagle and Northedge, the officers were as trifling as the men; and these New-York volunteers, as they called themselves, had not been in the country ten days before they began to desert in numbers. The promise of free quarters and rations seemed to have carried the most of them to Nicaragua; and the idea of performing duty could scarcely have entered their minds when they left the United States. Of course such trash as these men proved to be were far worse than no men at all; for their vices and corruptions tainted the good materials near them.

While these recruits were arriving at Granada, Belloso, having received reinforcements from San Salvador and Guatemala, was marching from Leon toward Managua with a force of about eighteen hundred men. He was accompanied by General Zavala, the second in command of the Guatemalan officers, Paredes remaining sick at Leon. Jerez also followed the allied camp; nor was he unattended by such Leoneses as Mendez and Olivas, éager for any disorder which held out the prospect of plunder. Valle, having ventured back to the Occidental Department after the June changes, with the view of raising the people against the Rivas authority, was arrested and afterward kept under the eye of the police. He waited at Chinandega hoping for the turn in affairs which might render his presence there useful to the Americans. By remaining in the Occidental Department he aided to keep the people of that region from joining in the crusade the Allies preached against the "filibusters."

Major Waters watched closely the advance of the Allies, and by the firm front he showed at Managua delayed them for several days on the road between that place and Leon. When, however, Belloso approached within a few miles of Managua Waters received orders to fall back to Masaya. At the latter place, Lieutenant-Colonel McIntosh was commanding, and the garrison consisted of about two hundred and fifty men; these had been increased in numbers, though not much in strength, by the Second Rifles from Tipitapa. Subsistence for many days was collected at Masaya, and the commandant began to build barricades and other defences near the main square of the city. While these works were going on, Captain Henry, who had been confined to his bed for many weeks from a painful wound received in a duel, came out, and by the skill he evinced inspired the soldiers with confidence in his judgment and sagacity. The commanding officer, Lieutenant-Colonel McIntosh, was sadly deficient both in knowledge and force of character; and the effect of his irresolution was such that it was clear the force at Masaya could not be depended on for holding the town against the advancing enemy. Had Henry been in command the condition of the garrison would have been far different ; and it was unfortunate that his long confinement had prevented his capacity from being known until the last moment. As will be seen hereafter, his disposition to get into danger kept him on the list of wounded nearly the whole time he was in Nicaragua. During the war in Central America, there was no better soldier engaged in it than Henry ; and by reading and study, as well as by practice and habit, he was familiar, not only with the details of military administration, but also with the deeper and more difficult principles of the art of war.

After halting a short time at Managua, Belloso continued to advance ; and at Nindiri, a league from Masaya, he was joined by Martinez and his followers from Chontales and Matagalpa, thus swelling the allied force to twenty-two or twenty-three hundred men. The moral condition of the command at Masaya was such that McIntosh received orders to retire on Granada ; and the state of his men may be judged from the manner in which they left Masaya. Such was the haste and confusion that Capt. Henry was left behind, and his safety was the result of accident, being due to the good-will of the women who attended him during his illness. A brass six-pounder was left on the road, about three miles out of Masaya, and the enemy afterward got possession of it. McIntosh might have been deliberate, even slow in his movement with entire safety ; for Belloso did not enter Masaya for some hours after it was abandoned by the Americans.

13

Walker, had he desired it, might probably have prevented for a time, or at least much embarrassed the junction of Martinez with Belloso. But a war against scattered guerillas was more exhausting to the Americans than a contest with the enemy gathered in masses. The Allies were less formidable when united than when acting in detached bodies at several distant points. Hence, no obstacle was put in the way of Martinez in his march toward Belloso. In fact, the best manner of treating a revolutionary movement in Central America, is to treat it as a boil, let it come to a head, and then lance it, letting all the bad matter out at once. It was an object for the Americans to let all the dissatisfied elements in Nicaragua gather about the Allied force, so that the question at issue might be decisively determined. The accession of Martinez really added little, if any, to Belloso's military strength.

Meanwhile the force in Granada was increased by the arrival, on the 4th of October, of Col. Sanders, with Capt. Ewbanks, and about seventy recruits from California. Three days after, Col. John Allan landed with nearly one hundred fresh men; and at the same time two twelve-pound mountain howitzers, with a small supply of shells, and four hundred Minié rifles were received from New-York. By some blunder, however, the carriages of the howitzers did not accompany them; and several days elapsed before Capt. Schwartz was able to have temporary carriages prepared. The arrival of the howitzers and shells had been anxiously expected, since it was hoped with their aid to drive the enemy more readily from the towns they were in the habit of barricading with adobes, thus making it difficult to carry them by assault, unless with the loss of large numbers of men.

General Hornsby, with his command, was ordered from the Meridional Department to Granada; and thus nearly the whole force of the Republic was concentrated at this point. The effective strength was about a thousand men, including those employed in the several departments of the army, as well as those in the line. A very large proportion of these, however, were newly arrived in the country; many of them had no military training whatever and still more had never seen an enemy during the whole course of their lives. Nevertheless it was necessary to strike a blow at the Allies, if for no other purpose than to show them that the Americans were not thrown entirely on the defensive. Accordingly, as soon as the howitzers were mounted on their rather clumsy carriages, and the new men, suitably armed and equipped, were distributed in the several corps, orders were issued for a march.

On the morning of the 11th October, Walker marched to Masaya with about 800 men. It was near midday when the First Rifles formed in the Jalteva and thence proceeded along the middle road to Masaya. In advance of the Rifles was Major Waters, with two companies of Rangers, and in their rear was the Cuban body-guard of the general-in-chief. Next after the guard came Capt. Schwartz with the howitzers; then the ammunition mules. The Second Rifles followed; and after them were the two Infantry battalions, under command of Gen. Hornsby. A small body of Rangers brought up

the rear.   The march was quiet and uninterrupted ; and
a little after nine o'clock in the evening the force encamped on the edge of the town of Masaya, occupying
the high ground flanking each side of the Granada road
as it enters by the plazuela of San Sebastian.   Some irregular firing took place during the night, between
mounted scouts of the enemy and some of the American
pickets, but the skirmishing was slight and unimportant.
Soon after daybreak on the 12th, Capt. Schwartz threw
a few shells into the plazuela of San Sebastian, and then
Capt. Dolan, with his company of rifles, proceeded at a
brisk pace, to occupy the square, finding it entirely abandoned by the enemy.   Belloso had withdrawn his whole
force into the houses near and around the main Plaza ;
and the mouths of all the streets leading into the large
square were strongly barricaded.   After the main body
of Nicaraguans had reached the plazuela of San Sebastian, a few sappers and miners who had been hastily
organized by a civil engineer, Capt. Hesse, were ordered
to cut through the walls of the houses on both sides of
the main street leading from the plazuela to the Plaza.
Hesse worked quite vigorously, supported by the Rifles
on the right side of the street and by the Infantry on the
left.   From time to time Capt. Schwartz tried to throw
shells into the midst of the main Plaza, but the fuses
were too short-timed, and the shells, for the most part,
burst in the air.   Besides the unfitness of the fuses, one
of the howitzers was dismounted after a few discharges,
and the carriage of the other was ill-adapted for its purposes.

The Rifles and Infantry, however, preceded by the

working party, steadily advanced toward the Plaza, sometimes encountering the enemy in their progress through the houses, and always driving them back. Capt. Leonard, with Capts. McChesney and Stith, were the foremost and most active among the Rifles; while on the left of the street, Dreux, of the Infantry, took and kept the lead. By dark the houses fronting on the Plaza were all that divided the Americans from the enemy; and then the men, tired out by their labors of the day were obliged to suspend work until morning. In the meanwhile, also, the Rangers on the Granada road reported heavy firing in the direction of the lake, and it became necessary to ascertain the meaning of it. Col. Fisher, the quartermaster-general, accompanied by Lieut.-Col. Lainé and Major Rogers, with an escort of Rangers, was sent to Granada in order to procure some stores, and also to ascertain whether or not the road was clear of the enemy. Not long after midnight Rogers returned, with the report that the enemy had attacked Granada, and were occupying much of the town, with the hope of getting entire possession of the place.

It seems that when Zavala, who, with his Guatemalans and some Legitimists, was occupying Diriomo, a small village between Masaya and Nandaime, heard of Walker's march from Granada, he determined to attack that place, supposing it to be left entirely defenceless. Gen. Fry had, however, command at Granada; and although the regular force under his orders was small, the citizens of the town, and the civil employees of the government, brought the number of the Americans to about two hundred. The force of Zavala was not less than seven hundred when he entered the town, and it was probably swelled to nine hundred before the morning of the 13th. Among his followers was a renegade named Harper, who, in the previous April, had fled from Granada to join the Costa Ricans, because his known character of pardoned convict from the California penitentiary had prevented him from securing the position he expected in the Nicaraguan army.

When Walker heard of the attack on Granada he immediately ordered his whole force to prepare for marching, and early on the morning of the 13th he was proceeding with rapid steps to the relief of Fry and his little garrison. Not long after nine o'clock, A. M., the returning Americans heard frequent volleys of small arms in the town; and, on approaching the Jalteva, they found a strong body of the enemy, with a small brass gun, occupying both sides of the barricaded road. Colonel Markham, with the First Infantry, was in advance; and the fire of the Allies was so sharp and well-directed that, for a time, it arrested the progress of the Infantry. In a few minutes, however, the Americans were brought to a charge, and then the enemy disappeared, scattering in all directions and leaving their gun behind them. Then the main body of the Nicaraguan force proceeded rapidly toward the main Plaza, where they saw their flag yet flying, and the town was soon cleared of the Allies. Zavala left another piece, besides the one taken at the Jalteva, behind him: and the streets were strewn with the bodies of his dead. Several prisoners of rank and some wounded remained in the hands of the Nicaraguans.

After Walker reached the Plaza, he ascertained that Zavala had attacked the town early the day before, and that the little garrison had been fighting the Allies for nearly twenty-four hours. The citizens of the place acted with commendable courage, and some of them received wounds they will carry to their graves in defence of their new homes. Major Angus Gillis, acting recorder of the Oriental Department, had gone to Nicaragua to revenge the death of a noble son who fell fighting at Rivas on the eleventh of April; and while with all the vigor of youth he was acting against the hated foe which had robbed him of his son, he received a severe and painful wound in the face, injuring permanently the sight of one eye, if not of both. John Tabor, the editor of the *Nicaraguense,* had his thigh broken while defending his right to print and publish his opinions in Central America. Douglass J. Wilkins had defended the hospital, threatened almost every instant with assault, and he had infused something of his own unquailing spirit into the weak and wasted forms of those stretched on the beds and gathered up in the hammocks of the several wards. The officers, too, attached to the several departments of the army had been very serviceable in repulsing the attacks of the Allies. Colonel Jones, paymaster-general, had directed the defence of the government house on the corner of the Plaza; while Major Potter, of the ordnance, was serviceable at many points, and particularly at the guardhouse near the church. It was on this occasion, too, that Captain Swingle first displayed the skill and courage which made him so useful in future operations.

Nor did those, whose usual avocation was to preach peace, deem it unworthy of their profession to strike a blow in defence of a cause reviled and persecuted of men, but just and sacred in the eyes of those familiar with the facts of the contest. It may not appear singular that the judge of the Court of First Instance, Thomas Basye, used his rifle in defence of the authority by which he held his commission ; but the conduct of Father Rossiter, a Catholic priest who had lately been appointed chaplain of the army, is more likely to attract attention and inquiry. But when we ascertain the acts of the Allies on their entrance to the town, it will not surprise us to see even a priest of the church arm in defence, from the attacks of those who acted like savages. This brings us to some incidents which occurred during the attack on Granada, indicating the character of the war the Allies were waging.

Among the old American residents at Granada was John B. Lawless, a native of Ireland but a naturalized citizen of the United States. He had been for a number of years engaged in trade on the Isthmus, principally in the purchase of hides and skins for export to New-York. Of a mild temper and inoffensive manner he had conciliated even Granadian jealousy by the honesty of his dealings and the integrity of his character. During the first weeks of the occupation by the Americans he had been of much service to the Legitimists by bringing their little grievances and complaints to the attention of the general-in-chief; and his intercessions were uniformly in favor of the native race, and in order to protect them from the thoughtless conduct of the new-comers. So entire was his faith in the good will of the Legitimists toward him, so perfect was his confidence in the protection of his American citizenship, that he refused, when opportunity offered, to repair to the Plaza to seek the safety afforded by Nicaraguan arms. He remained in his house when the soldiers of Zavala entered the town; and he was in the very act of unfolding the American flag before his door, when the Guatemalans tore him from his house, took him to the Jalteva, and there riddling his body with bullets, vented their savage passions in stabbing the lifeless body with their bayonets.

Nor was Lawless the only victim of their violence. An agent of the American Bible Society, Rev. D. H. Wheeler, was taken from his house and murdered after the same fashion as Lawless. Rev. Wm. J. Ferguson, also, a preacher of the Methodist denomination, was torn from the arms of his wife and daughter, and met the same fate as Lawless and Wheeler. Not satisfied with murdering these harmless persons, the brutal soldiers of Carrera had robbed them of their clothes and thrown their naked bodies, like dogs, into the public places. And in the house where Father Rossiter was quartered, a crime even darker still was committed by the followers of Zavala. When the Guatemalan troops entered the town the children of an Englishman, who had lately arrived at Granada from New-York, were seated at dinner. The group at the table consisted of a boy six years old, two girls one four and the other two years old, and their nurse. A soldier passing by the window pointed his musket at the innocent party, and firing deliberately, killed the boy instantly. The nurse saved the girls by

13*

flight to the next house, while the soldiers were forcing
the doors and windows of the room, where the dead boy
lay.

These injuries were done to persons claiming the protection of the American flag; but that flag itself was the
scoff and scorn of the soldiers an unlettered savage had
let loose on the plains of Nicaragua. The American
Minister, when the Allies attacked the town, lay nigh
unto death from the effects of a sudden illness, which
had seized him a few days previously. The ladies and
other non-combatants had been sent to the Minister's
house at the first moment of alarm; but it was well
that a small body of riflemen was also sent to protect
them. The Minister was not in a condition to take
charge of the helpless persons at his house; but his flag
was waving its ample folds in front of the door, and this
was deemed sufficient protection from the Guatemalans.
When the enemy, however, got possession of the houses
near the American legation, they began firing at the
"star-spangled banner," and called on Mr. Wheeler to
come forth into the street. All the choice phrases of
Spanish ribaldry were poured over the name of the *Min-
istro filibustero*—the filibuster Minister; and no epithet
of hatred or contempt for the race of the North was left
unuttered by the old Legitimists of Granada. It was well
for Mr. Wheeler that the American Secretary of State
about this time gave him leave to return to Washington
in order to report the condition of affairs in Nicaragua—
a civil way of telling the Minister his government had no
further need of his services.

The loss of the Americans during the action of the

12th and 13th at Masaya and Granada, was something upward of a hundred—twenty-five killed and eighty-five wounded. The loss at Masaya was very slight: most of the casualties occurred at Granada. A few were missing, principally those belonging to the party Col. Fisher had taken from Masaya on the evening of the 12th. Fisher returning toward Masaya by a different road from that Walker took on the morning of the 13th, was surprised when he reached the outskirts of the town to find himself in the presence of a large detachment of the enemy. Hastily taking a side path toward Diria and Diriomo he succeeded for a time in evading the enemy; but it was not long before he again fell in with them, though not in such force as previously. Then the Rangers and officers with Fisher found that the heavy night-dew had made the Sharp's carbines they carried unreliable, the moisture getting in between the chamber and the barrel. Finally the party separated, some soon finding their way to Granada, while it was several days before others returned. Lieutenant-Colonel Lainé, aide-de-camp to the general-in-chief, was taken prisoner by the Allies and shot. As soon as his execution was certainly known at Granada two Guatemalan officers, Lieutenant-Colonel Valderraman and Captain Allende, were there shot in retaliation.

The loss of the enemy at Granada was heavy. On the night of the 12th they probably buried their dead of that day, as many new graves were found in the neighborhood of the houses the Allies occupied. In addition to these, nearly a hundred bodies were buried by the Americans after Zavala retired to Masaya. The reports also stated that there were large numbers of wounded not only carried from Granada but also of those hurt at Masaya on the morning and afternoon of the 12th.

The lake steamer, La Virgen, was lying near the wharf at Granada during the action of the 12th and 13th; and late in the evening of the 13th she left for Virgin Bay, carrying several officers who were returning to the United States, and also Father Vigil for San Juan del Norte. The curate of Granada was wiser in the ways of Central American warfare than the Bible Society's agent, Mr. Wheeler, or the Methodist preacher, Mr. Ferguson: for as soon as he heard the Guatemalans were in the Jalteva he fled into a swamp near the town and remained hid away until the retreat of the enemy was entirely certain. Late in the afternoon of the 13th he came to congratulate the general-in-chief on the victory obtained over the Allies; and his congratulations ended in a request for a passport to go aboard the steamer about to leave for Virgin Bay. Nor did the good father feel easy until he was safely on the steamer beyond, as he thought, the reach of the dreaded *Chapines*.

A few days after the action of the 13th, the army received a valuable accession in the person of Col. C. F. Henningsen, who arrived at Granada in charge of arms and ordnance stores from New-York. When not more than nineteen, Col. Henningsen had commenced his military career under the Carlist leader, Zumalacarregui; and his service in Spain was well fitted to qualify him for war in Nicaragua. Although an Englishman by birth, he had spent most of his life on the continent of

Europe ; and after the death of Zumalacarregui he had resided for some years in Russia. Finally in 1849 he espoused
the cause of Hungarian independence and came about the
ame time as Kossuth to the United States. A day or two
after he reached Granada he was appointed brigadier-
general, and charged specially with the organization of
the artillery and with directing the practice with the
Minié musket. Much dissatisfaction was evinced by
many officers at the rank given to Henningsen ; nor
were efforts wanting to create prejudices against him
because he was not an American. But his own worth
and merits soon overcame most of these prejudices,
though in the breasts of some officers jealousy lurked
to the last. Walker, however, never had reason to re-
gret the confidence he early placed in the capacity of
Henningsen.

The efficiency of the new brigadier-general was soon
felt in the organization of two companies of artillery
and of a company of sappers and miners. Full and detailed instructions for tho uso of tho Minió musket were
written by Henningsen, and practice with this arm was
carried on for some days under his supervision. He had
much to combat in the idleness and indifference of the
officers, too many of whom valued their rank more as an
excuse for indulging their ease than as an incentive to
difficult and arduous duty. He was more successful in
the artillery practice than with the new rifle-muskets ;
for among the officers of artillery were several who had
much pride of profession. The skill and experience of
Major Schwartz have been mentioned, and besides him,
Capt. Dulaney and Lieut. Stahle deserve mention. Capt.

Ferrand had courage and little else ; his laziness was intolerable. Stahle was particularly useful in the practice with howitzers and cochorn-mortars. The proper carriages for the howitzers having arrived they were more fit for service than before, and the mortars, being light and easy of transportation, carried the same shell as the howitzers. The practice with the mortars was much simplified by always using the same charge, and determining the distance the projectile was to be sent entirely by the angle of elevation of the piece.

Meantime the Meridional Department was unprotected save by the schooner Granada, lying in the port of San Juan del Sur. During August and September Lieut. Fayssoux had been cruising first about the gulf of Fonseca and then in the gulf of Nicoya, and finally off Realejo ; but he had not been able to see anything with a hostile flag. The presence of the schooner at several points on the coast had kept the enemy in constant fear, and the Granada had, in many ways, embarrassed the action of the Allies. As the time, however, for the arrival of the steamer from San Francisco approached it became necessary to send a guard for the specie across the Transit and also to afford protection for the passengers on the Isthmus. Hence Gen. Hornsby was, on November 2d, sent from Granada to Virgin Bay with one hundred and seventy-five men. He reached the Transit just in time to guard the specie brought down by the Sierra Nevada.

It was known that a detachment had been sent from Masaya for the purpose of occupying Rivas ; while the reports of a fresh force from Costa Rica, with a view of co-operating with the Allies in the Meridional Department, were frequent and continued. Therefore Hornsby was ordered to remain at Virgin Bay with a view of holding the wharf, so that a force from Granada might at any moment be landed ; while Fayssoux remained in the port of San Juan del Sur to keep the enemy uneasy in case they attempted the occupation of that place. The log of the Granada shows how she performed her part. On the 7th of November, " At 4 30 P. M.," so the log reads, " received a notice, dated 4 P. M. at one mile from San Juan, and signed José M. Cañas, commanding vanguard of Costa Rican army, to surrender the post without firing a shot ; if I did so the citizens should be protected, if not, no protection would be given ; to which I paid no attention. At 5 P. M. Mr. G. Rozet—United States inspector at San Juan—came on board with a message that Gens. Bosque and Cañas were in the Plaza with six hundred Costa Ricans ; that they demanded the surrender of the schooner without my firing a shot ; if I did not the citizens would not be protected. I replied I would not surrender, but not having the power to drive them from the town I thought it would be prudent to run out of the harbor. At 5 45 P. M. cast loose from the buoy, ran out and lay off the harbor." Then on the 8th the log proceeds : " Lying-to off the harbor. At 3 30 P. M. received letters from the officer in command of San Juan, Guardio, offering protection to all citizens that would deliver up their arms to him, and from Mr. Rozet praying me not to come in, that if I did all Americans would perish. My answer to Rozet was that I did not intend to come in and for him to say to Guardio that I would not communicate with the enemy. The persons who

came off to me reported that the Costa Ricans were looking hourly for a bark and two brigs, the latter armed
and carrying troops, the former with provisions and troops."
On the 10th : "At 12 M. close in the mouth of the harbor.
Saw a number of mounted men, and apparently about
one hundred and fifty foot soldiers leave the town." The
cause of their departure will appear by returning to the
movements of Gen. Hornsby at Virgin Bay.

Although the nominal numbers of the infantry at
Virgin Bay was 175, their real strength was much less ;
and when, on the 10th, Hornsby was reinforced by Sanders with 150 rifles and a howitzer under Capt. Dulaney,
he was not able to march against the enemy with more
than 250 men. Cañas had taken up a position on the
hill over which the Transit road passes about a mile beyond the Halfway House toward San Juan del Sur.
Just beyond the Halfway House there is a deep cut in
the road, and some hundred and fifty yards farther on
there is a slight bridge thrown across a deep ravine.
The enemy had barricaded near the bridge, and thus
commanded a long stretch of the road, flanked on one
side by rising ground and on the other by the ravine.
Captain Ewbanks, with a detachment of Rifles, turned
the right flank of the Costa Ricans defending the bridge ;
and thus Hornsby was enabled to reach the foot of the
hill where the main body of Cañas was posted. When,
however, the American general reconnoitred the hill
the Costa Ricans occupied, and saw the effect produced
on his men by the fire they had just passed through, he
deemed it prudent to retire without hazarding an attack.
He therefore withdrew to Virgin Bay, and repairing to

Granada reported in person to Walker the result of his march against Cañas.

It was all-important to keep the Transit clear of any formidable force of the Allies. The enemy were well aware of its importance to the Americans when they styled the Transit the " highway of filibusterism." Accordingly, on the 11th, Walker repaired with 250 Rifles to Virgin Bay, taking also a howitzer, a mortar, and a squad of sappers and miners. General Henningsen accompanied the force with a view of directing the new corps which had been formed under his supervision. The Artillery had not acted well on the 10th, and the general was anxious for it to redeem its character.

Walker landed on the afternoon of the 11th; and marched the same night to the Halfway House, which he reached just before daybreak. After a short rest, the advance resumed its march and had proceeded as far as the cut in the road when the enemy opened fire from the same barricades near the bridge they had occupied on the morning of the 10th. Captain Ewbanks, being familiar with the ground, was ordered to make a large detour to the left, and he thus succeeded as before in dislodging the Allies from their barricades. The whole column then pushed forward without interruption to the foot of the hill where Cañas held his whole force, probably 800 strong.

The enemy, chiefly Costa Ricans, occupied the very ground on which the Democrats, a little over a year previously, had awaited in ambush the approach of Corral from Rivas toward San Juan del Sur. Colonel Natzmer, acting as aide to Valle in September, 1855, was therefore acquainted with the sides of the hill on which the Democrats had then been placed. Accordingly he was ordered to take the sappers and miners along the hillside to the right of the road and cut a path toward the top of the hill and in the rear of the first barricades of the enemy. Captain Johnson, with a company of Rifles, followed and protected the working party. Captain Green was also sent in the rear of Johnson's company ; but getting separated from those in advance, Green lost his way in the thick undergrowth and was not seen for several hours afterward.

The movement of Natzmer was covered by advancing the howitzer toward the curve in the road fronting the first barricades of Cañas, and by sending several shells into the works of the enemy. The fire of the allies was, however, so fierce and well-directed as to make it prudent to withdraw the howitzer, under cover, after a few rounds. On this occasion, the artillerymen behaved with commendable coolness, and recovered, by their steadiness under fire, some of the reputation they had lost on the 10th. In the meanwhile, the Costa Ricans kept up an irregular fire of musketry and rifles—for they had a number of riflemen with them—and Capt. Stith lost his life by exposing his tall person for a moment in the middle of the road.

In the course of an hour and a half Col. Natzmer had succeeded in reaching the point at which he aimed ; but in the meantime the enemy, becoming aware of his movement and fearful of its effects, prepared for retreat. When Johnson and the Rifles reached the barricades, they were already deserted, and Cañas was on his way toward

San Juan del Sur. The Americans then pushed on in pursuit, and as some of the Rangers were well mounted, they, acting under the orders of Henningsen, pressed on the rear of the enemy. Cañas conducted his retreat with deliberation as far as San Juan, taking advantage of several points in the road to delay the progress of the Americans; but, finally, near where the little stream that runs into the sea on the edge of the town crosses the Transit road, Henningsen, followed by Capt. Leslie, Lieut. Gaskill, and a few of the Rangers, charged on the retreating foot soldiers and breaking them completely, drove them at a rapid pace through San Juan and across the river up the coast trail to Rivas. The enemy were so scattered after passing San Juan that further pursuit would have been fruitless.

Numbers of the Costa Ricans had, in the confusion of the retreat, escaped from their ranks and taken the road to Guanacaste. Thus Cañas reached Rivas with a force not only thinned by deaths and desertions, but also discouraged and demoralized by defeat. It was evident, therefore, that he could not soon take any measures to trouble the Transit; he could scarce venture to show himself out of the barricades of Rivas. Hence Walker was anxious to return immediately to Granada and again attack Belloso, while Cañas was calling on him for aid in the Meridional Department. On the 13th, then, Walker marched from San Juan to Virgin Bay, and embarking his force on the lake steamer, arrived the same night at Granada. Col. Markham, with the First Infantry, was left at Virgin Bay.

On the morning of the 15th, the Americans were again on the road from Granada to Masaya. The force consisted of Sanders' Rifles, and a company of 2d Rifles, together with Jaquess' Infantry, a body of Rangors, under Waters, a few sappers and portions of the two companies of Artillery. The whole strength was about 560 men. The Artillery consisted of a twelve-pound howitzer, two small brass pieces, taken from the Allies, and two of the small mortars. As the train of pack-mules, carrying the ammunition, was long, and the day hot, the march was slow and fatiguing; nor had the force passed over more than half the distance to Masaya, when Walker ascertained that Jerez had marched toward Rivas with seven or eight hundred men. In consequence of this information Jaquess, with his Infantry, was ordered to return to Granada, and take a lake steamer for Virgin Bay. Thus Walker reduced his own strength to less than 300 men.

Major Henry, although scarcely able to walk, had mounted his mule and followed the column marching on Masaya. Two or three miles from the edge of the town he and Col. Thompson succeeded in passing the advanced guard, and coming on a picket of the enemy charged it at full gallop. The picket fled like deer, one of them leaving his hat, with a hole made by a bullet from Henry's revolver, and the blood sprinkled over the coarse straw of the crown. This incident, while it shows the excess of courage animating some of the officers in Nicaragua, also proves how difficult it was to restrain their valor within the limits of order and regularity; though it is probable Henry and Thompson were not aware of the fact that they had passed the guard, owing to the neglect of the officer in charge of the advance to perform his duty.

As the Rangers in front approached the small huts on the edge of Masaya, the enemy opened a heavy fire of musketry, and Waters drawing his men to the right of the road, in order to cover them with the heavy tropical vegetation, gave room for the Rifles to pass. In entering by the plazuela of San Sebastian, the road passes through a cut, on each side of which are scattered small reed huts, in the midst of plantain patches. The Allies, posted in the plantain patches, poured a most destructive fire into the Rifles as they advanced. Sanders, however, contrived to move toward the plazuela, deploying his men on each side of the road ; while Henningsen, pushing the howitzer close to the enemy, poured into them a rapid rain of canister. For several minutes the fighting was furious ; but finally the firing became less and less, and the enemy falling back into the main part of the town, left the Americans in possession of the suburbs.

But the ground had not been gained without severe loss. The Nicaraguans had lost more than fifty—six killed, and more than forty wounded. Lieut. Stahle, a valuable officer of artillery, had fallen beside his gun, and Major Schwartz had been wounded. Besides this, several of the best officers of the Rifles had been severely hurt. Capt. Ewbanks and Lieut. C. H. West had received painful and dangerous wounds ; and Col. Natzmer was struck down by a spent ball hitting him back of the ear. The approach of night, too, no less than the nervous state of the command, exhausted by the excitement and heavy loss, made it expedient to encamp on the high ground abandoned by the enemy. Hence orders

were given to unpack the mules, and post the pickets
for the night.

In the condition, however, of the force, it was far
easier to issue orders than to have them executed.
Owing to the darkness, it was some time before the
wounded could be got together near the centre of the
camp, and the surgeons had some difficulty in dressing
their wounds in the dark.   As the general-in-chief passed from one point to another, in order to see his commands executed, he found so many of the officers in such
a state of languor and exhaustion, that they were in capable of controlling their men.   Some of them during
the long march had taken a great deal of liquor, and
this, as well as the excitement of the conflict dying out,
left them utterly deprived of moral strength.   It was
only by his personal exertions that Walker obtained any
security for the camp ; and never, during the whole
time he was in Nicaragua, did he find it so difficult, as
on that night to have his orders executed.   The will of
the force seemed to be momentarily paralyzed by the
fierce fire through which it had passed.

The night was long and tedious ; but finally day
broke, and the men somewhat refreshed by the short and
interrupted sleep they had procured, were again ready for
action.   Major Schwartz, with admirable accuracy,
threw a few shells from the howitzer into the houses
near the plazuela of San Sebastian ; and then Major
Caycee advancing with a few of the Second Rifles, got
possession of the little square apparently just abandoned
by the Allies.   Soon the wounded were comfortably
quartered in the small church of San Sebastian ; and

after the troops had taken a hearty breakfast, their spirits were as good as ever. The sappers began their work cutting through the houses on each side of the street running into the right-hand corner of the main Plaza as you approach from San Sebastian. The cuts made through the adobe houses, during the attack of the 12th of October, were also found serviceable.

The work of the sappers was, however, slow ; and while they were advancing in front under the protection of a company of Rifles, it was several times necessary to defend the plazuela from the attacks of the Allies. But the enemy, after several repulses with loss, seemed to conclude that they were exhausting their strength fruitlessly by these demonstrations against the rear of the Americans. Then, too, the front having got so far toward the Plaza that it was inconvenient to keep up communications with San Sebastian, Walker pushed his whole available force close up to the enemy, burning the houses behind him so as to protect his rear. Moving thus during the 16th and 17th, the Americans had on the evening of the latter day, got within twenty-five or thirty yards of the houses on the Plaza held by the enemy.

General Henningsen had established a mortar battery in a hut near the enemy, and a few shells thrown from it were quite effective. But the fuses were, as before noticed, too short-timed, and the shells at the disposal of the Nicaraguans were too few to justify any lavish use of them. This, in fact, was a main reason for the small effects produced by the mortars and howitzers (when shells were used in the latter) during the whole campaign. In addition to the defective fuses, and the small supply of shells, the effects of three days' labor and fighting were seen in the lassitude of the men and the almost utter impossibility of having guard duty properly performed. Although the Allies were clearly disheartened by the approach of the Americans, it would have required some time longer to drive them from the town ; and Walker, anxious about the Transit, resolved to retire to Granada, preparatory to an abandonment of the Oriental Department.

Accordingly, near midnight of the 17th, after a few hours' rest in the early part of the evening, the Americans silently abandoned the houses they held and took up the line of march for Granada. In the darkness of the night the force was divided for a little while, but it was soon re-united and pursued its way toward the lake. The loss during the three days was nearly a hundred—one third of the whole number which attacked Masaya ; and the long line of the wounded mounted on horses, necessarily impeded the march to Granada. But in spite of the exhaustion of the command, the march was regular and the force was kept compactly together. General Henningsen, with a howitzer, kept the rear well closed up, and secured it from any annoyances the enemy might have attempted. The Allies, however, did not trouble the retiring Americans ; they were probably glad enough to be rid of such troublesome neighbors. On the morning of the 18th, Walker again entered Granada; and he soon after announced to Henningsen his determination to abandon the place.

Chapter Tenth.

THE RETREAT FROM GRANADA.

THE obstinate resistance of the Allies at Masaya was due mainly to the fact that they had received a reinforcement of about eight hundred Guatemalans the very day they were attacked. It was these Guatemalans who had been placed in the plantain patches a few hours after they reached Masaya; and ignorant of the effects of American rifles they had kept their ground longer than any other portion of the allied force would have maintained it. During the three days' fighting, however, the fire had been taken from the new men of Belloso; and his losses had been such that it was supposed he would scarcely be able to move without fresh troops. Hence Walker imagined the evacuation of Granada might be effected without any interruption from the enemy. He had, however, determined to destroy as well as abandon Granada; and as this duty required skill and firmness, he decided to intrust the task to Henningsen.

Preparations for the retreat from Granada were begun on the 19th. The sick and wounded in the hospital

14

were placed on a steamer for transportation to Omotepe Island. In order to make the movement as rapid as possible, both the lake steamers, the San Carlos and La Virgen, were engaged for the service. On the 20th Walker repaired to Virgin Bay with the view of having all ready for a march to San Jorge or to Rivas, after the destruction of Granada. He supposed that the government property and stores would be at Virgin Bay on the 21st or the 22d, at latest : but several causes delayed the movement. There was a great deal of property scattered through Granada, belonging to officers and soldiers, and each one tried to save everything he owned. Besides, as soon as the idea got abroad that the town was to be destroyed the work of plunder began, and liquor being abundant, nearly every man able to do duty was more or less under its influence. Henningsen found it impossible to restrain the passions of the officers, and these, in turn, lost all control over their men. On the 22d, however, Fry had removed the women and children, as well as the sick and wounded, to the island, and had with him a guard of about sixty men. Henningsen had removed most of the ordnance stores to the steamer, and was proceeding with the destruction of the city. As the burning went on the excitement of the scene increased the thirst for liquor, and soldiers thought it a pity to waste so much good wine and brandy. In spite of guards and sentries, orders and officers, the drunkenness went on, and the town presented more the appearance of a wild Bacchanalian revel than of a military camp. Of course, Belloso soon knew the state of affairs at Granada, and on the afternoon of the 24th the town was attacked by the Allies.

At Virgin Bay the Infantry of Markham and of Jaquess were in a very disorganized condition.   It being
the close of the rainy season there was much fever in the
camp ; and the contrast between the quarters at Granada and at Virgin Bay, as well as the scarcity of vege-
tables in the rations at the latter point, depressed the
spirits of the officers no less than of the soldiers.   There
were some choice men who seemed more cheerful at
the prospect of difficulty and danger and privation; but
such organizations are rare in every time and among
every people.   They are, unfortunately, the exceptions
and not the rule.

To add to the general gloom, on the morning of the
23d, news came from San Juan del Sur that the schooner
Granada had gone out of the harbor to engage a Costa
Rican brig, and the people of the town had watched the
fight by the flashes of the guns, until a broad bright
light, accompanied by a loud noise as of thunder, led
them to suppose one of the vessels had been blown up.
Couriers arrived at Virgin Bay from time to time during the night of the 23d, announcing it as the general
impression at San Juan that Fayssoux had blown up his
schooner rather than let her fall into the hands of the
enemy.   This report, while it shows the opinions held
by the people as to the inevitable result of a conflict
between a vessel of the size of the Costa Rican brig
and the little schooner, also indicates the idea they had
formed of the character of the commander of the Granada.   The failure of the schooner to enter the harbor
during the night confirmed the impression of the towns-
people ; and at Virgin Bay few, besides the general-in-

chief, doubted the correctness of the conclusions drawn from the light and the explosion.

On the morning of the 24th, however, the schooner was seen coming into port, and although her deck seemed covered with more than her complement of men, she cast anchor as usual in the harbor. In a little while the news spread that it was the enemy's vessel which had been blown up the night before. The log of the schooner for the 23d tells the story thus : " Commences with light breezes from the N. and E., and pleasant. At. 4 P. M. saw a sail off the harbor ; hove up anchor, and stood out to her. At 5h. 45m. she hoisted Costa Rica colors. At 6, within four hundred yards of her ; she fired round shot and musketry at us. At 8 we blew her up. At 10 we had taken from the sea her captain and forty of her men. Her name was Once de Abril, Capt. Antonie Villarostra ; crew, 114 men and officers ; guns 4, 9 lbs. calibre. The captain states that he was about surrendering when she blew up. All were lost and killed but those that I picked up. I had one man, Jas. Elliot, killed ; Mathew Pilkington dangerously wounded, Dennis Kane seriously, and six others slightly. Light breezes ; stood in for the harbor."

The simplicity of the narrative reveals a feature in its author's character ; but it needs the commentary of the schooner's size, and crew, and armament, to make its full force felt. The Granada was about seventy-five tons burden, and had on board during the action with the Once de Abril twenty-eight persons all told, and among them were a boy and four citizens of San Juan. She carried two six-pound carronades, and had not more than

180 rounds of ball and canister. No wonder the people on shore imagined that a fight of two hours at close distance (for they knew, they said, Fayssoux would bring the brig to close work), had disabled the Granada to such an extent as to induce her commander to blow her up.

The destruction of the brig was caused by a ball fired into her from the schooner, the shot probably striking some iron or caps in the magazine. The Costa Ricans, however, and the people of Nicaragua, imagined it was effected by some new missile the Americans had invented. Many of the prisoners were badly burned; and they appeared grateful and somewhat surprised at the care the surgeons bestowed on their wounds. The captain was badly hurt, but after some time his burns were healed, and passage was given him on the steamer to Panama. The prisoners who could walk were soon released, and passports were given them for Costa Rica. When they reached home their reports did much to correct the prejudices the Moras had created against the Americans; and the released prisoners were finally silenced by the orders of the government. None of them, however, could ever be forced to march to Nicaragua.

The day after the action with the Once de Abril, Fayssoux was promoted to the rank of captain, and the estate of Rosario, near Rivas, was bestowed on him for the signal services he had rendered the republic. The result of this first sea-fight with the enemy, the disparity of numbers and guns, as well as the decisive character of the contest, gave new life to the men at Virgin Bay. Even the mean quarters and scanty rations of the village were, for a while, forgotten in the new glory the Granada had won for the red star flag of Nicaragua. And when, late in the evening of the 24th, news came that Henningsen was attacked at Granada, it did not interrupt the cheerfulness inspired by the success of the schooner off San Juan.

About three o'clock in the afternoon of the 24th the Allies attacked Henningsen at three points almost at the same moment.* One body of the enemy appeared in the Jalteva, another on the side of the San Francisco church, while a third body attacked the Guadalupe church on the street leading from the main Plaza to the Playa of the Lake. Major Swingle with a few cannon-shot soon caused the force in the Jalteva to disappear ; while O'Neal resisted the advance of the enemy on the side of San Francisco. At the Guadalupe, however, the Allies were more successful. They not only gained possession of the church of Guadalupe, but also commanded the church of Esquipulas, about half way between the former and the Plaza. Thus a small body of men at the fort and on the wharf engaged in sending freight aboard of the steamers were entirely cut off from Henningsen and the main body of Americans.

Soon after the enemy appeared around Granada Lieut. O'Neal had fallen ; and his brother Calvin, half frantic from the loss, called on Henningsen to permit him to charge the enemy forming near the church of

---

* The writer is principally indebted for the incidents of the operations at Granada between the 24th November and 12th of December to the " *Personal Recollections of Nicaragua*," *by Gen. C. F. Henningsen, author of "Recollections of Russia," and " Twelve Months' Campaign in Spain.*"

San Francisco. The Allies were between four and five hundred strong ; but O'Neal, in his fury, thought not of numbers, and every other feeling was drowned in grief for a brother's death. At a convenient moment the general gave him thirty-two picked Rifles and let him loose on the enemy. O'Neal, barefooted and in his shirt sleeves, leaped on his horse, and calling on his Rifles to follow, dashed into the midst of the Allies as they formed near the old church. The men, fired by the spirit of their leader, followed in the same fierce career, dealing death and destruction on the terrified foe. The Allies were entirely unprepared for O'Neal's sudden, dashing charge, and they fell as heedless travellers before the blast of the simoom. The slaughter made by the thirty-two Rifles was fearful, and so far were O'Neal and his men carried by the " rapture of the strife" that it was difficult for Henningsen to recall them to the Plaza. When they did return it was through streets almost blocked with the bodies of the Guatemalans they had slain. This charge well closed the fighting on the first day of the attack.

At daybreak on the 25th, Henningsen had concen-trated his force and was able to ascertain his real strength. He had only 227 men capable of bearing arms, and was encumbered with 73 wounded and 70 women, children, and sick persons. Twenty-seven had been cut off on the wharf, while Capt. Hesse with 22 men had been lost, either killed or taken prisoners, at the Guadalupe church. Henningsen had also seven guns and four mortars ; but his supply of ammunition for these was so short as to make them of much less service than they might have been. This force was, during the night of the 24th, concentrated near the Plaza, and it held the adobe houses on each side of the principal street leading from the main square by the churches of Esquipulas and Guadalupe to the lake. A breastwork was built from the parish church on one side of the mouth of this street to the guard-house on the other side ; and the Americans were also partially protected from the enemy by the burning buildings around and near the main Plaza.

During the 25th, Henningsen, while repelling the advances the enemy were constantly attempting to make, pushed on toward the Esquipulas, driving the Allies from the huts and small houses of the neighborhood ; and in the afternoon he succeeded in getting possession of the church. The hot embers had prevented the enemy from occupying Esquipulas ; but they had loopholed several huts near, and thus, for some time, kept the Americans from getting possession. After a second charge, however, the Allies were driven from their barricades in the brush as well as from the huts they held ; and thus the way was open for the advance of the Americans toward Guadalupe. The losses during the day were small ; and the wounds slight.

On the 26th, all the houses on the Plaza were destroyed, except the church, the guard-house, and one or two others. Still the operations were delayed by the too free use of liquor ; and it was difficult to get work done at the time and in the way it was ordered. The general commanding found himself unable to keep together a sufficient force to aid in the attempts he made against the Guadalupe church. In the efforts to gain this point much of the slender supply of shot and shell were exhausted without making any impression on the defences of the enemy ; and the Americans, on the contrary, were somewhat discouraged by the success of the Allies in knocking away the works they hastily built. About sunset Henningsen gave up the attempt on Guadalupe, with a loss of sixteen killed and wounded. In addition to this loss several officers had been hurt during the day at different points ; and Col. Jones had received a wound which kept him on his back for many weeks afterward. Fortunately, after this, the supply of brandy in the American camp was scanty ; and the allied soldiers having got some of the liquor left in the town, it is probable, that Belloso found difficulty in managing its distribution.

Soon after giving up the attempt on Guadalupe, Henningsen heard heavy firing, as he supposed toward the north ; and then prolonged shouts coming apparently from the same direction. He fancied, at the time, it might be a relieving force, which had been landed to the north of the town ; but it was really the firing and shouts of the Allies at the attack they made on the men at the old fort, which had been partially destroyed for the purpose of building a wharf. This point was held for two days by the captain of police, Grier, assisted by some twenty-five of his men and of other civil employees of the government. On the evening of the 25th, Walker hearing no news from Granada after the attack, took the steamer San Carlos, which anchored off the wharf early on the morning of the 26th. The general-in-chief seeing the red-star flag flying on the parochial church, and

14

the smoke of the burning houses constantly rising in new directions, inferred that Henningsen, not having completed the destruction of the town at the time of the attack, was delayed on the Plaza more through choice in the complete execution of orders, than by any necessity the Allies had imposed. But perceiving the importance of holding the fort for Henningson's ready communication with the lake, Walker sent to the wharf in order to ascertain the state and the wants of its defenders. Grier sent word that his men were in good spirits, confident of holding the position, and that all they wished was, after a while, some provision and ammunition. At dark, a boat was sent from the San Carlos to the wharf with the articles required; but then the aide, who went in the boat, reported, on his return, that the spirits of the men were failing. The change was due to the desertion of a young Venezuelan, Tejada, who had been released from chains by the Americans, on the 13th of October, 1855. The consciousness that their exact number and condition were reported to the enemy by Tejada, made the men nervous of an attack on the fort. By their courage and skill in the use of their weapons they had given the Allies the idea, that they were much stronger than they really were; but now, the deserter, by destroying the delusion of the enemy, also destroyed the confidence of Grier and his men.

Scarcely had the aide-de-camp returned to the San Carlos before the heavy firing Henningsen heard on the evening of the 26th was also heard aboard of the steamer. The frequent flashes of dischargiug small arms formed a circle of fire around the wharf, and the deep, prolonged

volleys of musketry, so distinct from the short, sharp
crack of the rifle, told that the enemy were doing most
of the work ; nor were the shouts from the shore such
as come from the lusty lungs of defiant or triumphant
Americans. In a short time, too, a man swam to the
steamer, and saying he had escaped from the wharf, told
the story of its capture by the allies. The deserter, Tejada,
had not only given the number of Grier's men to the
enemy, but had also pointed out how the wharf in the
rear of the Americans might be reached with a large iron
launch on the beach. At the same time Grier was
assailed in the rear, a large force attacked him in front,
and, paralyzed by the combined assault as well as by the
number of the enemy, the Americans were nearly all
killed or wounded, and taken prisoners without a serious
struggle. Well does the conduct of these men, before
and after the desertion of Tejada, illustrate the oft-re-
peated remark of the great captain, " that in war the
moral is to the physical as three to one."

On the 27th, Henningsen moved his wounded from
the parochial church, and the difficulty with which
the labor was begun shows the indisposition of his
force to do any work except fighting. Some of the Jamaica negroes, who had been at work on the lake
steamer, and were caught in the town accidentally, were
of service for fatigue duty ; nor were prisoners from the
guard-house entirely useless. After the wounded had
been removed, a few hundred pounds of damaged powder
were put under one of the towers of the church, and all
the houses remaining on the Plaza were fired. The
enemy tried to press on the Americans as they left the

main square, but they were kept back by a few riflemen
in the church towers until Henningsen was ready to
withdraw.   When all was prepared, the Americans
abandoned the Plaza, and as they retired put a match to
a train reaching the damaged powder under the church.
The fire reached the powder, blowing the tower high into
the air just as the too eager enemy were crowding into
the Plaza, of which they had so long strove to get the
mastery.

The town was now almost entirely destroyed, and Henningsen having got his force completely together, determined to make another attempt on the Guadalupe
church.   He was now able to control sixty good men
for the assault, and the spirits of his command were
raised by the success of previous operations.   Besides
the sixty riflemen for the attack, there were twenty-four
artillerymen at the three six-pounders, and after seven
rounds from each of the guns, rapidly fired into the
Guadalupe, the Rifles rushed to the assault.   But the
enemy had abandoned the church before the Americans
reached it, and thus the most important point between
the Plaza and the Lake was carried without the loss of
a single man.   Immediately the wounded, ammunition,
stores, and guns, were moved to the Guadalupe, and Major Henry was ordered, with twenty-seven men, to take
possession of two huts in the low ground between the
church and the lake.

Henry forthwith executed the order, and soon reported
that, from appearances, he expected an early attack by
the enemy.   He also advised the abandonment of one
of the huts, adding that he could hold the other during

the night. Henningsen urged him to hold the single hut as long as possible, and promised reinforcements; but the confusion of the move to the Guadalupe not being yet over, only ten riflemen, with Col. Schwartz and his howitzer, could be sent to Henry's assistance. Nor was it long after dark when the enemy, under the shade of the thick plantain walks and mango trees, crept up toward the huts, with the hope of surprising the Americans. But a vigilant eye was watching their movements, and Henry, sending a few rifle shots among them, discovered their position and strength by the answering volleys of musketry. Then the howitzer threw its canister into the allied ranks, spreading death and confusion among the numerous body attacking Henry's position. The enemy were driven back with severe loss.

After this repulse of the Allies Henningsen re-organized his force and found it stronger than he had supposed. He formed forty of the best men into a main guard, holding them in reserve for immediate and urgent use. A company of fifteen were detailed to guard the doors and windows of the Guadalupe church; while twenty were selected for the defence of the enclosure in the rear. Ten men were assigned to each of the six guns at the church, and besides these it was found there were yet thirty to spare. The latter were formed into a lower main guard and sent to report to Henry at the hut in the low ground. It will thus be seen that the fighting men, then for duty, numbered two hundred and ten.

Nor was the increase of strength by the new and more efficient organization the only added force Henningsen now had. The men recovering from the effects of debauchery in the town and seeing the necessity for laborious effort were more willing to work than they had hitherto been. During the night of the 27th, they worked with a vigor which surprised their commander, and by daybreak of the 28th, they had finished an adobe breastwork the general had scarcely hoped to see completed. Major Swingle, by his industry and intelligence, did much to forward the labors of the men, and it would have been difficult for Henningsen to find a man more capable than Swingle of directing the execution of any orders he might issue. But the concentration of the force at the Guadalupe, while it enabled Henningsen to complete an organization whereby his men were more readily handled, had its inconveniences and dangers. The crowding together of more than three hundred persons, many of them sick and wounded was calculated to affect the health of the camp; and the exposed nature of the ground where Henry was posted, commanded as it was by several points in the hands of the enemy, made it impossible to move non-combatants thither until it was properly entrenched.

On the 28th the enemy, under cover of a flag of truce, sent into the American camp a renegade by the name of Price, together with an aide of Zavala, bearing a letter to "the commander-in-chief of the remains of Walker's forces." This letter invited the commanding officer, for humanity's sake, to surrender himself and soldiers prisoners-of-war, promising them safety and passports to leave the country. Price, too, at his entrance into the camp urged the men to give up their arms as they were surrounded by three thousand of the Allies, but Price was immediately arrested and silenced, and a defiant reply to their insulting invitation was forthwith despatched to the leaders of the hostile forces. The aide was evidently sent as a spy, for he entered without being blindfolded or duly introduced, and Henningsen showed his contempt for the Allied leaders by telling the officer he might pass through his camp and observe all his defences.

The enemy, finding it was necessary to use more vigorous means than words in order to get the Americans out of the positions they held, made several efforts to regain the church of Guadalupe. At three o'clock in the afternoon of the 28th, they tried to storm the church, but were repulsed with severe loss. Then at eight the same evening they attempted to surprise the position. The night was dark, and a large force got within eighty yards of the breastwork in the rear of the church before they were discovered. Major Swingle with two six-pounders poured canister rapidly into the approaching columns, and the blaze of the enemy's musketry showing their position, the guns were used with deadly effect. In a short time the Allies were again repulsed, and without the waste of rifle caps, now becoming scarce in Henningsen's camp. Several other faint attacks were afterward made on the church, but it was clear that the officers of the Allies could not drive their soldiers to an assault.

The entrenchments near Henry's position were not sufficiently advanced to admit of the removal of the sick and wounded until the 1st of December. In the meanwhile cholera and typhus broke out in the Guadalupe. The crowded state of the church, the numbers of sick and wounded, and the bad air from the decaying bodies of the enemy's dead, tended to produce sickness; and the tendency was increased by the exposure to night air and rains. The camp was now subsisting on mule and horse meat with small rations of flour and coffee; but this diet, sufficiently wholesome, had little to do with the disease which appeared. The Allies also perished in large numbers by cholera and fever; yet they had an excellent quality and great variety of subsistence. Among the allied officers who died of cholera was the commander of the Guatemalan forces, Gen. M. Paredes. His death left Zavala in command of the Guatemalan contingent.

The cholera was a more fearful enemy to the Americans than any by which they were surrounded. Hence it was important to hasten the removal of the sick and wounded to the entrenchments in the low ground; and after they left the Guadalupe disease diminished and the cholera almost entirely disappeared. About seventy men remained in the church; but its garrison was gradually reduced to thirty rifles under the command of Lieut. Sumpter Williamson. His steady courage and cheerful spirits made him competent, even with the small force at his disposal, to hold the position against any attempts of the enemy; and it was always easy for Henningsen, in an emergency, to strengthen him with fresh men.

But the cholera did not leave until it had taken off some of the most useful persons in the American camp. Among these was Mrs. Bingham, the wife of Edward

Bingham, the actor. While the disease was worst in the Guadalupe, she had been constantly employed in the care of the sick; and her unwearied kindness and attention had probably enabled many to overcome the fatal epidemic. But she was herself finally seized and carried off by the disease in a few hours.

After moving the main part of his force to Henry's position, Henningsen endeavored to work his way to the lake while keeping open his communications with Williamson in the church. For several days the enemy strove constantly to interrupt these communications. But all their attempts failed; and while the Americans held their ground against the enemy, the ordnance officers were increasing the supplies of ammunition. Major Rawle, one of the original fifty-eight, was possessed of untiring industry; and Major Swingle was fertile in resources and most ingenious in all mechanical contrivances. They made round shot by piling up small pieces of iron in sand hollowed on a six-pound ball, and then pouring lead over the iron pieces so as to hold them together. Thus the effective strength of the artillery was much increased; and the general was enabled to count on it as a means for breaking through the enemy's lines in case such a step became necessary or advisable.

On the 8th Zavala sent another letter to Henningsen, imploring him to surrender, and saying that he need expect no assistance from Walker, as the steamers had arrived at San Juan del Sur and San Juan del Norte without bringing any passengers for Nicaragua. But the Nicaraguan general did not condescend to give a written reply to the Guatemalan officer. He merely sent the message that he could parley only " at the cannon's mouth." The men now began to be discouraged at the frequent appearance of the steamers on the lakes without the landing of a relieving force ; and the enemy not moving it was necessary to send the Americans to attack some indigo vats on their right to keep them from dwelling on the condition in which they were placed by the Allies. The provisions were nearly exhausted ; and the men had commenced discussing among themselves the necessity of breaking through the enemy's lines, when, on the morning of the 12th, the steamer, La Virgen, again appeared off the port.

While the retreat from Granada was thus embarrassed by the large and constantly recruited force the Allies had brought against Henningsen, the troops in the Meridional Department were not prepared to relieve their beleagured comrades. Walker was almost constantly on the lake, watching the progress and attempting to ascertain the position of Henningsen ; and when, at intervals, he returned to Virgin Bay, he usually found the force there nervous and apprehensive of an attack from Cañas and Jerez who then held Rivas. Jaquess, commanding at Virgin Bay, had more knowledge of tactics than of other branches of the military art more important in the operations of irregular war ; and he permitted the most alarming reports as to the strength and resources of the enemy to be circulated in his camp. His men were worn out by heavy guard duty, and all the spirit was taken out of them by being kept in a state of constant anxiety and watchfulness.

Nor was the camp at Omotepe, whither the main

hospital of the army had been temporarily removed, in a less uneasy mood than the Infantry at Virgin Bay. Fry had some sixty men capable of duty, and there were with him several efficient officers. It was impossible for the enemy, in any numbers, to reach the island, even if they had been able to spare the force from the position they held. But there were constant rumors of barges passing from San Jorge to Omotepe with arms for the use of the Indians on the east side of the island. Knowing well that but few of the Indians on Omotepe could be used against the Americans, even if the Allies had been able to furnish them all with arms, Walker felt confident that no serious attack could be made on the little village where the hospital had, for the time, been fixed.

On the morning of the 2d of December the general-in-chief went aboard of the lake steamer, with a view of visiting Granada. Just before the anchor was hove, a courier from San Juan del Sur announced the arrival of the Orizaba with eighty men for Nicaragua. The steamer was getting under weigh when a small canoe, with three men in it, approached the vessel from the direction of Omotepe. The men from the canoe were taken aboard the steamer, and they reported that the Americans on the island had been attacked the night previously by a large body of Indians. The tale of these three persons was indistinct, but as they had been out during the night and were shivering from exposure to the damp, chilly air, it was more charitable to impute the confusion of their story to cold than to fear. The steamer was forthwith ordered to the island, and the general-in-chief took the most intelligent of the three fugitives to the cabin and dosing him with a half-tumblerful of whiskey, tried to get out of him the true state of affairs at Omotepe. All he could get out of the man was that every soul on the island, sick and wounded, women and children, had probably been murdered. The cowardly fellow was not ashamed to live and tell the tale.

As the steamer approached the island one of the large iron launches used by the Transit Company for loading freight and passengers was seen drifting in the lake, without sail or rudder, and filled with a crowd of men, women, and children, in all varieties of dress and humor. It was some comfort to see that everybody on the island was not killed ; though the forlorn condition of the launch's passengers was well fitted to excite pity and compassion. Among them, two or three ladies who had been delicately brought up, bore their trials and sufferings with more patience than the stoutest men ; while some of the women, viragos in appearance, as soon as they were safely aboard the steamer, loosened their tongues and gave free play to their long-restrained feelings. Soon the steamer anchored off the village where Fry was quartered ; and he immediately reported that the Indians had attacked the Americans merely to get a chance of rifling their trunks, and that they had disappeared not long after daylight. Some of the men capable of bearing arms, and even some officers, had disgraced themselves by deserting women and children, as well as the sick and wounded, at the first alarm. Two or three of these men, as they might by courtesy be called,

escaped to the main land before the passengers by the
Orizaba left Virgin Bay ; and thus the report was sent
to the United States that all the people of Omotepe had
been massacred by the Indians.

Leaving the island and going to Granada, Walker
remained there only long enough to see that Henningsen
had reached the huts half way between the Guadalupe
and the lake ; then, returning to Virgin Bay, he proceeded to organize the new men who had arrived from
California on the Orizaba. The spirits of Jaquess' men
had been revived by the arrival of these fresh recruits ;
and in a short time the main portion of the troops at Virgin Bay were ready for a march to San Jorge. On the
afternoon of the 3d December, the Americans occupied
San Jorge, without any opposition from Cañas, then at
Rivas with some seven or eight hundred men. The sick
at Virgin Bay, as well as the army stores and government property collected there, were carried to San Jorge
on the lake steamers ; and the fine air of that village,
together with the improved quarters and rations, diminished the sick list and increased materially the effective
force of the several companies.

When nearly the whole American strength in the
Meridional Department had been concentrated at San
Jorge, the hospital at Omotepe, together with the women
and children there, were removed to the main land.
Many of the native women and families had followed
the army in its retreat frnm Granada, and many of these
were supplied with quarters and rations by the proper
officers of the Nicaraguan forces. The trunks and chests
of most had suffered from the foray the Indians made on

the island; but the delightful air of the isthmian December rendered the loss less severe than might be imagined.

In the meanwhile the steamer from New-Orleans arrived at San Juan del Norte with nearly two hundred and fifty passengers for Nicaragua. On the afternoon of the 6th these persons reached Virgin Bay; and on the morning of the 7th they arrived at San Jorge. They were mostly under the direction of Lockridge, who had gone to the United States during the previous summer te encourage emigration to Central America. A small company of these men, commanded by Captain G. W. Crawford, was assigned to the Rangers; while the remainder were organized into a new corps, called the Second Rifles, (the old Second Rifles being dissolved,) and placed under the command of Major W. P. Lewis. Crawford's company were, for the most part, supplied with saddles and revolvers they had brought from the United States; and the rifle, commonly called Mississippi, was issued to them. Major Lewis' men were armed with Minié muskets.

Lockridge had brought to San Jorge about 235 men; and these, together with the men from California, raised the number of recruits to more than 300. The men from California were, for the most part, distributed into two companies, commanded respectively by Capt. Farrell and Capt. Wilson. Farrell was ordered to report to Waters for duty with the Rangers; while Wilson was attached to the new command of Lewis. These fresh men were in good spirits, and all anxious to see some fighting. Nor had they long to wait for active service. Sanders was ordered to take Higley's company, the strongest of Lewis's command, and proceed to Granada with a view of ascertaining Henningsen's position. It was supposed that Henningsen had probably been able to reach the lake ; and if such were the case, Higley's company would suffice to aid his embarkation. But Sanders returned and reported that Henningsen appeared not to have advanced further than the position he held between Guadalupe and the beach on the 2d ; and it was certain that he was altogether unable to communicate with the lake shore. Rumors also came by the way of Nandaime, through native channels, to the effect that the Americans were suffering from disease and famine in the church of Guadalupe.

Accordingly on the 11th, Higley's and Wilson's companies were ordered to report to Waters ; and these, together with Leslie's, Farrell's, and Crawford's companies of Rangers, formed a body of 160 men. Waters soon had his men embarked on the steamer La Virgen ; and the general-in-chief accompanied the command. Besides the Rangers and the two companies of Rifles, several volunteers requested leave to act under Waters. Lockridge appeared anxious for action ; and although no definite rank was assigned him, he was, for the occasion, placed next in command to the chief of the Rangers. Early on the morning of the 12th, the steamer was anchored off Granada, out of range of the enemy's shot ; and the officers were instructed to keep the men carefully concealed in the lower part of the vessel. During the day, the positions of the enemy were as far as possible observed ; and the anxiety of the Allies to prevent a landing, was proved by their parading soldiers in numbers along the beach. These soldiers would march and counter-march; and the effort was manifest to arrange them in such a manner as to make them appear more numerous than they really were.

Between eight and nine o'clock in the evening, the steamer quietly and with all her lights covered, moved-up the lake to the same point where the Democrats landed on the night of the 12th of October, 1855. This point was more than a league from the fort and wharf of Granada; and the depth of water was such as to allow the steamer to approach near the shore. The disembarkation was immediately begun; and when the first boat reached the beach, a picket of the enemy fired a single volley and fled. In about two hours the whole force was ashore; and Waters received orders to proceed to the relief of Henningsen, keeping as close as possible to the beach, in order not to lose his power of communicating with the general-in-chief who remained aboard the steamer. Then the La Virgen withdrew, and resumed as nearly as possible the anchorage she held during the day.

Not long after the steamer anchored off the wharf, and near midnight of the 12th, the long lines of fire from small arms followed by the reports of heavy volleys of musketry and answered by quick and angry retorts from the rifles announced that the conflict of Waters with the enemy had begun. Then the flashes and the reports ceased; but in a short time the fires again appeared and the sounds yet louder and more distinct told that the bold chief of the Rangers was driving the enemy before him. For several minutes the flashes and the reports were even fiercer and heavier than before; but they soon ceased, and their sudden cessation again told the tale of the yet advancing Americans. Soon after the last firing was heard, a noise from the water, crying as if for help, announced a messenger with news. A small boat was let down, and in a few moments a dusky form was seen scrambling over the rail of the steamer. At first Walker was apprehensive the news might be from Waters, and, it being dark and the messenger not a white man, the general-in-chief commenced his questions in Spanish. But the answer was English, and spoken in the thick broken accents of a Kanaka boy who had come to Central America on the Vesta in 1855. Kanaka John had been for several hours in the water, and bore, in a sealed bottle, a note frou Henningsen, giving information of the state of his force and indicating certain signals to be made in case a landing was attempted. The signals were made as soon as the note was read; but they were not seen by those for whom they were intended.

After landing Waters proceeded along a narrow strip of land with the lake on his left and a lagoon on his right. As he approached a point where the lagoon reaches within thirty or forty yards of the lake, he was fired on by the enemy, who were stationed behind a barricade they had built from one body of water to the other. The heaviness of the volleys showed that the Allies were in force; and the Americans for a moment wavered. Waters had ordered Leslie to assault the barricades with his company; but his men hesitated, and some confusion

15

arising, Leslie took the first who offered and leading them up to the barricades drove the enemy from their position.   The march toward Granada was resumed ; but when Waters reached a place called the " coal pits" he was again arrested by a large body of the Allies.   The numbers of the enemy were greater than at the first barricade ; the position, however, was not so good and they were soon driven from it by the vigorous charge of Higley and his company.

Waters, as he approached the town, turned to the right in order to gain the Tipitapa road which passes over higher ground than that nearer the lake.   About day-break he had gained the suburbs and was approaching some small cane huts when he again received the fire of the Allies.   The enemy were behind strong barricades ; but Capt. Crawford, passing with his company to some rising ground on the right, was enabled to turn the left flank of the Allied lines.   A prisoner taken at this point gave Waters such information as decided him to proceed at once to the Guadalupe.   He was encumbered with thirty wounded and it became an object to join Henningsen without further loss.   Leslie was, therefore, sent in advance to advise Henningsen of Waters' approach ; and thus early in the morning of the 13th the Americans in the Guadalupe were strengthened by the entrance of the force landed the night previously.

It was well for Henningsen that Waters arrived ; for the commissary stores of the former were nearly exhaust-ed, and, as fearful a plague as cholera, desertion, had begun to thin his enfeebled ranks.   Even after Waters' arrival, the difficulties of Henningsen's position were not slight. But the vigorous fighting of the Americans during the night had impressed the Allies with an exaggerated idea of their strength ; and Belloso was discouraged by the fierceness with which his barricades had been assailed. He began to think that wood and earth were no safe protection from the soldiers who had carried three well-defended positions in the course of almost as many hours ; and the movements of his force soon showed his weakness and irresolution. The fort was abandoned, and the sheds built on it were set afire. Of course, as soon as Henningsen discovered the fort was given up by the enemy he took possession of it ; and thus, without further difficulty, communication with the steamer was established.

Preparations were immediately made for embarking the whole command on the La Virgen. The number of sick and wounded made the movement slow ; and the men for duty were exhausted, some by their long fatigues and exposures, and others by the march and actions of the previous night. Of the 419 under Henningsen when Granada was surprised, 120 died of cholera and typhus, 110 were killed or wounded, nearly 40 deserted, and 2 were made prisoners. Of Waters' force, 14 were killed and 30 wounded. Leslie was unfortunately shot in the head after he reached the Guadalupe, and his death was a loss not easily repaired, for his services as a scout were inestimable. Lieut. Tayloe, who was absent, by leave, from his post at San Carlos, had obtained permission to march with Waters, and he fell at one of the barricades outside the town.

It was near two o'clock on the morning of the 14th

before everything was aboard the steamer. At leaving, Gen. Henningsen stuck up on a lance the words *"Aqui fué Granada"*—" Here was Granada"; and these were well calculated to re-kindle the passions of party, not yet extinct among the old Legitimists and Democrats. While the voice of one party was that of wailing and woe, at the loss of its cherished city, the other party could not suppress its feelings of triumph and exultation. Nor has the destruction of Granada failed to call forth censure elsewhere than in Central America. It has been denounced as an act of vandalism, useless in its consequences to the authority which ordered it. As to the justice of the act, few can question it; for its inhab· itants owed life and property to the Americans in the service of Nicaragua, and yet they joined the enemies who strove to drive their protectors from Central America. They served the enemies of Nicaragua in the most criminal manner; for they acted as spies on the Americans, who had defended their interests, and sent notice of all their movements to the Allies. By the laws of war, the town had forfeited its existence; and the policy of destroying it was as manifest as the justice of the measure. It encouraged the Leonese friends of the Americans, while it gave a blow to the Legitimists from which they have never recovered. The attachment of the old Chamorristas to Granada was strong and peculiar. They had for their chief city a love like that of woman; and even after years have passed tears come to their eyes when they speak of the loss of their beloved Granada. And well did it become them to have such affection for the town; because it furnished them with the resources which enabled them to maintain power, and to keep under the excitable passions, as they called them, of the Leonese Democrats. The destruction of Granada was, therefore, a long step toward the destruction of the Legitimist party ; and thus the Americans of Nicaragua were able to cripple their most bitter and consistent foe.

As the steamer left her anchorage a strong north-easter rose, and the vessel was obliged to seek the shelter of Omotepe, and to lie for several hours under the lee of the beautiful volcano which springs, as it were, from the waters of the lake. When the wind fell the La Virgen ran across to San Jorge, and everything was soon got ashore. The enemy at Rivas, hearing of the relief of Henningsen, and fearful of the artillery now at the disposal of the Americans, stealthily abandoned the place, and marched hastily to join Belloso at Masaya. On the morning of the 16th the Americans were again in possession of Rivas.

Chapter Eleventh.

In the retreat from Granada much of the type and printing materials, as well as the paper belonging to the office of the *Nicaraguense*, had been destroyed or lost. Hence, a few days after the headquarters of the army were moved to Rivas, the sub-secretary of Hacienda, Rogers, went to San Juan del Norte for the purpose of purchasing the materials necessary for the publication of the suspended newspaper. A number of officers, on leave of absence, went down the river on the same steamer with Rogers. Lockridge also, who had shown himself active in procuring emigration to Nicaragua, was aboard the steamer on his way to New-Orleans. He seemed anxious to serve the cause of the Americans in Nicaragua, and as there was no place in the army he could suitably fill, he was sent to the United States with the hope that he might be useful there. Emile Thomas, too, and his brother Carlos, repaired to San Juan del Norte at the same time.

As these passengers for the mouth of the San Juan steamed down the river they saw some suspicious looking rafts floating out of the San Carlos, and Emile Thomas, a watchful and discreet man, familiar with the country and its people, advised a scrutiny into the meaning of the singular appearance. Some have sought to place on Rogers the whole blame of the neglect to follow the advice of Thomas, and there were not wanting persons who attributed the negligence to design. But whatever may have been the previous faults of Rogers, it must be admitted that he served the cause of Nicaragua with a singleness of purpose and honesty of action which might have shamed the conduct of those who spoke evil of him. And on this occasion there were aboard the steamer officers whose duty it was to ascertain the meaning of the rafts, whereas such was no part of the duty specially pertaining to Rogers' office or orders. The responsibility of neglecting the rafts must rest on other shoulders than those of the sub-secretary of Hacienda.

It was not long after the steamer passed the mouth of the San Carlos before the meaning of the rafts became apparent. On the 23d of December, while the company stationed at the mouth of the Serapaqui were at dinner, they were surprised by a body of Costa Ricans about 120 strong, led on by a man named Spencer. When Thompson, who commanded at the Serapaqui, was attacked by Spencer, he had no sentries posted, and the arms of the men were at some little distance from the place where they were dining. Spencer had got to the rear of the American camp, and by placing a soldier in the top of a tree he was able to know accurately the state of Thompson's camp. The surprise was complete, and most of the Americans were either killed or wounded.

Thompson was made prisoner; his conduct and courage were praised by the Costa Ricans, and he himself was liberated soon after being taken to San Juan del Norte. Well might the Costa Ricans afford to laud Thompson, for it was his criminal neglect of duty which enabled them to get possession of the point at the mouth of the Serapaqui, and thereby secured the success of their subsequent operations.

Spencer had marched with his Costa Ricans from San José to a point on the San Carlos river, some miles above its mouth, and had thence floated his men on rafts down to the mouth of the Serapaqui. In addition to the force which attacked Thompson on the 23d, a large body of soldiers had been marched to the San Carlos, under the orders of General José Joaquin Mora, brother of the President, Juan Rafael Mora, and commander-in-chief of the Costa Rican army. The march was very difficult from the nature of the country through which it was made, the region between San José and the San Carlos being entirely uninhabited, and wholly destitute of subsistence. The road over which Mora marched was a mere trail, and his soldiers had at times to cut their way with machetes through the thick undergrowth. The results of the march depended wholly on the success of Spencer's efforts to get possession of the river San Juan and of the boats plying on it, and Spencer, as we have seen, owed his first and most important success to the gross and criminal negligence of Thompson at the Serapaqui.

After the surprise of Thompson, Spencer again took to his rafts and floated to the harbor of San Juan del Norte.

He reached there during the night of the 23d, and on the morning of the 24th he had possession of all the river steamers at Punta Arenas. The United States commercial agent at San Juan del Norte called on the commander of the English forces off that port to protect American interests from the soldiers of Costa Rica. To this request Capt. Erskine of the Orion replied that " he had taken steps, by landing a party of marines from one of Her Majesty's ship, to protect the persons and private property of Capt. Joseph Scott, his family and all citizens of the United States of America ;" but as regards the capture of the steamers he adds : " To prevent all misapprehension, I think it, however, right to state that the steamers and other property belonging to the Accessory Transit Company being at this moment the subject of a dispute between two different companies, the representatives of which are on the spot, and one of them authorizing the seizure, I do not feel justified in taking any steps which may affect the interests of either party. With respect to the participation of a force of Costa Ricans in the seizure and transfer of the steamers alluded to, I must observe that these steamers having been for some months past employed in embarking in this port and conveying to the parties with whom Costa Rica is now carrying on active hostilities, men and munitions of war, it appears that as a non-belligerent I am prohibited by the law of nations from preventing the execution of such operations by a belligerent party." Of course it was a mere act of comity for a British officer to protect American property at Punta Arenas ; but the subtlety of distinguishing between American property in dispute and

15*

that not in dispute, was a convenient invention for the occasion. If Capt. Erskine desired to protect American property his plain course was to maintain those in posses- sion. As to the question of the right of Costa Rica to seize the steamers it will more properly come up when we inquire why the United States had, at this time, no naval force at San Juan del Norte.

When Spencer had secured the river boats in the har- bor of San Juan he proceeded to the mouth of the San Carlos and communicated to General Mora—then at the embarcadero, some miles up the latter river—the success of the operations below. As the small steamer Spencer sent up the San Carlos approached a picket of Costa Ricans posted on a raft, the soldiers, frightened by the noise and appearance of such a boat as they had never before seen, plunged into the river and were drowned in their efforts to reach the shore. At the embarcadero Mora had, according to Costa Rican accounts, eight hundred men, with a rear guard of three hundred more expected each moment to arrive. To supply this force with subsistence six hundred men were employed in carrying provisions from the capital to the river. Much of the transportation between those points was done on the backs of men, as the trail is difficult for even mules.

Castillo was forthwith occupied by the Costa Ricans ; and Spencer, taking the steamer which runs over the Toro Rapids, easily succeeded, by concealing his men, in getting possession of the lake steamer, La Virgen, then lying at the mouth of the Zavalos, awaiting the return of Rogers from San Juan del Norte. Then proceeding to Fort San Carlos he lured aboard the steamer Capt.

Kruger, commanding that post. The first-lieutenant of Kruger had been sent to headquarters on business connected with the garrison at San Carlos ; and his second lieutenant, Tayloe, had been killed at Granada, while marching as a volunteer under Waters to the relief of Henningsen. Hence, after Kruger's capture by Spencer, the post was in charge of a sergeant, and Kruger so far forgot his duty as to permit Spencer, under a threat of death, to extort from him an order directing the sergeant to surrender the post to the enemy. The sergeant, taken by surprise, was less to blame for obeying the order than was the captain for signing it.

Thus the Costa Ricans were in possession of the San Juan river from Fort San Carlos to the sea, and they also held the smallest of the lake steamers, the La Virgen. On the latter steamer they had also taken some arms and ammunition intended for the service of Nicaragua. But the occupation of the river and the seizure of the La Virgen would have been comparatively useless to them and harmless to Walker without the capture of the steamer San Carlos. The loss of the river might have been easily repaired by the force then at Rivas, but the loss of the control over the lake was a much more serious event. Spencer well knew that he could not venture on the lake with the La Virgen as long as the larger and faster steamer remained in the hands of the Americans, and, therefore, he prevailed on Mora to keep his Costa Ricans quiet until the San Carlos got into the river with passengers from California for the Atlantic States.

Early in the afternoon of the 2d of January, 1857, the Sierra Nevada arrived at San Juan del Sur from San

Francisco. Her passengers were in a few hours aboard of the San Carlos ready to cross the lake. Some anxiety had been felt at Rivas on account of the long delay of the La Virgen in the river, but it was easy to imagine causes why she had not yet returned to Virgin Bay. Therefore the steamer San Carlos, with the passengers aboard, unsuspectingly approached Fort San Carlos and passed into the river without seeing any cause for alarm on shore. But when the steamer had passed the fort, Spencer, who was aboard a river boat with a force of Costa Ricans, hailed the San Carlos, demanding her surrender. There were a number of Nicaraguan officers on the San Carlos, going to the United States, but in the midst of the confusion, created by the surprise, Spencer got aboard of the lake steamer and soon had possession of her. The captain of the San Carlos, a cool, bold Dane, proposed to run the steamer back into the lake under the guns of the fort, and the movement might have been made without any great danger or loss of life. But Harris, jointly interested with his father-in-law, Morgan, in the transit contract across Nicaragua, happened to be aboard the steamer, and he refused to permit Capt. Ericsson to make the attempt. By the surrender of the San Carlos the Costa Ricans got control of the lake, and thus they were enabled to communicate rapidly and readily with the Allies at Masaya, while Walker was cut off from any direct communication with the Caribbean sea.

It is clear that the success of Mora's movement to the San Juan river was due to the skill and daring of Spencer. The march to the San Carlos with all its expense and all its fatigues would have been useless without the aid of the bold hand which got possession of the river steamers. And the success of Spencer was the reward of a rashness which, in war, sometimes supplies the place of prudent design and wise combinations. The fortune which proverbially favors the brave certainly aided Spencer much in his operations. Mora afterward attempted to depreciate the value of the services Spencer rendered him ; and the brutality of the man toward the soldiers soon made it an object for the Costa Rican General to get rid of him. But it would be difficult to overestimate the advantages the Allies derived from the services of the base and murderous man who did not scruple for the sake of lucre to imbrue his hands in the blood of countrymen straggling to maintain the rights of their race against a cruel and vindictive foe.

Unfortunately for the honor of human nature, Spencer was not the only American who co-operated with the Costa Ricans for the purpose of robbing the naturalized Nicaraguans of the rights they had in Central America. As to Spencer's immediate employers their conduct need not excite surprise ; for gain is the god of their idolatry, and at Ephesus they would have persecuted the Apostle to the Gentiles for teaching a religion which destroyed their trade in shrines. From such as these he is but a fool who expects aught high in principle or unselfish in action. But we are entitled to expect loftier sentiment and nobler actions from the men who aspire to govern states and control policies. As Spencer's operations closed the American transit across Nicaragua, it is not unimportant to ascertain if any public persons besides the Moras of Costa Rica and their Allies in Central America are directly or remotely responsible for the act. Especially is this becoming in view of the fact that no less a person than the President of the United States* has, in a grave annual message to the Houses of Congress, declared with most indecent inaccuracy that the Transit was closed in February, 1856, by the revocation of the charters of the Ship Canal and of the Accessory Transit Companies.

As early as the month of April, 1856, the American Secretary of State, Mr. Marcy, had been advised by the Costa Rican government that it meditated the seizure of the river and lake steamers and the consequent destruction of the Transit. At that time Mr. Marcy replied such an act would not be regarded with indifference by the United States. The language of the Secretary implied that the American government would deem it a duty to prevent such acts. And such a position was worthy of an American Minister. Undoubtedly Costa Rica, at war with Nicaragua, had a right not only to prevent the latter from using the property of neutrals for the purpose of transporting military persons and stores ; and she might also take possession of such property and use it, as lawfully as Nicaragua, for the conveyance of her own troops and military equipments. But this did not involve the right of Costa Rica to confiscate the property of neutrals used by her enemy for purposes of transportation. Neutral ships at sea are liable to capture by a belligerent if they are found hav-

---

* His Excellency James Buchanan.

ing aboard military stores or persons belonging to the enemy ; for at sea, such an act on the part of a neutral is one of choice and not of compulsion. But on land, or within the territory of a country at war, where the property of neutrals is entirely under the control of the belligerent sovereign, the involuntary act of the neutral certainly cannot subject him to the loss of his property. Hence Mr. Marcy was right when he told Costa Rica, to all intents and purposes, that the use of American property by Nicaragua did not make it forfeit if taken by the enemy ; and still less could it justify the destruction of a franchise, such as the Transit across the Isthmus, held by the owners of the lake and river steamers. When Walker saw the declaration Mr. Marcy made to the Costa Rican Minister, he felt assured the Allies would not attempt to interrupt the Transit and thus risk a rupture with the United States. Nor, in the face of this declaration, is it probable that Costa Rica would have attempted to break up the Transit without assurances of the act not provoking active hostilities from the American Republic.

Heretofore we have seen the decided opposition of the Secretary of State to the American movement in Nicaragua. But he was reluctantly compelled to give way to the President in reference to the reception of Father Vigil. Mr. Pierce was, in May, 1856, seeking the nomination of the democratic party for a re-election ; hence he was able to resolve on a policy displeasing to his chief minister. After the Cincinnati Convention, it was easier for the Secretary to manage the President ; and the departure of Father Vigil from Washington having been procured, Mr. Marcy was relieved from the presence of a Minister of Nicaragua. He immediately ordered Mr. Wheeler to demand the causes of the revocation of the Accessory Transit charter; but in August he was disappointed at a reply which entirely justified the act of the Rivas administration. If, however, Mr. Wheeler proved not pliant to the purposes of the Secretary, it was easy to secure British aid for getting the Americans out of Nicaragua. And if Mr. Marcy would silently permit British power to accomplish this object, he might hope for a strong interest in the city of New-York to aid his ambitious schemes.

It is difficult to imagine that an American Secretary of State would thus connive at a plan for driving his countrymen from the Isthmus; but pride of opinion and desire for office were Mr. Marcy's leading passions, and one of these had been hurt by the reception of Father Vigil and the other was pleased at the hope of conciliating a strong influence in his own State. The evidences, too, of this connivance, are too palpable to escape the notice of the least observing. By the middle of September, 1856, the British had stationed off San Juan del Norte a strong fleet, of eight vessels, carrying several hundred guns, and evidently with a view of influencing the result of the war in Central America. No United States vessels were sent thither to watch the movements or ascertain the intentions of the British fleet. The objects of the fleet had been foreshadowed in the previous April by the attempt of the British vessel Eurydice to prevent the passengers of the Orizaba from going up the river. At that time the commodore of the American squadron in the Caribbean had been instructed to show the United States flag at San Juan del Norte; and if it was expedient for the American flag to be displayed when only a single British man-of-war was in the harbor, how much more pressing the necessity when several hundred British guns were pointed at the Isthmian transit.

Not only did the American Secretary of State quietly permit a strong British fleet to take its station off San Juan del Norte and there await a favorable opportunity to act against the naturalized Nicaraguans; but he was also advised by Costa Rica of her intention to close the transit if she had the requisite military force. On the first of November the President of Costa Rica published a decree, declaring in its second article: " The navigation of the river San Juan del Norte is prohibited to all kinds of vessels while hostilities against the invaders of the Central American soil continues." And the fourth article of the same decree orders : " The officers and military forces of the Republic will carry out this decree, using for that purpose every means within their reach." Here was a public and explicit declaration to Mr. Marcy notifying him that if he desired to keep the Transit from being closed during the hostilities between Nicaragua and Costa Rica, he must have United States vessels at San Juan del Norte to resist force with force. The United States had a consul in Costa Rica to advise it of the acts of the government there; and so well aware was her Britannic Majesty's consul, Allan Wallis, of the movement against the Transit that with evident reference thereto he published, at San José, on the 26th Nov., the following notice : " All persons residing in this Republic, claiming to be British subjects, are requested to send into this office with as little delay as possible, and not later than the 20th prox., their names, professions or occupations and places of residence, with the names of the members of their family, if any." Singular, too, as it may seem, the Secretary of State did not, after the order of Mora's decree of the first of November was executed, take any steps to re-establish the Transit or protect those who were aiming to re-open it from the interference of the British naval forces. These facts, together with others to be hereafter related concerning the acts of American naval officers on the Pacific coast of Nicaragua, lead irresistibly to the conclusion that Mr. Marcy co-operated with the British government in its Central American policy.

An insight into the policy of the American Secretary of State is necessary to a due understanding of the events which followed Spencer's operations on the San Juan river. The Costa Rican soldiers who accompanied the passengers from California to Punta Arenas were scarcely able to leave on their return up the river before the steamer Texas arrived in the port of San Juan del Norte with nearly two hundred men for the service of Nicaragua. But these men not having been received by the State could not act in the name of the government. Hence Mr. Harris, the agent of the owners of the lake and river steamers, selected Lockridge, who was at San Juan del Norte, as a proper person to regain possession of their property for the Transit contractors. As before stated, Lockridge had been ordered to New-Orleans on

special duty ; and had the task of re-opening the Transit
been a strictly military enterprise, the duties of command would naturally have devolved on Lieut.-Colonel
Rudler, the senior officer present at San Juan del Norte,
and lately charged with the defence of the River frontier. Rudler had a leave of absence to visit the United
States ; but he had only to tear up his leave and resume
his right to command on the river in order to have full
authority over any expedition attempted in the name of
Nicaragua. But merit is modest and unobtrusive, while
pretension is forward and presumptuous ; therefore,
Lockridge was put in command of the men who were
expected to clear the river of the Costa Ricans, and
Rudler left for New-Orleans. In addition to the men by
the Texas, General C. R. Wheat, and Colonel Anderson,
with some forty others from New-York, arrived at Punta
Arenas on the ninth of January by the James Adger.
Arms and ammunition were not wanting for the whole
of Lockridge's command ; and the supply of provisions
was abundant.

Lockridge remained for some days at Punta Arenas,
engaged with Joseph N. Scott in fitting up one of the
old disused river steamers for purposes of transportation.
But he was not allowed to work without interruption by
the British naval officers. On the morning of the 16th
of January, Capt. Cockburn, of H. B. M.'s ship Cossack,
went ashore at Punta Arenas, and inquired for the commander of the armed men occupying the point. On
meeting Lockridge, Capt. Cockburn informed him he
had received orders from Capt. Erskine, of Her Majesty's
ship Orion, and " senior officer of Her Majesty's ships

and vessels employed on the coasts of Central America,"
to offer protection to any British subjects who might be
detained and compelled to bear arms against their will.
In accordance with his instructions, Capt. Cockburn demanded a list of all the men at Punta Arenas, and required them to be paraded in his presence, that he might
read to them the orders of Capt. Erskine. The men
were accordingly drawn up on the beach, and Cockburn
read to them the order of Erskine. The concluding sentences of the order were : " Should any of the party in
question claim protection as British subjects, and their
claims appear to you to be well founded, you will acquaint
the officer commanding, that these men must be permitted
to withdraw from their present position ; and you will
(in the event of his acquiescence) either give these men
a passage to Greytown, or take them on board Her Majesty's ship under your command, to await my decision
as to their disposal, as they may desire. In the event of
the aforesaid officer resisting such a course as I have
pointed out, you will inform him that, in the first place,
no person whatever under his command will be permitted
to leave their present position, to proceed up the river or
elsewhere, until my demands shall be complied with ;
and, secondly, that I will adopt such measures to enforce
the rights of British subjects as I may think best adapted
to the purpose." Ten men claimed and received protection under the order of Erskine, and were taken from
the point in Cockburn's boat. The instructions of Her
Majesty's government must have been indeed stringent,
when they induced honorable officers to degrade themselves to the work of inciting men to desert a cause they

had voluntarily embraced ; for Cockburn, not satisfied with reading Erskine's orders, had also advised the whole of Lockridge's command of the dangers they ran in attacking the large force the Costa Ricans had concentrated on the river.

Thus the demoralization of Lockridge's men was commenced before they left Punta Arenas. The Americans —at least the good men among them—were, of course, indignant at the course the British pursued ; but all the Europeans were more or less affected by this English interference. Nor is it in the nature of men long to respect those claiming authority over them, when they see such persons humbled by the actions of others. Hence it was all-important for Lockridge to get beyond the reach of British interference. Not only was he daily losing men by the policy the British practised ; but the effectiveness of those remaining with him was constantly diminished. Finally the small steamer was got ready for going up the river, and Lockridge moved his whole force to a point several miles below the mouth of the Serapaqui.

On the morning of the 4th of February the Texas again arrived from New-Orleans at San Juan del Norte, having aboard H. T. Titus, known in Kansas as Col. Titus, in charge of about one hundred and eighty men. Many of the persons with Titus had been his companions in Kansas, and probably most of them were made of better stuff than their leader. But his swaggering air had imposed on many people ; and the contest in which he was said to have been engaged, gave him a sort of newspaper notoriety, thus making his name familiar as the

leader of the " border ruffians." Lockridge organized
Titus and his men in a separate body, and soon a jealousy rather than rivalry sprang up between the new-comers and those acting under Anderson. Attached to the
command of the latter was Capt. Doubleday, formerly of
the Nicaraguan service ; and several others who were
yet in the service, acted under Anderson's orders. All
of Titus' men were entirely new to the country.

Soon after Titus arrived, Lockridge, by a sharp skir-
mish, got possession of Cody's Point, a piece of high ground
just opposite the mouth of the Serapaqui; and Wheat
thence opened a cannonade on the defences the Costa
Ricans had built on the opposite side of the San Juan
river. But the fire of Wheat's guns was not of such a
character as to make a serious impression on the enemy ;
and it was only after Col. Anderson had crossed the river
and succeeded in harassing the Costa Rican flank and
rear with riflemen, that the Americans drove the enemy
from the Serapaqui, and got possession of both sides of
the river. The Costa Ricans left behind a number of
killed and wounded, besides two guns, some small-arms
and ammunition, and a supply of military clothing. A
yet more important portion of the articles captured were
certain letters from General Mora detailing the condition
of his force on the San Juan, and urging the necessity
for fresh troops, in order to hold his position on the river.

The Costa Ricans were driven from the mouth of the
Serapaqui on the morning of the 13th of February ; and
the next day Titus, with some hundred and forty men,
ascended the river on the little steamer Rescue with the
view of attacking Castillo. Anderson was placed in

charge of Hipp's Point; and the contest between him and Titus, as to rank, had increased the disorganization and disorder already existing in Lockridge's command. Desertions were frequent, and were, of course, encouraged by the protection and assistance the English gave to the deserters. The heavy rains made camp l'fe disagreeable, and its duties arduous; and much labor was necessary in order to protect the men from the weather. Thus the movements were impeded; and much care was necessary to keep the ammunition in a state fit for use. Numbers were sick with fever; but considering the exposure and fatigues to which the men were subjected, their health was not bad.

On the other hand the difficulties of the Costa Ricans were not slight. After getting possession of the San Juan and of the lake, Mora had communicated with the Allies at Masaya; and movements were undertaken which will bo more particularly described hereafter. Suffice it to say here, that these movements entailed heavy draughts on the force Mora held on the river; and in addition to this the Costa Ricans coming from the high lands about San José, suffered much with fever when they reached the low country on the San Juan. Thus by the necessities of the Allies for troops in the western part of Nicaragua, and by the effects of disease in the force occupying the river, the garrison at Castillo was reduced to a trifling figure; and when Titus appeared before the fort Cauty, an Englishman commanding at Castillo, had, according to some, twenty-five, and according to others, fifty men.

When Titus landed near the fort of Castillo Viejo, he

found the houses of the village in flames, and the small steamer Machuca also rapidly burning. He succeeded, however, in cutting loose the steamer J. N. Scott, and although her machinery was somewhat damaged, it was easily repaired in the course of two or three days' work. Soon after he appeared at Castillo, Titus sent to Cauty a demand to surrender the fort; and the reply was a proposal for an armistice of twenty-four hours, with a promise of surrender in case the garrison were not relieved by the expiration of that time. Strange to say the proposal of Cauty was accepted; and it was not difficult for him to send a courier to Fort San Carlos with news of his position. Of course, before the armistice expired, reinforcements for Cauty were landed a short distance above the fort; and on the appearance of the fresh Costa Ricans, Titus retreated in great disorder and confusion. The retreat was made before the number of the relieving party was even approximately ascertained; and the fact, that the Americans were able to escape without any protection to their rear, shows the enemy did not arrive with much force.

After the Americans withdrew, or rather fled, from Castillo, they halted at San Carlos Island, a few miles below the fort. On this island Lockridge threw up some works for defence from the enemy, and also built, with much labor, sheds for protection from the weather. The repulse at Castillo, shameful in its character, added to the demoralization of the whole command on the river, and desertions accordingly increased. Such, too, was the feeling against Titus that he gave up his command and left for San Juan del Norte, with the intention of going by Panama to Rivas. When he arrived at San Juan del Norte his insulting language to one of the British officers led to his arrest and detention for a few hours. At the same time Titus was arrested the steamer Rescue was detained ; but she was soon released when the U. S. sloop of war Saratoga was seen coming into port.⎺ This single fact shows how different might have been the conduct of the British naval forces had there been a few United States vessels stationed off San Juan del Norte.

In the latter part of February Walker sent an aide, Major Baldwin, from Rivas by Panama, to Lockridge, confirming the latter in his command on the river, and also informing him of the importance of early communication either around or across the lake. The orders sent to Lockridge were, if he found it impossible to take Castillo and San Carlos without great sacrifice, to cut a road from the river either to Chontales or the southern shore of the lake, and march by land to Rivas. The cause of these orders will hereafter appear ; and it is sufficient here to say, that one chief reason for Walker's holding Rivas was, the apprehension that Lockridge, reaching the Meridional department, might be placed in an awkward position by finding the town in the possession of the Allies. Baldwin arrived at San Juan del Norte about the middle of March, and nearly at the same time with some hundred and thirty fresh men, principally from Mobile and Texas, and directed respectively by Major W. C. Capers and Captain Marcellus French.

With this reinforcement under Capers and French,
16

Lockridge's numbers had been so reduced by desertion and sickness, that his effective force scarcely reached four hundred. The men, however, were for the most part of excellent quality, and in other hands might have accomplished much. French's command particularly was, by general consent, composed of fine materials. But these men arrived too late; and they met on the river bands which had been disorganized by bad conduct and ill fortune. Lockridge, however, determined to make another effort to get possession of Castillo Viejo; and with this purpose he prepared nearly his whole command for an attack on the fort.

Landing his force a short distance below Castillo and out of sight of the enemy, he led his men by a trail through the woods to a position near an elevation, known as Nelson's Hill. This elevation commands the fort, and the Costa Ricans having entrenched it were occupying the summit. Along the sides of the hill they had cut some trees and formed a sort of chevaux-de-frise; and by clearing away the undergrowth for some distance around the summit, they had made the approach difficult and dangerous. After reconnoitring the position of the enemy, Lockridge deemed it imprudent to hazard an attack; and calling the principal officers together and asking their opinions, he received the concurrence of all as to the expediency of retiring without engaging the enemy. The resolution was wise, for defeat would almost inevitably have been the result of an attempt on the Costa Rican defences. The opportune moment for taking Castillo had been lost through the incapacity of Titus, and with a month to prepare for a second attack, the enemy had not been idle. Even if the Costa Ricans had been less strongly posted, the moral condition of Lockridge's force was not such as to warrant ordering them on any hazardous service.

After Lockridge retired from Castillo the men began to discuss plans for the future, and all appear to have agreed on the propriety of abandoning the river. It was clear that the effort to re-open the Transit had entirely failed, and the leader of the enterprise drawing up the men informed them that he proposed to try to reach Rivas by the Isthmus of Panama, and called on all who wished to follow him to step from the ranks. Near a hundred persons agreed to take this course; and the remainder of the men were deprived of their arms and virtually discharged. Then the disarmed men sought means to reach the mouth of the river. Not waiting for the steamer they took the boats they could put their hands on, and some floated on logs to the harbor of San Juan del Norte. The panic-stricken crowd thought the Costa Ricans were hot in pursuit; and each over-anxious for his own safety added to the fright of his fellows.

The men who had agreed to go with Lockridge to Rivas descended the river more leisurely than the fugitives; but ill luck pursued them to the last. On the way to San Juan del Norte, the steamer J. N. Scott was blown up, and several of those proposing to go to Panama were killed and others were painfully and dangerously scalded. This accident entirely discouraged the men who yet adhered to Lockridge, and forthwith the idea of crossing the New-Granadian Isthmus was abandoned by them. It was an absurd plan at any rate; for it was folly to suppose, under the existing circumstances, that known enemies of Costa Rica, either armed or unarmed, would be permitted in numbers to cross the territory of a neutral State, or rather of a Republic, hostile to those called " filibusters."

Of course the English were glad to furnish means to all the men who reached San Juan for leaving Central America. Accordingly a large number of the destitute and disappointed expeditionists were sent to New-Orleans on H. B. M's steamer, Tartar; and the passages of others were paid with drafts drawn by Capt. Erskine who held the arms of Lockridge's command to secure himself against the loss on the drafts. In a few days nearly all the remains of Lockridge's force had left the shores of Nicaragua; and most were bitter in their expressions concerning the weakness and incapacity of the man who attempted to lead them up the river. It may not be amiss, however, while concluding the narrative of Lockridge's operations on the San Juan to say that Walker refused to listen to the censure passed on the unfortunate commander until he heard fully the facts of the case; and it was not until he heard from Lockridge himself the story of his undertaking that Walker formed an opinion as to the merits of the leader of the San Juan expedition.

During the attempt of Lockridge to open the Transit the efforts of the friends of Nicaragua in the United States were more active and fruitful than at any previous period. The Southern States, satisfied of their inability to carry slavery into Kansas, were then prepared to concentrate their labors on Central America; and not only were the men who went to the San Juan of good quality, but they were also furnished with excellent supplies and equipments. Had the same effort and expenditure been made three months earlier, the establishment of the Americans in Nicaragua would have been fixed beyond a peradventure.

Since the failure of Lockridge numerous agencies have been employed to re-establish the line of American travel across the Isthmus of Nicaragua: but all without avail. At the very time American youth was engaged in the attempt to force open the Transit for the benefit of those holding the Rivas grant of the 19th of February, 1856, these parties were treacherously dealing with the government of Costa Rica and attempting to secure the franchise from a power having no shadow of a right to bestow it. There have been rumors of grants from Costa Rica and grants from Nicaragua; and the authorities of the latter republic have actually made bargains with several different companies to re-open the Transit. The persons in Nicaragua who desire to keep the Americans out of the country are well aware of the importance to them of keeping the "highway of filibusterism" closed; and all their negotiations for transit grants are "a delusion and a snare." Often, too, it has been semi-officially announced that the United States government was determined to force open the road across Nicaragua; but as no justification for so violent an act on the part of the United States has been presented, it must be presumed that such declarations are intended merely for popular effect. In fact the American authorities, by an arbitrary act of force, interrupted the only effort which, since December, 1856, has promised successfully to restore the passage across Nicaragua to citizens of the United States. In December, 1857, Col· Anderson, at the head of forty-five men, took the river boats and one lake steamer from the Costa Ricans and restored them to the agent claiming for the American owners; and but for the acts of the United States naval forces the transit across the Isthmus might have been re-established in thirty days. It was the enemies of the naturalized Nicaraguans who closed the Transit; and it is they also who keep it closed.

But it is time for us to return to Rivas, and follow the course of events on the Pacific side of the Isthmus.

Chapter Twelfth.

On the 20th of December, 1856, nearly the whole body of Americans in Nicaragua was concentrated at Rivas, and the health and moral condition of the troops were favorably affected by the movement thither. The hospital was established in a large building, situated on a slight elevation near the edge of the town, known as the house of Maleaño. Under the efficient administration of Dr. Coleman, acting surgeon-general, the wards were kept clean, and the surgical attendance was good. The diet of the patients was of the best sort, and although the number of wounded was large, no disagreeable results followed from placing them all in the same building. The supplies of medicine and surgical instruments were ample, and the strength of the surgical staff was far greater than usual in any armies either of the eastern or western continent. The fictions which have been published concerning the want of medical and surgical attention to the inmates of the hospital were created for the purpose of pandering to a morbid public opinion, and of excusing the faults and crimes of those who deserted their countrymen in Central America. The quarters of the troops were comfortable, the subsistence varied and abundant, and the spirits of the force were cheerful and buoyant.

The reports from the enemy also tended to increase the confidence of the Americans. After the retreat of Henningsen from Granada was so triumphantly achieved, Belloso sullenly retired to Masaya, and there attempted to gather the remains of the shattered force which had attempted to cut off the troops charged with the destruction of the Legitimist stronghold. But the other Allied generals were no longer willing to act under Belloso. Defeated in their efforts to destroy Henningsen, the chiefs of the Allied army were naturally inclined to throw the responsibility· of their discomfiture on the Salvadorian general. They accused Belloso not only of want of skill, but also of want of courage ; and they intimated that his hasty withdrawal toward Masaya, soon after Waters reached the Guadalupe, was due to an over-anxiety for his own personal safety. The dissensions which thus arose in the Allied camp promised in a short time to dissolve the whole force, and the charges then made against Belloso were afterward examined by a military commission in his own State of San Salvador.

These dissensions were also increased by the disheartening effects on the Allied officers of the great losses they had sustained in the campaign against the Americans. It is difficult to estimate the numbers the Allies had actually brought into the field before the retreat from

Granada was accomplished, but it is certainly no exaggeration to place the troops they had employed from the beginning of October to the middle of December at seven thousand. In addition to the losses at Granada on the 12th and 13th of October, on the Transit road, by the affairs of the 11th and 12th of November, and at Masaya, during the three days fighting there, the Allies must have lost near two thousand men by the attack they made on Henningsen. Reports concur in the fact that Belloso had not more than two thousand under his command after he retired to Masaya. Thus, even placing the deserters at fifteen hundred—and you must place these at a high figure, considering the forced character of the service in Central America—the enemy must have lost thirty-five hundred in killed and wounded during the ten weeks immediately succeeding their march from Leon.

Nor did Belloso entirely escape the cholera after he reached Masaya. Hence fear of the pestilence as well as of the deadly rifles of the Americans, stimulated desertion among the Allies. So disorganized did Belloso's force become, that the propriety of a retreat on Leon was discussed among the chiefs of the several contingents ; and the Salvadorian troops, particularly, were disposed to withdraw from the contest. The Salvadorian cabinet were, it seems, not well pleased with the censures some of the generals of the other States had passed on the commander-in-chief ; and a large portion of the Liberal party of that State, unmoved by the passions which prompted Cabañas' friends to revenge themselves on the Americans for the refusal to re-establish his power in Honduras,

16*

consistently refused to support the war waged against the naturalized Nicaraguans.

Such was the general condition of the respective parties on the 2d of January, 1857, when the steamer San Carlos, as heretofore narrated, crossed the lake with the passengers from California to the Atlantic States. The morning report of the troops at Rivas on the 3d will give an accurate idea of the American force at that time. The total, including those employed in the several departments, is reported at 919. Of these, 25 were employed in the ordnance department; 15 in the quartermaster's department; 20 in the commissary's and 12 in the band; thus leaving an aggregate in the line of 847. Of the aggregate 8 were of the post and division field and staff, while 1 captain and 29 privates were on detached duty; 3 captains, 3 lieutenants, and 2 privates, on furlough; and 2 privates absent without leave. Thus the aggregate present was reduced to 788; and of these 60 were on extra duty, and 197 sick. The number for duty, officers and men, was 518; but many of those reported sick had only chigoës in their feet, and were fully able to aid in the defence of the town. Laziness and a disposition to shirk duty placed many on the sick list, who in an emergency might have proved among the best fighting men in the garrison.

Henningsen had been promoted to the rank of major-general, and Sanders to that of brigadier; so that O'Neal had command of the First Rifles, with Leonard as lieut.-colonel, and Dolan as major, while Jaquess was in command of the Infantry, and Lewis of the Second Rifles. The Artillery, as well as the Rangers were very much thinned by the hard service through which they had passed ; and Col. Schwartz, being in bad health, soon after reaching Rivas, obtained leave of absence to visit California. Col. Waters kept the small companies of Rangers under his command, riding constantly in search of supplies and information.

In a few days after the San Carlos left Virgin Bay with the passengers, uneasiness was felt on account of the non-arrival of the steamers from the river. There were several causes which might be assigned for their detention, one being the misunderstanding between the two agents of the company, Scott and Macdonald. The improbabilities, too, of all the steamers falling into the hands of the Costa Ricans were so many, that in the event of the enemy's appearance on the river, it was supposed some news of the fact would soon reach Rivas. It was many days before the steamers finally appeared on the lake, and then their movements indicated that they were in the hands of the Allies. In the meantime, the steamer Sierra Nevada, which had been waiting at San Juan del Sur for the passengers, sailed for Panama ; and it was not until her return on the 24th of January, that Walker heard definitely the events which had transpired on the river, and of Lockridge's presence at Punta Arenas, with a body of immigrants for Nicaragua.

Previous to the return of the Sierra Nevada from Panama, Capt. Finney had been sent with about fifty Rangers as far as Nandaime, in order to ascertain what news the people near Masaya had in reference to the steamers ; and also to learn whether or not the enemy were making any movements of importance. Finney returned, reporting that he had gone as far as Nandaime without seeing the enemy or hearing any news indicating either an advance of Allies or a knowledge on their part of the capture of the steamers. The country between Nandaime and Rivas was quiet ; the people were engaged in their usual domestic pursuits, and had not been troubled by detachments of the Allies.

In the meantime Rivas was prepared for defence. Soon after occupying the place, in December, Walker had given orders to Henningsen to strengthen the natural advantages of the position, so that a small garrison might be left there without risk to the military and other stores gathered in the town. In fulfilment of these orders, Henningsen had burnt most of the small huts on the edges of the town, and had cut away the thick tropical undergrowth which might conceal and protect an attacking foe. The nature of the ground in and about the place was well ascertained, and the numerous trails and by-paths of the neighborhood were examined. Strobel was, at the same time, engaged in surveying a more direct road than the one usually travelled from Rivas to Virgin Bay ; and for this service he principally employed natives, who, with their machetes, are able to clear away rapidly the dense brushwood of that luxuriant soil and climate.

A small schooner, which had once belonged to the chief of the Mosquitos, was brought up the river and across the lake during the month of December ; and having been purchased by the government, this vessel was undergoing repairs at the time the steamers made their appearance at Omotepe. On the 16th of January,

Walker sent for Fayssoux to come to Rivas, in order to have his opinion as to the feasibility of using the schooner for re-taking the steamers. Fayssoux, although suffering at the time from fever, reached Rivas a few hours after he received the message ; and on his arrival he said he thought the schooner would be of very little use for such a purpose. Afterward the vessel was burned, to prevent her from falling into the hands of the enemy ; to hold the vessel securely it would have been necessary to keep a strong garrison at Virgin Bay.

Of course, the knowledge that the enemy held the river and the lake, diminished greatly the spirits and confidence of the troops at Rivas. But, although difficulties appeared to gather about the Americans in Nicaragua, they never for a moment relaxed their resolution to maintain strict order and discipline wherever they held sway. An extract from the log of the Granada for the 19th of January, shows the assistance her commander gave to a vessel of the very power which in a few short weeks manifested its gratitude for such services by capturing the Nicaraguan schooner. The log reads : " Crew employed on ship's duty. Sent five men and an officer to assist the civil authorities to place the mutinous crew of the Narraganset (an American ship) on board of her. Lent her four hand-cuffs to iron them." The fact may appear trifling, but, when read by the light of after events, it becomes instructive and characteristic.

After Mora had secured the San Juan river and the lake steamers, he established his headquarters at Fort San Carlos. Some days elapsed before he communicated with the Allies across the lake. His object, probably,

was to get all the force he could command to the river,
and so secure his communications between San Carlos
and San José, previous to taking any step which might
give Walker an opportunity of ascertaining the occurrences on the San Juan. When, however, he had, as he
supposed, put the river in a proper state of defence, he
crossed to Granada, and there met the chiefs of the allied forces. By the success of Costa Rica on the San
Juan, she had obtained a preponderating influence in the
counsels of the confederates ; and hence there was little
difficulty in having Cañas placed in command of the
army at Masaya. The possession of the lake and river,
and the closing of the Transit, gave new life to the leaders of the allied troops, and they determined to advance
into the Meridional Department.

On the 26th of January Walker received news of the
advance of the Allies toward Obraje, a small village on
the south side of the Gil Gonzales, and about three
leagues distant from Rivas. The same afternoon O'Neal
with his Rifles, about 160 strong, and with a twelve-
pound howitzer and a small four-pound brass piece,
went to meet the enemy, reported as numbering 800 or
1,000 men. A company of Rangers also accompanied
O'Neal ; and Finney riding to the edge of Obraje came
suddenly on a strong picket of the Allies and received
their fire, himself mortally wounded, almost before he
was aware of their presence. When O'Neal ascertained that the enemy held Obraje he halted for the night
about a mile from the village. The next morning he
sent forward a skirmishing party to feel the strength of
the Allies, and the latter came out to meet the skir-

mishers in such force that O'Neal judged it prudent to recall his riflemen. In the skirmishing with the enemy O'Neal lost several men ; and when his report of the apparent strength and confidence of the Allies reached Rivas, Henningsen was sent to Obraje to reconnoitre the position of the enemy. After a short time Henningsen reported the Allies occupying the principal square of the village, strongly barricaded and also protected by earthworks ; and that the place could not be carried without a loss entirely disproportionate to its value and importance. On the receipt of Henningsen's report Walker ordered the Rifles to fall back to Rivas.

The enemy remained in Obraje during the morning of the 28th ; but about nightfall of that day some Americans from San Jorge brought the news of small bodies of the Allies being seen in the outskirts of this village, situated near the lake shore and about two miles to the east of Rivas. By eight o'clock in the evening Cañas was in San Jorge, and his force was busily engaged in building barricades and other defences. The rapidity with which Central American troops throw up barricades is almost incredible, and long practice has made them more expert at such work than even a Parisian mob. Hence, in a few hours, all the streets leading into the square of San Jorge, as well as the houses around the Plaza, were strongly barricaded. The secrecy, however, of the march from Obraje, no less than the rapidity with which the barricades at San Jorge had been built, showed that the Allies were not disposed to meet the Americans in the open field or to come to a decisive action. It was clear that they desired to hold San Jorge in order to communicate with Mora on the lake, and thus to secure more strength for future offensive operations. Therefore, Walker determined to attack them at once.

On the morning of the 29th, Henningsen marched to San Jorge with the 1st and 2d Rifles, Jaquess' Infantry, some Rangers, a twelve-pound howitzer, and a six-pounder. Next in command to Henningsen was Sanders. They soon succeeded in driving the enemy behind the barricades of the Plaza; but by some misunderstanding of Henningsen's orders, Sanders, with a part of Lewis' Rifles, became separated from the rest of the command, and reached a position to the north of the main square and near the road leading to the lake. Confusion ensued; and as the Americans had suffered rather severely from the enemy's fire, they were drawn off to gain time for new dispositions. It appears that several of the officers had taken too much liquor during the morning, and did not apprehend clearly the purport of the orders they received. Besides this, there was a jealousy on the part of Sanders toward Henningsen, and the latter averred that the former afterward admitted he had done all in his power to frustrate the attack on San Jorge. It is certain Sanders was of a jealous disposition; and though he denied having made the admission above referred to, there can be little doubt that he was not altogether displeased at any incidents which tended to diminish the confidence of the general-in-chief and of the army in the skill and capacity of Henningsen.

After getting his force as far as possible out of the enemy's fire, Henningsen reconnoitred more exactly the position of the Allies with a view of another attempt to carry their defences. Early in the afternoon, and before Henningsen had prepared for a second attack, the enemy sallied in strength from the barricades and made a vigorous effort to drive the Americans out of some plantain patches they were occupying. The number of riflemen among the plantains was not large at the time the Allies came suddenly and rather unexpectedly upon them; but the 12-pound howitzer was on the spot, and its discharges of cannister were very destructive to the enemy. Nothing can be more effective than this arm for brushing away a harassing foe from the plantain fields scattered around the edges of the towns and villages of Central America. On the occasion of the sortie the enemy made at San Jorge, the howitzer did the service—to make a moderate estimate—of at least fifty riflemen.

The repulse of the enemy among the plantains raised the spirits of the men; and late in the afternoon Henningsen again attacked the barricades. Lewis was to attempt to get a foothold on the north and east side of the Plaza, near the church, where the enemy kept its ordnance and other stores, while Jaquess with the Infantry was to try to effect a lodgment on the south side near the road leading toward Virgin Bay. Lewis' men could not be brought to advance nearer than within eighty or a hundred yards of the barricades; but the Infantry made a gallant effort, though an unsuccessful one, to perform the part assigned it in the general assault. The Infantry had hitherto lacked opportunities for meeting the enemy; and some jests had been passed at their expense among the other corps of the army.

Therefore Jaquess was now put on his mettle. He, followed by Major Dusenberry, led the men up toward the barricade with more courage than conduct ; and for several seconds the Infantry received, without wincing, a most galling fire from the Allies. Jaquess was struck down by a ball in the loins, while Dusenberry fell at about the same moment mortally wounded. Thus losing their chief officers, the Infantry were checked at a critical moment and were obliged to retire, leaving several killed near the barricades and bringing off a number of wounded.

From the reports Walker received he was led to suppose that the ill success of the attack on San Jorge might be due in some degree to the want of cordial co-operation on the part of Sanders and other officers with Henningsen. There was always some little prejudice against the latter because of his European birth and education ; and it is impossible even with the aid of long military habits to conquer or destroy such prejudices. Therefore Henningsen was recalled ; but as Walker had little confidence in the capacity of Sanders for independent command, Waters was sent to San Jorge with orders which gave him the real control of the troops there. Soon, however, Waters reported that he thought it impossible to carry the place with the force then before it ; and Sanders was accordingly ordered to return to Rivas.

The loss of the Americans on the 29th January was about eighty killed and wounded. Captains Russell and Wilkinson, both valuable officers, were killed ; while Major Dusenberry died in a short time after he was

brought to Rivas. Jaquess' wound made him unfit for
duty for many weeks; and Lieut. Col. Leonard was
confined to his bed for months from the effects of that
day at San Jorge. The loss of the enemy was also
large, especially in the plantain patches where they met
the howitzer. But it was difficult to get even an ap-
proximative report of the losses of the enemy. They
kept their wounded carefully out of sight, sending them
to Omotope and other points, and scattering them so as
to make the numbers seem less than they were. So,
too, when inquiries were made for men who disappeared,
instead of letting it be known they were killed, the
officers would represent that they had been ordered to
some distant point. Thus the lake steamers were very
serviceable to the Allies by enabling them to keep their
wounded out of sight, and to prevent their large losses
from affecting the spirits of those who escaped the
American rifles.

On the afternoon of the 30th, Walker marched with
the 1st and 2d Rifles (about 250 men in all) and a 12-
pound howitzer to San Juan del Sur, with the double
view of inspiring the troops with confidence by showing
them that the Allies feared to meet them in the open
field and of communicating with the steamer Orizaba,
expected in port about the first of February. The
march to San Juan was made in good time and with
cheerful spirits, and no signs of the enemy appeared on
the road. On the evening of the 1st of February the
Orizaba arrived from San Francisco, bringing Captain
Buchanan and some forty others for Nicaragua. The
vessel was coaled, as usual, by men in the service of the

State ; and without aid from the government it might have been difficult for the steamers to get labor at reasonable rates. A marginal note in the log of the schooner Granada, written by Captain Fayssoux, shows whether or not American commerce had reason to be thankful to the authorities then at San Juan. In the body of the schooner's log for the 2d of February we read, " Eleven of the crew employed coaling the Orizaba ;" while in the margin we find the note : " M. Mars being drunk on board the Orizaba, and urging our crew to strike for higher wages, which they did, the captain and he got into a fight ; I separated them, and sent Mars on shore, and persuaded the men to go on coaling."

About 4 o'clock in the afternoon of the 2d, Walker marched from San Juan to Virgin Bay. At the latter place he ascertained that Cañas had been there with some four or five hundred men, and had retired as soon as he heard of the approach of the Americans. Early on the morning of the 3d the steamer La Virgen appeared off Virgin Bay, and the troops then in the village were carefully concealed, with the hope that the steamer might come up to the wharf. When, however, she got within a few hundred yards of the wharf, she stopped her engines, yet did not drop anchor, as if regarding the aspect of affairs on shore. After a while several tried to strike her pilot-house with the Minié musket ; but their efforts were not very successful ; and in a short time the steamer turned away from the wharf and proceeded toward San Jorge. Then the Americans resumed their march and reached Rivas about midday of the 3d.

On their return to Rivas the Rifles were ordered to get as much rest as possible during the afternoon and the early part of the night, since their services might be required before daybreak of the 4th. Not long after midnight of the 3d, Walker marched with about 200 of the Rifles toward San Jorge ; and near a mile from Rivas, taking a road to the left, he entered the village, where the enemy lay, at 4 o'clock on the morning of the 4th of February. The Allies were taken entirely by surprise, and a select corps of volunteers, led on by Dr McAllenny, penetrated to one of the main barricades of the Plaza and fired over its top at the enemy, running hither and thither across the square. But the main body could not be brought to sustain the advancing party before the enemy recovered from their surprise. Then it was too late to carry the barricades without great loss, and the Americans were drawn off to the edge of the village beyond the reach of the enemy's small-arms. During the assault on the barricade Lieutenants Blackman and Gray were mortally wounded ; and while the Americans were ou the edge of the village O'Neal received his death-wound. By eight o'clock A. M. on the 4th, the Americans had returned to Rivas.

During this attack on San Jorge, Jerez was wounded in the face, and for some days there were reports of his death ; but the hurt was less dangerous than represented, and he soon recovered from its effects. The loss of O'Neil was a more severe blow to the Americans than any they inflicted on the Allies. Young and enthusiastic, he was not without the quick perception and rapid decision which fit a man for command in moments of

danger.   He was almost a boy in age, not twenty-one, at
the time of his death; but the mind matures rapidly on
the battle field, and he had by nature the true sentiment
of the soldier which tells him that it matters little
whether death comes soon or late, so it finds him in the
performance of duty.   He lingered for several days after
he was carried back to Rivas, and probabaly his gallant
spirit would have preferred to go forth from the world
amid the storm of battle.   But anxious eyes watched
over his last agonies, and there was none in camp who
was not saddened when the news of his death spread
through the town.

It was while Walker was at San Juan del Sur that
printed proclamations from Rafael Mora — promising
deserters protection and free passage to the United States
—were first scattered in the suburbs of Rivas.   At the
same time letters were addressed to Americans, signed
by those who had deserted from Granada and elsewhere,
urging officers and men to desert Walker and go over to
the enemy.   This was an entire change in the policy of
Costa Rica.   Not a year before, Mora had declared a war
of extermination against the " filibusters;" now he
attempted to make the war one against a single person,
and besought the Americans to desert their leader.   This
change of policy, while it tacitly admitted that the war
had failed in its objects, was also indicative of new
counsellors in the cabinet of Costa Rica; it proved
that other than Central American heads were busy
in plotting the removal of the naturalized Nicaraguans
from their adopted country.   All Americans, however,
are interested in having the names of these counsellors
remain in the obscurity their deeds deserve.

While barricades were being built at Rivas and the town was more thoroughly prepared for defence, Col. Swingle was engaged in labors which added much to the efficiency of the artillery. The mechanical genius of Swingle was extraordinary. Besides the well-organized work-shops he established at Rivas, he got a small engine from San Juan del Sur and succeeded in producing a blast of air which enabled him to smelt iron, and thus he cast the first cannon-balls ever made in Central America. The scanty supply of balls had been a serious obstacle to the employment of the artillery, and for some time it was necessary to use such as could be moulded with lead. As the supply of lead was limited, it would not do to put a great deal of it into the shape of cannon balls. A number of bells had been gathered from the towns and villages of the Meridional Department, and from these Swingle cast round shot, more effective, though also dearer, than those made of iron.

On the morning of the 7th of February, a supply of round shot having been procured, Henningsen, supported by the Rifles, proceeded to San Jorge to give the enemy a cannonade. He prepared some empty musket-boxes in order to construct a breastwork rapidly and without annoyance from the enemy. While it was yet dark he reached a point about six hundred yards from the lines of the Allies, and before daybreak his work was so far complete as to enable the men to proceed without interruption by the fire from the Plaza. The breastwork being finished, the six-pounders were fired rapidly and with much accuracy. The impression made on the Allies was apparent, though they affected to say that the balls did small damage. None of the Americans was hurt, and they returned to Rivas in good spirits at the work which had been done with so little expense. The object of these frequent attacks on the enemy was to keep them in a state of constant alarm, and besides the actual loss of the Allies in killed and wounded, the confusion into which they were thrown by the appearance of the Americans always enabled a few of the soldiers to desert. It was important, also, for Walker—while waiting the result of Lockridge's effort to open the Transit—to let his troops see that they were not thrown entirely on the defensive.

It was necessary to inspire the Americans with confidence in their own strength, and to show them the weakness of the enemy in order to cure, if possible, the fearful epidemic—for it is a disease—of desertion which had begun to demoralize the force at Rivas. Early in February a number of Rangers, with a commissioned officer, deserted and took the road to Costa Rica, carrying off their horses, saddles, and arms. The morning report of the 6th of February shows twenty desertions in twenty-four hours; that of the 8th of the same month shows six. Desertions at that time were the result of pure fright and restlessness; for the subsistence was unexceptionable, a large supply of flour and other provisions having been received from California during the month of January. Besides, the Rangers were then passing in bodies of ten and twelve through most parts of the Meridional Department and were able to bring in supplies of corn, tobacco, and sugar, for the troops. The spirit of desertion was rifest among those who had been in California; and the wan-

dering habits there engendered made them restive under
the restraints of military life. Americans, too, are accustomed to discuss public affairs with entire freedom;
and it is difficult to cure them of the habit—most dangerous in camp—of expressing their opinions about public acts and events. Such discussions may often be fatal
to the safety of an army; and thus, the habits of freedom,
while they add to the courage of the citizen, may also
diminish the fortitude unlicensed speech too often shakes.
Foolish speech and the spread of absurd reports did
more to foster desertion among the troops at Rivas than
all the promises of the enemy or any privations to which
they may have been subjected. Unfortunately, many
officers were not much wiser than the men in this respect, and their discouraging remarks produced most
pernicious effects. Such military faults, too, on the part
of officers are hard to deal with; for the punishment of
them may increase the evils they produce.

On the 6th of February, the United States sloop-of-
war St. Mary's, Commander Charles Henry Davis commanding, cast anchor in the port of San Juan del Sur;
and a few days thereafter, on the 10th, Her Britannic
Majesty's steamer Esk, Commander Sir Robert McClure
commanding, also anchored in the same harbor. On the
11th the log of the Granada reads: "At 9 A. M. the
commander of the English ship sent on board to know
my authority for flying a flag. He was answered by the
authority of our government. At 6 P. M. he again sent
on board using threats that he would take me prize or
sink me if I did not proceed on board of him with my
commission, which I refused to do. After making me

17

three visits and threatening everything, the lieutenant insisted on my making a friendly visit to the commander, which I did." As soon as the conduct of Sir Robert McClure was known at Rivas, orders were sent to Fayssoux not to hold or allow any of his officers or men to hold communication with the English commander, his officers or crew, and not in any manner to notice the presence of the Esk in port. In a few hours Sir Robert was in Rivas; and when informed that his conduct should be properly reported and brought to the attention of Her Majesty's government, he was profuse in his apologies, saying he had not intended any insult to Fayssoux or his flag. After his apology, the order to Fayssoux was revoked. In the schooner's log for the 13th we find: "At 11 A. M. Capt. Davis of the American sloop-of-war paid us an official visit. At 12 M. Capt. McClure returned my friendly visit." The course of Sir Robert McClure illustrates the conduct of the British naval officers toward Nicaragua. Whenever they were properly met and resisted in the first instance they would draw back from their arrogant demands; but if they found only hesitation and concessions they pressed their interference with more determination after each successful act. On the 19th the Esk left for Punta Arenas.

Commander Davis, having sent word that he desired to visit Rivas on business, an escort was ordered to conduct him to the town, and on the 18th he arrived at headquarters. He spent the afternoon and night in Rivas, and in his conversations with Walker studiously addressed him as President. During his stay the officers who accompanied him passed freely through the camp, and seemed surprised at the cheerful aspect of the place. The commander stated to Walker that the captain of the Narraganset, a coal-ship at San Juan, would require her small boats, then in Rivas, before going to sea. These boats had been brought from the Transit some weeks previously, with a view of using them on the lake, but as they were now useless for this service, Walker told Davis he did not object to return them to the Narraganset. At the same time Walker mentioned to Davis that the lake and river steamers, belonging to the American owners of the ocean steamships between Nicaragua and the United States, were precisely analogous to the boats of the Narraganset, and if he asked for the latter he should also demand the former from the Allies. Morgan and Garrison could no more carry on their business of transporting passengers between the Atlantic and Pacific ports of the United States without the property then in the hands of the Allies, than the Narraganset could go to sea without her small boats. Davis appeared to see the analogy of the cases, and said he would visit San Jorge after leaving Rivas, and speak with the Allied general on the subject.

From Rivas Davis went to San Jorge; but if he mentioned the lake and river steamers it must have been casually, and it was certainly without any result. He demanded to know from the Allied general whether the Americans on the small steamers were held against their will, for such was the current report through the country at the time. But he was satisfied with the simple assurance that these men served the Allies voluntarily. Of course any one familiar with the character and morals of Spanish-American officers, know that such assurances are readily given and really mean nothing. Davis, however, took no farther steps to ascertain the facts in relation to the Americans on the steamer, and this, with other facts, led Walker to see that the United States commander was more desirous of pressing demands against him than against the Allies. Hence, when the lieutenant of the St. Mary's came up for the Narraganset's boats, Walker told him he could not give them up unless Davis treated both parties to the war alike, and pressed his demands against the Allies with as much vigor as those he might make on the Nicaraguans.

During the latter part of February there were several encounters between the Rangers and small parties of the enemy. A few riflemen, too, would go out at night and alarm the camp of the Allies by firing on their pickets, and the enemy would, in the same manner, scatter small parties through the plantain patches and fire up the streets of Rivas. The Rangers in the employ of the commissary (of whom at one time there were about thirty) had some skirmishes with the Allies while the former were collecting subsistence for the Americans, and on the afternoon of the 4th of March the enemy took two wagons, several carts, and a number of oxen which had been sent out, in charge of the Rangers, for corn. This capture was made not more than a mile from Rivas, and on an estate belonging to the family of an officer in the Allied army.

On the evening of the 4th of March, Caycee, with some forty Rangers, was sent to San Juan del Sur as an

escort to Col. Jaquess, Mrs. Dusenberry, the widow of
the major mortally wounded at San Jorge, and others
going to the United States. They arrived at San Juan
without seeing the enemy ; but on the 5th, as Caycee
was returning to Rivas, he found himself unexpectedly
in the presence of 200 of the Allies, just after he passed
the Half-way House, and was about to leave the Transit
road. The enemy took Caycee by surprise, and he lost
six of his men, four killed and two wounded, before he
was able to extricate himself from the fire of the Allies.
He fell back to San Juan, and remained there until the
7th. In the meantime, Walker having learned, through
a native boy, that a Costa Rican force had left San
Jorge, and was on the way to the Transit, ordered Sanders to get the Rifles ready for marching. The boy who
brought the information to Walker had seen the Costa
Ricans pass along the hill-side while he lay hid in the
bushes, and he had thus been able to count almost every
man. He reported them about 200 strong, and Sanders
was sent out to join Caycee with 160 of the Rifles. In
the afternoon of the 5th, Sanders, while on the march toward the Transit, met the enemy near a league from the
Jocote farm. The Rifles were much scattered when the
Costa Ricans first appeared, and Captains Conway and
Higley were engaged in deploying their companies on
either side of the road when they received the enemy's
attack. The Costa Ricans came on briskly and with
confidence ; the Rifles, on the contrary, hesitated, and
in spite of the efforts of their officers began to give way.
Waters, who was with Sanders, made several ineffectual
attempts to check the disorder into which the Americans

fell, but he could not get the Rifles to make head against the Costa Ricans, and the latter continued to press the rear of the Americans until they reached the point where the road forked—one fork leading to Rivas, the other to San Jorge. The enemy took the road leading to San Jorge; and no doubt the idea that they were cut off from their main body, and the necessity of forcing their way back to Cañas, increased the vigor of their attack, and made them fight with more appearance of courage than was usual to them. Sanders' loss was 28, of which there were 20 killed and 8 wounded. The large proportion of killed is explained by the fact that a number of the wounded were left on the field, and the enemy killed these when they came up. Higley and Conway, both excellent officers, were among the killed. For many hours there were numbers both of men and officers missing, but the most of these came into Rivas during the next day.

The Allies, elated by the result of the conflict with Sanders, marched a strong body into the plantain patches, to the east of Rivas and near the Plaza, about ten o'clock P. M. of the 5th. A deserter, who was with them, called out to the sentry not to fire as "they were Rangers;" but the fellow's over-anxious tone betrayed his plans and the alarm was given. Some rounds of canister fired among the plantains soon scattered the allied force stationed there; and though the bugles continued to sound the charge, the spirit of the enemy did not seem equal to the attempt. The fire into the town had been short and rambling; but a musket-ball struck Dulaney, of the Artillery, in the throat, inflicting a painful though not dangerous wound.

On the afternoon of the 7th Caycee returned to Rivas with his Rangers and 70 footmen from California, in charge of Capt. Stewart. Arms had been furnished to the new men from the supply aboard of the Granada ; and the steamer which brought these immigrants from California, also bore a quantity of arms and ammunition for the service of Nicaragua. Stewart's men were formed into a corps called the Red Star Guard, and they were put under the command of Major Stephen S. Tucker, formerly of the U. S. Mounted Rifles. Tucker was an excellent officer, punctual in the discharge of his duties, and rigid in exacting from others the performance of theirs. The captain of the Guard, Stewart, was a noisy, talkative man, whose ideas about public affairs had been derived principally from grogshop assemblies in the mining villages of California ; and Tucker's ideas of discipline and duty were quite distasteful to a man whose habit it was to fawn on people in order to secure their good-will and favor. From the beginning, Tucker was strict with his men, and aspired to make them the best soldiers in Rivas. For a time he succeeded admirably ; and it is probable he might have done more with the Guard in the end, had it not been for the foolish talkativeness of its captain.

The day after Stewart and his men arrived, the whole force in Rivas was paraded on the Plaza, and Walker addressed them with a view of raising their spirits after the depression of Jocote, and Caycee's mishap on the Transit. He reviewed the course the Costa Ricans took in the opening of the war, and contrasted it with the policy the Allies had since adopted, thereby showing that they had been humbled in their conflict with the Americans. He also alluded to the efforts made to seduce the troops from their allegiance to the flag, by representing their chief as selfish and ungrateful. It was, he said, an insult to Americans to suppose, that they served a chief; they served a cause and not a man; and when the Allies asked, what reward they had received or what thanks had been bestowed for the sufferings at Rivas, at Masaya, and at Granada, they recalled names that should fill the souls of soldiers with devotion and enthusiasm to the cause in which they were engaged. The address was brief; but it had an effect on those who heard it, and for several days the spirit of the garrison was better than it had been.

On the 13th, Caycee, with his Rangers, went to San Juan for the purpose of bringing to Rivas the letters and papers brought by the Sierra Nevada from Panama. Titus was a passenger on the steamer, and had been intrusted, so Lockridge afterward said, with the official report of events on the river; but Walker did not get this report until many days after Titus' arrival at Rivas, and then in the shape of duplicates by the next vessel with mails from San Juan del Norte. Hence, for some time, the chief information as to affairs on the San Juan was derived from Titus, and this, as may be readily imagined, was of very inaccurate character. This person, Titus, had not been at Rivas long, before his reports were regarded as wholly worthless; for, during the sickness of one of Walker's aides, Titus was requested to act, for the time, on the staff of the general-in-chief. The first duty on which he was sent, required him to approach a point where the Allies and Americans were in presence of each other; and Titus, not venturing within range of the enemy's fire, received a statement from a soldier and brought it to headquarters as a report of facts. A moment after Titus' return, Henningsen rode up, and reported to Walker a state of facts entirely the reverse of Titus' report. Of course, the services of Titus were immediately dispensed with.

From the first, Walker placed no confidence in the statements of Titus about affairs on the river. No commission was given to Titus; on the contrary, when he requested to be sent to the United States with authority to act for Nicaragua, his application was refused. Although possessed of some plausibility, he could lead only superficial observers astray as to his real character. He had too much the air of the bully, to gain credit for either honesty or firmness of purpose. His future conduct will hereafter be related; and from it may be learned something of the man who, when he left New-Orleans, boasted that in not many days the San Juan river would be open to the Americans.

At two o'clock on the morning of the 16th, Walker marched for San Jorge, with about 400 effective men, two iron six-pounders, one twelve-pound howitzer, and four small mortars. Henningsen accompanied the force with the view of directing the operations of the artillery. The force of the enemy had been swelled to upward of 2,000 men, by fresh troops from Guatemala and Costa Rica; and only the day before a body of 400 or 500 had been carried on the lake steamer from Tortugas, about ten leagues south of Virgin Bay, to the camp at San

17*

Jorge. By daybreak, however, the Americans had possession of a small church, about six hundred yards from
the Plaza, where the enemy lay. Soon after the position
was secured, the six-pounders opened on the Allies, men
being stationed in the trees so as to watch where the
balls struck ; for the dense vegetation about the town
made it impossible to get an open view of the square, and
thus the pointing of the guns was to some extent con-
jectural. Twelve-pound shells were also thrown from the
mortars ; and had there been a larger supply of shells,
the fire of the mortars would have accomplished much.
Even the small number of shells thrown were not without effect on the enemy. As one of the characteristic
incidents of the day, it may be mentioned, that while
the artillery firing was going on, Col. Henry, who had been
left in bed at Rivas, rode up on his mule, and received
another bullet from the enemy before the day was over.

While the artillery was engaged in pouring round shot
and shell into the Plaza, Tucker, with the Red Star
Guard, was throwing up a breast-work some seventy or
eighty yards to the left, and in advance of the church
Walker occupied. The ground where Tucker was at
work touched the road leading straight into the Plaza ;
and he was preparing it for the reception of a gun which
might thence have told with much effect on the Allies.
The enemy, however, observed Tucker's men, and before
the breastwork was complete, several hundred of the
newly-arrived Costa Ricans sallied from the Plaza, and
advancing through the plantain walks, fell with fury on
the Red Star Guard. Tucker fought fiercely for several
minutes, his men showing fine spirit, and doing good

work with their Minié muskets. But the strength of the enemy was such, as to force him to retire to the church, after the loss of several killed and wounded.

The several roads and bye-paths in the rear, and on the flanks of the American main position at the church, were well watched and guarded by the Rangers, as well as by some companies of Infantry and Rifles. Captain Northedge's company on the left, was assailed about the same time with Tucker; but he held his position, and the enemy retired. There was more or less skirmishing on the flanks and rear, while the Artillery was exhausting its supplies of shot; after some three hundred and fifty rounds had been fired, it was clear that few of the enemy remained in the Plaza, and that they were taking positions on the road between San Jorge and Rivas, with a view of harassing, if not of preventing the return of the Americans to the latter place. The delay in the reappearance of some Rangers sent to Rivas to ascertain whether the road to that place was open, showed that the Allies were attempting to occupy it. The enemy thus having almost entirely deserted San Jorge, and offering action along the road to Rivas, Walker decided to accept the offer.

Placing, then, Waters with the Rangers in front, and Henningsen with the twelve-pound howitzer in the rear, while the wounded and the six-pounders occupied the centre of the column, Walker took the main road from San Jorge to Rivas. As he approached a small rise in the road, near a mile from San Jorge, the general-in-chief found Waters engaged with the enemy, posted some hundred and fifty or two hundred yards in advance, on each side of a deep cut in the road. The Rangers had been engaged for several minutes when the general-in-chief came up; and when Walker saw how the Allies were posted, taking the nearest company, which happened to be that of Captain Clark of the Infantry, he made a detour to the right, and coming suddenly on the enemy's left flank, drove them across the road, and then from their whole position. Thus sweeping the road as they passed over it, the Americans reached the point known as Cuatro Esquinas, near half a mile from Rivas, without further serious interruption from the Allies. Several times they tried to close on the rear but the resolute and defiant air of Henningsen, kept them at a safe distance.

While Walker was at San Jorge, Swingle remained in command at Rivas; and the enemy had once during the day approached the barricades, thinking they might enter the town with small risk. But Swingle was not a man to be trifled with; and the Allies soon gave up their efforts to get a foothold in the place. Then they occupied a house some six hundred yards from the Plaza of Rivas. and near the road between the town and the Cuatro Esquinas. The enemy had, during the afternoon, strongly barricaded this house, and as the head of the American column approached it, the Allies opened a sharp fire of musketry from the loop-holes they had cut through the walls of the building. The Americans were, to some extent, protected by the shelving ground between the house and the road, and many of them thus passed without much danger from the enemy's fire; but several were hurt before they got under a steep bank which

entirely screened them from the balls of the Allies.
Walker himself pushed on to Rivas, and ascertaining
that the road to the left from Cuatro Esquinas was clear
of the enemy, sent orders to Henningsen to have the
wounded brought in by that road.   He also sent orders
to have the guns brought in the same way ; but before
these orders reached Henningsen, the guns were already
on the narrow road the main body had taken, and
could not be withdrawn.   After the general-in-chief
passed the house the Allies occupied, Dolan, coming up
with his Rifles, rode almost on to the muskets of the
enemy, calling to his men to follow.   His characteristic
impetuosity carried him too far; he fell bleeding and
apparently nigh dead, from several severe wounds ; and
he is indebted to a remarkably tough body for his re-
covery from the effects of that day's rashness.   Soon
after dark nearly all the American force had reached the
Plaza of Rivas ; but it was not before morning of the
17th that the guns and mortars were safely within the
barricades.

The loss of the Americans on the 16th of March was
thirteen killed and sixty-three wounded, four of the latter
mortally.   Among the mortally wounded was Lewis, of
the Second Rifles.   He received a musket-ball through
the chest as he rode into the midst of the enemy near
San Jorge ; and among his last words were, " Tell my
mother that I died as I have always wished to die."
Tucker was wounded in the sword hand ; but not so
seriously as to prevent him from reporting for duty a few
days afterward.   The Red Star Guard suffered severely,
they reporting on the 17th two killed, four mortally

wounded, and nearly half their number more or less hurt. The loss of the Allies was, according to the reports of their own officers, five hundred killed and wounded. An Italian, acting as an officer with the Allies, and afterward taken prisoner, put their loss at this figure; and a Costa Rican officer, who arrived at San Jorge on the 17th, and was made prisoner by the Americans on the 11th of April, stated that the sight of the numerous wounded being carried to the lake steamer, as the new men from Tortugas landed, made a deep and gloomy impression on the minds of the latter.

On the 19th, Colonel Waters, with fifty Rangers, marched to San Juan del Sur to communicate with the steamer Orizaba, which arrived that day from San Francisco. The steamer brought Captain Chatfield, with twenty others, for Nicaragua, and also some arms and five hundred 6lb. shot. Waters had three hundred of the shot carried to Rivas; and Chatfield, with his men, accompanied the Rangers on their return. By the Orizaba, Walker also received letters from his California correspondents, more than intimating doubts of Garrison's fidelity to his contracts and compromises. The regular day for the sailing of the Orizaba was the 20th of March; and the friends of Nicaragua in San Francisco had made their arrangements expecting she would sail at that time. Two or three days, however, before the 5th of March, letters were received from Morgan and Garrison by their agents at San Francisco, ordering the Orizaba to be despatched two weeks in advance of her regular day. The change was damaging to the plans of Walker's friends in California; and the inference was

that the Transit contractors were about to play false
with the men who had risked much to advance their interests.

The day after the action at San Jorge and along the
road between that town and Rivas, the Allies received
fresh troops, and also brought across the lake one of the
old 24-pound pieces the Spaniards left in the country.
They took a position on a slight eminence, about 1,200
yards from Rivas, just beyond the Cuatro Esquinas;
and, on the 22d of March, planting the twenty-four
pounder there, they opened a scattering and irregular
fire on the town. The 24-pound balls were, at long intervals, sent into the place, doing, however, little or no
damage. They were picked up by the men and carried
to the arsenal; and Swingle afterward melted them into
6-pound balls and sent them back to the enemy. But
the cannonade—if such it might be called—of the 22d,
was preliminary to an attack the Allies made early on
the morning of the 23d.

On Monday, the 23d, just before daybreak, a body of
some four or five hundred of the enemy crept under the
thick shades of the cacao walks, behind the Maleaño
house, and getting almost to the back gate of the hospital before they were discovered, made a vigorous attempt to get within the building. But Dr. Dolman,
with a few half-sick men, resisted the enemy with such
firmness and composure, that time was afforded Dr.
Callaghan, who had charge of the point, to get the hospital ready for defence. The Allies thus foiled in their
efforts to surprise the Maleaño house, were driven back
with much loss and more disgrace: for they had unsuc-

cessfully, no less than cruelly, attacked a building occupied almost exclusively by the sick and wounded.

The attack on the hospital was, however, part of a general assault on the positions held by the Americans. On the north side of the town, Cañas, with some six or seven hundred men, tried to get up to the houses near the barricades, but his men were driven back by the deadly fire of the riflemen stationed behind the adobe defences. Finding the efforts of the infantry to approach the barricades ineffectual, Cañas had a four-pounder, in charge of an Italian, pushed within less than two hundred yards of the American lines. This was a bolder movement than the enemy were in the habit of making with their artillery, and it was the result of a mistake rather than of design. The gun was fired two or three times; but when it got within range of the Mississippi Rifles the men at the piece began to fall rapidly, and finally abandoned it. The Italian commanding the piece was dangerously wounded and made prisoner; and Rogers, with a few of the native Nicaraguans, took the gun and dragged it into the town. Cañas was forced to retire, leaving many of his wounded, as well as a large number of his dead, on the field.

The south side of the town was attacked by Fernando Chamorro with some six hundred men. He succeeded in getting possession of some empty houses not more than a square from the Plaza, and commenced with the usual rapidity to raise barricades at the points he occupied. The Red Star Guard was defending the portion of the town attacked by Chamorro, and Tucker was kept busy in repelling the advances of the enemy.

At one time a company of the Allies actually got possession of a house which had been occupied by the Guard ; but though a bold, it was a mistaken movement on their part, for the Guard cut them off from their main body, and killing several, and wounding others, as they attempted to leave the house, Tucker's men took the rest of the company prisoners. With some difficulty Henningsen succeeded with the six-pounders in driving Chamorro from the houses he had occupied early in the day, and after this was accomplished the fire of the enemy almost entirely ceased.

The loss of the Americans on the 23d was slight ; three killed and six wounded was the report made immediately after the action. The loss of the enemy must have been near 600. They left between 40 and 50 dead on the field ; and the wells about the houses Chamorro occupied were filled with freshly-slain bodies. The wounded taken by the Americans were sent to the hospital, and received the same attentions as the other patients. The other prisoners were set to work burying the dead of the enemy, building barricades, and doing the police duty of the town.

After the action of the 23d, the Allies took possession of the house of D. José Maria Hurtado, a fine large building, less than half a mile from Rivas, on the road to Granada ; and on the morning of the 24th, a body of the enemy, probably belonging to the troops stationed at Hurtado's house, attempted to set fire to the building of Santa Ursula, occupied by some of the Infantry. They used for this purpose some combustibles covered with resinous matter, and stuck on a bayonet fixed to the end of a long pole. Approaching the rear of the building, the enemy thrust the bayonet between the tiles of the roof into the cane on which they are placed, and thus the fire partially caught. But the Infantry drove off the troops which applied the fire, killing several and wounding others, and the flames were soon extinguished.

During the afternoon of the 25th Henningsen used a safer and more effectual method for setting fire to the enemy's barricades, made partly of wood and plantain stalks. He threw a number of hot shot from one of the six-pounders into the wood-work of the barricades, and the smoke which arose showed that the shot had been effectual. As a supply of round shot had been received from California, and Swingle was engaged in casting others, the Americans could afford to reply with their six-pounders to the fire of the enemy's guns, and yet retain a reserve of balls for any pressing emergency. This, of course, much increased the effectiveness of the artillery, and enabled it to keep the Allies at a safe distance from the lines of Rivas. After the repulse of the 23d, the enemy evidently aimed to invest the town and cut off its supplies ; and, in addition to the occupation of Hurtado's house, they took a position on the San Juan road. This last position was taken on the morning of the 26th, and in an unsuccessful effort made by some Infantry and Rifles, Capt. E. H. Clark was unfortunately lost. With their ranks already thinned by desertion, the Americans could ill afford to spare the lives necessarily lost in driving the Allies from their barricaded positions with small arms ; and the artillery, forcing the enemy to extend their lines, thereby prevented the investment from becoming complete. Hence Walker had no difficulty in constantly sending native couriers through the allied lines, in order to get the news circulating in the country.

The Allies were, however, strong enough to prevent detachments from bringing cattle and other supplies from a distance into the American camp. Col. Natzmer, who acted as commissary-general after Walker occupied Rivas in December, had been actively employed during January and February, and had brought in a supply of subsistence which, considering the means at his disposal, was creditable to his skill and efficiency. The post commissary, also, Capt. J. S. West, had much aided his chief in the duties of the commissariat; and even after the enemy had cut off supplies from a distance, West, by his cool, deliberate courage, did much to gather rations of plantains from the debateable and dangerous ground between the American and Allied lines. But on the 27th of March, it became necessary for the commissary to have two quartermaster's oxen killed; and these, with a slight mixture of mule meat, furnished the rations for the next morning. The mule meat was eaten by the troops as beef; and in two or three days none but horse or mule flesh was issued as the meat ration. The large number of horses and mules belonging to the Rangers and to the quartermaster, furnished full rations to the whole camp for more than a month, and the leaves of the mango trees, many of which grew around Rivas, furnished excellent forage for the animals. In order not to place Lockridge in a false position, should he succeed in reaching Rivas from the river, Walker was determined to hold the town as long as his provisions lasted. Besides this, although Cañas, in return for the care taken of his sick and wounded, after his retreat in April, 1856, had been placed under obligations to see that the Americans were treated in the same manner, Walker was averse, unless in the last extremity, to leaving his hospital to the tender mercies of the Allied generals.

During the last days of March and the first ten days of April, the enemy, having brought up another twenty-four-pound gun and placed it on the south side of the town, kept up an irregular fire with their large pieces, and from time to time they would fire volleys of musketry at random, the balls dropping on the houses and in the streets of the place. Few men were hurt by this irregular fire. Two officers, Capt. Mann and Lieut. Moore, were killed by twenty-four pound balls, and the officer of the day, on the 29th of March, Lieut. Graves, had his arm broken by a Minié ball, while he was visiting on horseback the several points on the edge of the town. The aides of the general-in-chief, Hooff and Brady, who were constantly, day and night, passing through different exposed quarters of the place—Brady, too, on a fine spirited white horse, which neccessarily attracted the attention of the enemy—escaped untouched. Every now and then, small parties of Americans were sent beyond the lines, and getting close to the enemy's pickets would drive them in, nearly always killing or wounding some of the sentries of the Allies. So, too, the enemy would sometimes meet the Americans when they ventured outside to gather plantains, and skirmishes, with more or less loss to each side, would ensue.

But it was not the scanty rations or the fire of the Allies which did most injury to the American force ; it was the shameful desertion which most affected the spirits and the strength of the defenders of Rivas. As long as the desertion was confined principally to those of European birth, it did not so seriously sap the confidence men had in each other ; but when the fatal infection spread among the Americans, it wrung bitter tears of agony from every true-hearted man who witnessed the shame and dishonor of his countrymen. Sometimes the deserters left in bodies of ten or twelve, and the sentries and pickets would leave with the countersign for the night. Let us pass the names of these with sorrow for the weakness of human nature, nor taint the air with the narration of their crimes and degradation. There is shame and infamy enough in the world without seeking for them on fields where glory should be won and honor achieved.

A day or two before the 10th of April the Allies received a body of fresh troops from Guatemala, and the quiet of the enemy on the 10th led to the surmise that they might select the anniversary of the action at Rivas, in April, 1856, for another general attack on the American lines. They supposed that the force in Rivas, weakened by its unusual food and disheartened by desertions might yield readily to a vigorous assault made on all sides at the same moment. But they underrated the spirit of their adversaries. The Nicaraguans really hoped that the Allies would find courage to attack them, and they were vigilant and well prepared during the night of the 10th and on the morning of the 11th.

As expected, the enemy came up a little before daybreak of the 11th, and made their first dash at a house
on the south side of the Plaza, occupied by a couple of
American ladies. The latter had been frequently warned of the danger of their position, but they persisted in
remaining where they were against the remonstrances
of several officers. This attempt of the enemy to
gain a foothold on the Plaza was made by a body of
Costa Ricans, and guided by a Legitimist, Bonilla,
familiar with the ground, they got close to the house and
were within it before the alarm was given. But as they
opened the door fronting on the Plaza, with a view of
getting to the house next on their right, and held by
some of the quartermaster's men, Sevier, of the Artillery, ran out a twelve-pound howitzer, not thirty yards
from the Costa Ricans, and one round of canister drove
the enemy behind the adobes. Thus the advance of the
Allies was checked on the south side, and the company in
the house, fronting the Plaza, was completely cut off by
the quartermaster's men on one flank, Williamson with
his company on the other, and by Pineda with Buchanan's
Rangers in the rear. In a few moments Henningsen
began to riddle the house with six-pound shot, and the
Costa Ricans, crouching on the ground, knew not how to
escape the danger which surrounded them. Finally
Pineda, addressing them in Spanish, called on them to
surrender, and those who escaped death were taken
prisoners.

But while the round shot were riddling the house
held by the Costa Ricans, the fresh Guatemalan troops,
half drunk with aguardiente, were driven up by their

officers close to the American lines. These soldiers, probably never before in action, and not aware of the danger from rifles, exposed themselves without reason, at a distance of sixty or seventy-five yards from the positions held by McEachin and McMichael. The men under these two officers poured a deadly fire into the foolish and ignorant Indians Carrera had sent to Nicaragua ; and it was with a feeling almost of pity for these forced levies that the Americans were obliged to shoot them down like so many cattle. The Guatemalan officers cared no more for their men than if they were sheep ; and when they finally drew off their troops the ground was thickly strewn with the dead and the wounded.

The third point of attack on the 11th was the house of Santa Ursula. Martinez directed the Allies on that side ; but he was not more fortunate than Mora—for José Joaquin Mora was now commander-in-chief of the Allies—on the south or than Zavala on the north. The men Martinez sent against Santa Ursula did not make as bold a dash as did the Costa Ricans at the house on the south side of the Plaza, nor did they expose themselves as unnecessarily as the Guatemalans in front of McMichael and McEachin ; but the number of dead they left on the field when they retired showed that Chatfield and the men at Santa Ursula had not missed opportunities for weakening the enemy. The repulse of the Allies was complete on all sides ; and when they fell back, it was clear that they were much exhausted and demoralized.

The loss of the Americans on the 11th of April was small, being the same as on the 23d of March three killed and six wounded. The loss of the Allies was even greater than at the previous attack. After the enemy retired 110 of their dead were buried by the Americans; the wounded prisoners were sent to the Allied camp under a flag of truce, and upward of 70 unhurt prisoners retained. In addition to the dead found by the Nicaraguans, nearly one hundred bodies were seen the day after in the Allied camp, so that the killed exceeded 200. The whole loss must have amounted to 700 or 800 ; and the weakness of the enemy for several days was very apparent to the troops in Rivas. In addition to the prisoners taken by the Americans, 250 small arms, many of them Minié muskets, and some ammunition, were picked up on the field. The Minié muskets were those which had been taken from the steamer La Virgen at the time of her capture by Spencer ; and the ammunition also was of that the Costa Ricans had got with the Minié muskets.

The night of the 11th, Capt. Hankins, with two native boys, was sent to San Juan del Sur to get the correspondence brought from Panama by the Orizaba. On the night of the 14th he returned to Rivas, and added to the commissary stores by riding in on horseback. The letters from the San Juan river gave the news of the arrival of Capers and Marcellus French with their respective commands ; while those from New-York too well confirmed the surmises of Walker's friends in California, for they gave notice of the intention of Garrison and Morgan to cease running their steamers. It is unnecessary to go into the reasons which induced these men to the course they took ; for it would involve an

investigation into transactions uninteresting if not posi-
tively distasteful. Suffice it to say that their conduct
was the result of weakness and timidity. As to their
treachery, Walker had expected them to remain faithful
to the Americans in Nicaragua only as long as their interests required fidelity ; he expected them, however, to
show more commercial nerve and sagacity than they
displayed. Their course evinced as much folly ' as
timidity, and jeoparded their reputation of skilful merchants fully as much as it damaged their character for
honesty and integrity.

From the 14th to the 23d, a number of skirmishes
took place between parties of the enemy and small
bodies of the Americans who went out to gather plantains ; but none of these was serious or deserving of
special notice. One of these skirmishes occurred on the
morning of the 23d ; and in the afternoon of the same
day, a flag of truce brought letters to Walker announcing that Lieut. Huston, of the St. Mary's, was at the
headquarters of the Allies, and was ready, under the
United States flag, to conduct the women and children
in Rivas to San Juan del Sur. A letter from Mora to
Walker proposed to send two of his aides with Lieut.
Huston to a convenient point between the camps, where
the United States officer might be met by two of Walker's aids, and be thus conducted into Rivas. In accordance with this proposition, Hooff and Brady accompanied
the native boy who bore the letters from Mora to a point
about half way between the camps, and there halted,
waiting the approach of Lieut. Huston. While these
two officers waited, a couple of deserters approached and

18

attempted to address them; but Hooff, drawing his pistol, warned the fellows off under peril of their lives. Then, indignant at the Allies for permitting such an insult as the approach of deserters to officers bearing a flag of truce, Hooff and Brady returned to Rivas without waiting longer the arrival of Lieut. Huston. Soon after, however, Lieut. Huston entered the town, accompanied by a corporal of marines.

Immediately after Lieut. Huston entered the Nicaraguan camp, he was told to forbid his corporal to speak with the soldiers about facts or events at San Juan del Sur. In spite of this injunction the marine told the most exaggerated stories about the number of men the Allies had at San Juan, and about their strength generally. Lieut. Huston remained in Rivas during the night of the 23d, and he frequently expressed his surprise at the cheerful and confident aspect of affairs in the place. Before leaving with the women, he informed Walker that Commander Davis had ordered him to say any communications he had to make to Macdonald, the agent of the Transit contractors at San Juan, should be faithfully delivered. Walker replied, "he did not desire to write to Macdonald"; but added that Lieut. Huston might say to Commander Davis—and as a communication for Macdonald—" he considered his position at Rivas impregnable to the force at the disposal of the enemy so long as his provisions lasted; if Lockridge did not join him in Rivas by the time his commissary stores were exhausted, he would abandon the place and join the force on the San Juan; and he considered himself wholly able to carry out such a movement." Macdonald afterward told Walker that he never received this message. From this fact, it would appear that Davis' offer was a mere effort to entrap Walker into writing something which might seem to justify the former in the course he afterward took.

On the morning of the 24th the women and children left Rivas in charge of Lieut. Huston and under the protection of the United States flag. Among them were several ladies who had encountered the dangers and privations of the camp with a courage and fortitude which might have made many of the men blush. Their departure was a great relief to Walker, as it removed one of the most serious obstacles to a movement from Rivas; and it was reasonable to suppose that their absence would inspire new spirit and resolution into the troops thus relieved of an anxious burden. Far from this, however, desertions, which had almost ceased since the 11th, re-commenced after the 24th; and by the 26th Johnson and Titus and Bostwick had disappeared from Rivas. Late in the afternoon of that day it was reported to Walker that Bell, commanding at Santa Ursula, had not been seen for several hours; and when he did reappear, his orders in regard to the change of the sentries' post, were suspicious. He was ordered to headquarters; but soon after the aid communicated the order, Bell mounted his mule, and riding hastily past the sentries, fled to the Allied camp.

But while Americans were thus proving false to themselves and false to their countrymen, the native Nicaraguans in Rivas were giving an example of fidelity and fortitude worthy the race which had been naturalized in

their midst. The natives in Rivas were mostly Democrats from San Jorge, and they were there by families—
fathers and sons fighting together against the Allied foes
who had violated their fields and their homes. They
bore the scanty fare of the camp with patience and
cheerfulness, saying they had not as much need of meat
rations as the Americans, who were accustomed to have
beef every day. During the frequent conversations, too,
which occurred between the men at the barricades of
the respective forces, Pineda reminded the native Nicaraguans who were with the Allies that he saw the flag of
his country flying on the walls of Rivas, while only the
Costa Rican colors floated over the camp without. Some
of the soldiers would reply to Pineda that they were
"agarrados"—caught up—and were tied to their barricades; and it was noticed that the Americans were
never annoyed by the fire from the points at which the
Leoneses were stationed. On the 27th, Pineda threw
among the Leoneses an address which, while it indicates
the loftiness of his character, also shows his opinion as
to the conduct of the Americans in Nicaragua. "Born,"
so the address read, "a citizen of Nicaragua like yourselves, fond of liberty, and desirous of seeing its flag
waving over our country, I early enlisted under that
standard. All the hardships tyranny can heap upon a
man, all the horrors of the civil war, which for so many
years has been our plague, I have suffered without com-
plaint. The scars I bear with pride are the best proof
of what I say. I feel my enthusiasm yet more strengthened by the testimony I find in my heart that none of
the heavy sacrifices I have made were made for low or

selfish interest.   Never, I believe, never have I been
found guilty, at your hands, of any misconduct; and I
call upon you to bear witness to the correctness of my
words.   You were my fellow-soldiers, and bestowed upon
me your confidence.   Under these circumstances, what
other object than your happiness and welfare could nerve
me?   My own happiness, my reputation, my private
feelings, and all that is mine, are involved in this struggle
for liberty.   Yes, and I call upon those leaders who drag
you into this murderous war of extermination, to say if
they have not been indemnified, if they have not accumulated profits by it, while you and I have received
nothing.   The flag of Nicaragua waves over this city,
and it is a painful disgrace to see it besieged by the
armies of Costa Rica and Guatemala, and you, my fel-
low-countrymen, assault it with them."   Then, remind-
ing them of the services they had received at the hands of
Walker, the address adds: "How is it that you, my friends,
should fight against him, thus giving a most striking instance of perfidy and ingratitude?   No: it cannot be.
My heart is filled with gloom, and, fellow-soldiers, believe me when I say that tears fell from my eyes on
hearing the voices of those who used to take my hand
with heartfelt demonstrations of friendship.   When I
see you where you are, I dare tell you to awake from
your slumber, and fly from the enemy's ranks to the
only man who will bring us in safety to the bosom of
peace and happiness, by putting an end to this, desola-
ting war.   But if you continue in your present course,
and remain the tools of barbarism, you will meet reproof,
though war may last some time and your own acts ob-
struct its termination."

Little occurred between the 27th and 30th to change the condition of the respective parties. In order, however, to understand the events of the 30th, it will be necessary to relate occurrences at San Juan del Sur previous to that date. Then may we perceive how efficiently the U. S. naval forces, on the Pacific side, co-operated in the policy the British ships pursued toward parties on the San Juan river.

For the facts which transpired at San Juan del Sur, the log of the schooner Granada will be principally relied on, and full extracts from the log will furnish the clearest and most accurate narrative. On Wednesday, the 8th of April, the schooner lying in the port of San Juan, we find : " At 9 A. M., 100 of the enemy came into the town and fired some few shots at the schooner and at one or two of the citizens, doing no damage ; we did not return their shots, on account of the steamer being in range full of passengers, but slipped our chain and dropped out of reach. Through the intercession of Captain Davis, of the U. S. sloop-of-war St. Mary's, we agreed to not fire upon each other, as we might endanger American life and property. At 2 P. M. the Orizaba left for California. At 9 P. M. the enemy left San Juan." Then, on the margin of the log for April 15th, we find : " At 9 A. M. one of the enemy came in and met Gottell." This Gottell was a German, claiming to be a naturalized citizen of the United States. On the margin for the next day Fayssoux remarks : " In conversing with Gottell he acknowledged that the above man came from the enemy's camp on Tuesday." On ⋅the 17th, in the body of the log :

" Made a formal charge to Captain Davis, of the U. S. sloop-of-war, St. Mary's, against Gottell, for his violating his neutrality, and received his assurance that Gottell should be punished if it occurred again. Mora requested Davis to go up and speak to the troops at Rivas, to get them to desert General Walker." Then in the margin for the same day : " Captain Davis read to me letters from Mora. Later in the day we heard that about 150 of the enemy were in and about town. Lieutenant McCorkle, of the St. Mary's, came on board and said that Colonel Estrada wished the former truce continued." On the 18th, the log says : "At 10 P. M. received a communication from shore, to the effect that Jerez was coming in with 200 more troops, and that they were going to fire on the schooner at daylight ; slipped my chain and dropped out of their reach." In the margin, for the same day : " The enemy offered Michael Mars $2,000 to place the schooner in their hands." On the 21st : " The enemy negotiating with Thomas Edwards to deliver up the schooner."

On the 22d Fayssoux notes in the log : " I met Col. Estrada, the commander of the enemy, on board of the U. S. sloop St. Mary's ; he expressed great gratitude for my treatment of his countrymen that I had taken prisoners, and offered his services to me." On the 23d : " Saw a letter from ex-Captain James Mullen, in which he stated that Roman Rivas wished him to see me, and offer $5,000 if I would deliver the schooner to the enemy. Colonel Garcia, second in command, requested an interview with me on board of the U. S. sloop, St. Mary's, to communicate something of importance—I suppose another attempt to bribe." Then, on Friday, the 24th, we have an account of a most singular scene aboard of the St. Mary's. Fayssoux's object in permitting the interview may be readily imagined, but it is more difficult to divine why Davis should permit his ship to be made the theatre of an attempt to seduce an officer from his allegiance. But to the log : " I met Colonel Garcia on board of the St. Mary's. He stated that Jerez had written to him (by order of General Mora), to see me and try to make some arrangement to bring the war to a speedy close ; that the schooner being in port, under General Walker's orders, she was much dreaded and might delay the close of the war. He asked if I had any proposition to make ; I told him that he had sought the interview, and that I was waiting to hear for what purpose. He then said that they wished the schooner taken from the port or given up to them. I asked upon what terms : he said that he was not prepared to offer any, but that a commissioner would be appointed for that purpose ; that his object was to see if I could be approached. I said that I would listen to any proposition from General Mora ; that the present interview had not effected anything ; that he had not proposed any mode of closing the war ; that we stood as we had done previously. I acted on the above occasion with the knowledge and approval of Captain Davis and Colonel Macdonald, and at no time lost command of my temper, although seeing the full extent of the dishonor offered me, and the insult of their sending such a noted thief and traitor to confer with me."

For the 25th, we find : " Sent word by Capt. Charles

H. Davis to Col. Estrada that if he did not discontinue erecting barricades which could be commanded by my guns that I would fire upon him ; he agreed to do so until Lieut. Huston of the St. Mary's should arrive from Rivas, where he had gone to escort the American ladies who were there, to San Juan.   Col. Estrada said that in erecting barricades he had nothing in view against this schooner, but put them up to prevent the landing of troops ; that he did it in ignorance, not meaning to violate the agreement between him and myself.   At 4 P. M. some thirty women and children arrived at the Pacific hotel.   The barricades not worked upon."   Then on the 26th : " Capt. Davis spoke again to Col. Estrada in regard to the barricades ; he said he would not do anything on them until he heard from Rivas.   Capt. Davis wrote to General Mora asking him to confirm the truce, as the number of women had largely increased, and that I felt it my duty to fire upon their barricades, if in reach of my guns.   The enemy mounted and brought to the beach an old gun that they found lying in the street Capt. Davis says that General Mora has written to him several times, appearing anxious for him to come to him and open a treaty with General Walker."   And in the margin : " I had to urge Capt. Davis at all times to interfere about the barricades."

On the 27th : " At 10ʰ 45′ saw the enemy erecting a barricade in the Columbia hotel ; I immediately prepared to haul in shore.   At the same time I sent to Capt. Davis, and said that as the enemy were acting in bad faith I would fire upon them.   He sent First Lieut. Maury to me to ask if I would not wait until he heard

18*

from Rivas. I replied that I would if Capt. Davis would then go on shore and destroy them (meaning the barricades). Lieut. Maury could not answer that question. I then told him that if they did not stop that in half an hour I would fire. Lieut. Maury then went to Colonel Estrada and said that Capt. Davis looked on the truce as at an end, and that I would fire in half an hour. Colonel Estrada wished to debate the question, and again pleaded ignorance; but Lieut. Maury said that he had nothing more to say, that I would fire. Estrada then agreed to let the barricade alone, and that the truce should be observed. The first note was sent to Col. C. J. Macdonald, and shown by him to Capt. D., who said that he would take me if I did fire, as he thought it would be his duty. Macdonald was asked to come on board and say that I must not fire, as Davis would take me; Macdonald asked for that threat in writing; Davis offered to give it, but after some more conversation on the subject, he sent the above message to Estrada. Capt. D. acknowledged to Macdonald that it would be my duty to fire if the enemy did not desist; his reasoning was entirely incomprehensible to me." And the reasoning is incomprehensible to any one, on the supposition of Davis' neutrality. The marginal note on the log for the 27th, says: " Although being perfectly aware of the treachery of the enemy at all times, and their violation of the truce in building barricades in reach of my guns, I permitted them to go to a certain extent, hoping to turn them to our advantage. And thinking it policy, I did not urge upon Capt. Davis his duty to destroy those already started or completed, though I took occasion to let his officers know my views on the subject, and that I thought he was easily satisfied with promises which were constantly broken ; that I had had opportunities of gaining advantages, but had scrupulously kept the truce."

Tuesday, April 28th : " Saw the enemy putting up a barricade on the Transit road. Although the fact was mentioned to Capt. Davis, he did not take any action upon it, but told me that General Mora, in reply to a letter from him, said that though he looked upon it as a matter of great importance to fortify San Juan, as Davis requested it, he would not put up barricades under my guns. Lieut. McCorkle visited the enemy's camp, to ascertain if reports brought by a man by the name of Titus from General Walker's camp were true, he, Titus, being thought a traitor." On the 29th : " At 2 P. M. Lieut. McCorkle returned from the Allied camp. He reports our men deserting in large bodies ; that General Mora says that General Walker will not be included in any treaty that may be made." Then on the 30th : " Capt. Davis visited the camp of the Allies for the purpose of treating between them and General Walker."

The facts plainly and simply told by the log of the schooner show that Davis was in constant communication with Mora, and that he was fully aware of the value of the Granada to Walker, and of the importance the Allies attached to her presence at San Juan del Sur. It was with a full and thorough knowledge of the ineffectual efforts Mora had made to get the schooner that Davis reached the headquarters of the Allies, whence on the afternoon of the 30th, he sent a letter to Walker by an aide-de-camp of the Costa Rican general-in-chief. The latter proposed that Walker should abandon Rivas and go aboard of the St. Mary's to Panama, Davis undertaking to guarantee his personal safety. Although the tone of the letter was offensive, Walker, thinking Davis might have some information he did not possess, and unwilling to let slip an opportunity of gaining knowledge as to what was passing between Davis and the Allies, replied that the proposition of the United States commander was vague, and suggested a visit on his part to Rivas. Davis answered that he was sorry Walker found his proposition vague ; that he proposed the latter should " abandon the enterprise and leave the country ;" that Walker might rely on the fact of Lockridge having left San Juan river ; and finally that he had maturely considered the invitation to enter Rivas, and had decided, unreservedly, not to take such a step. Thus did the United States commander refuse to see for himself the state of the force in Rivas before he determined on the course he should pursue. In reply to the second letter of Davis, Walker proposed to send two officers, Henningsen and Waters, to confer with the United States commander, provided they had safe conduct from Mora. The required safe conduct was forthwith sent, and with a short note in the handwriting of Zavala, but signed by Davis, saying that Henningsen and Waters should proceed at once to the headquarters of the Allies, as the commander of the St. Mary's was obliged to return speedily to San Juan del Sur.

Accordingly, Henningsen and Waters proceeded to the headquarters of the Allies, and what there passed may be best told in the words of the written report Henningsen made to Walker on the 2d of May. The report says :—

" In conformity with your instructions on the night of the 30th of April, I procceded with Col. Waters to the enemy's camp at Cuatro Esquinas, to confer on your behalf with Capt. Davis of the U. S. sloop-of-war St. Mary's. Capt. Davis remarked that he was in possession of information, which, in his opinion, rendered your position at Rivas untenable, and that he had, therefore, with the view of saving further useless effusion of blood, opened negotiations with the Allies for the evacuation of that place, in the event of his being able to obtain your concurrence.

" This information was, firstly, that Col. Lockridge had retired with all your forces to the United States, leaving the enemy in possession of the San Juan river ; secondly, that the Transit Company intended to send no more steamers to San Juan del Sur ; thirdly, that you were reduced to a few days' provisions, and that your ranks were being rapidly thinned by desertion. Under these circumstances, considering your position as desperate in Rivas, he had to propose that you should surrender Rivas to him, that you and your staff should accompany him to San Juan del Sur, to be transported by the St. Mary's to Panama ; that the rest of the army and citizens should be likewise transported via Tortugas and Punta Arenas to Panama, after surrendering their arms to him, the officers retaining their side-arms. I replied that your entertaining such a proposition would depend on your being satisfied with regard to the evacuation of the river by Col. Lockridge and his command, as your principal motive for holding Rivas to the last moment was the fear that he might arrive and find it occupied by the enemy : that with regard to your position being desperate, it was true that you could not, from want of provisions, hold Rivas much longer, but that you could break through the enemy's lines and march in any direction at present : that, if further enfeebled, you could always cut your way to the Pacific, and embark either at San Juan or at some other point on the coast, on your schooner Granada, which had on board two six-pounders and a store of arms, cartridges, cannon ammunition, powder and lead. On this Capt. Davis remarked, that he must at once inform me that it was his unalterable determination not to allow the schooner Granada to leave the port, and to take possession of her previous to his sailing from San Juan del Sur, which must take place in a few days ; that he was acting on instructions from his superior—from his commander-in-chief;* that, since the outgoing of the late administration at Washington, instructions had been received from the new, which contained nothing to induce him to alter the course which he intended to pursue; but that he preferred I would consider all this as unsaid, and that you would regard him as acting on his own and sole responsibility. I remarked, that his resolution was a most important one and would probably prove a determining fact,

---

* The commander-in-chief referred to was probably Commodore Mervine. The latter was an old and intimate friend, as the author has been told, of Secretary Marcy ; and both he and Davis were sent to the Pacific in January, 1857. Undoubtedly both of them received verbal instructions far more precise and definite, than their written orders. Soon after Davis reached Panama, direct from New-York, he took command of the St. Mary's and sailed for San Juan del Sur.

and therefore asked him deliberately to repeat whether
it was his fixed determination to seize the schooner
Granada. He replied that it was his unalterable resolution not to allow the Granada to leave the harbor of San
Juan, and to take possession of her before he sailed
With regard to the evacuation of the San Juan river by·
Col. Lockridge and his command, he said, that he had
entirely satisfied himself of the fact, both by the investi-
gations of his Lieut. McCorkle, and by perusal that
morning of a contract for passage to the United States,
signed by Scott and by officers of the British squadron,
besides other corroborative evidence. I observed that he
might have been imposed upon by a forgery, and asked
whether his conviction was shared by C. J. Macdonald,
agent of the Transit Company, whose experience rendered his opinion valuable. Capt. Davis replied that Mr.
Macdonald had been satisfied of the fact by Lieut. Mc-
Corkle's report, but that he (Capt. Davis), fully aware of
the responsibility he was assuming, pledged himself for
the authenticity of this statement. I thereupon agreed
to communicate to you this conversation, and to submit
the following offers from Capt. Davis, as the only propositions likely to be admissible, viz : That, under the guar·
antee of the American flag, you should, with sixteen
officers of your selection, with their arms, horses and
effects, leave Rivas to embark at San Juan for Panama;
that Rivas with its garrison, should be surrendered to
Capt. Davis; that the privates should deliver up their
arms, and, together with the officers, employees and citizens, be transported by another route to Panama, accompanied by a United States officer, and under guaran-

tee of the United States flag. At 2 o'clock, A. M., 1st May, I returned to Rivas, promising your answer at 10 o'clock, and personally to come back, if the negotiation was not broken off."

In the offers thus submitted by Henningsen, nothing was said of the native Nicaraguans then in Rivas. Walker, therefore, informed Henningsen that he would sign nothing, or agree to nothing, unless ample guarantees were given for the safety, both in person and property, of the native Nicaraguans. Hence, when Henningsen returned at 10 o'clock, A. M., on the first of May, with the draft of an agreement to be signed by Walker and Davis, it contained a clause protecting all natives of Central America then in Rivas.   The convention submitted to Davis, and signed by him, reads as follows :

" RIVAS, May 1, 1857.

" An agreement is hereby entered into between Gen. William Walker, on the one part, and Commander H. Davis, of the U. S. Navy, on the other part, and of which the stipulations are as follows :

" Firstly, Gen. Wm. Walker, with sixteen officers of his staff, shall march out of Rivas with their side-arms, pistols, horses, and personal baggage, under the guarantee of the said Capt. Davis, of the U. S. Navy, that they shall not be molested by the enemy, and shall be allowed to embark on board the U. S. vessel-of-war, the St. Mary's, in the harbor of San Juan del Sur, the said Capt. Davis, undertaking to transport them safely on the St. Mary's to Panama.

" Secondly, The officers of Gen. Walker's army shall march out of Rivas with their side-arms, under the guarantee and protection of Capt. Davis, who undertakes to see them safely transported to Panama, in charge of a United States officer.

" Thirdly, The privates and non-commissioned officers, citizens, and employees of Departments, wounded or unwounded, shall be surrendered with their arms to Capt. Davis, or one of his officers, and placed under his protection and control, he pledging himself to have them safely transported to Panama, in charge of a United States officer, in separate vessels from the deserters from the ranks, and without being brought into contact with them.

"Fourthly, Capt. Davis undertakes to obtain guarantees, and hereby does guarantee that all natives of Nicaragua, or of Central America, now in Rivas, and surrendered to the protection of Capt. Davis, shall be allowed to reside in Nicaragua, and be protected in life and property.

" Fifthly, It is agreed that such officers as have wives and families in San Juan del Sur, shall be allowed to remain there under the protection of the U. S. Consul, till an opportunity offers of embarking for Panama or San Francisco.

" Gen. Walker and Capt Davis mutually pledge themselves to each other that this agreement shall be executed in good faith."

It will be noticed that this agreement was made entirely between Walker and Davis, and the Allies were not mentioned in it except as " the enemy." Nor would it be necessary, unless for the singular conduct of Commander Davis afterward, to say that no other agreements were made or entered into, except the one which was signed by the respective parties.

After Davis had agreed to the terms of the convention, Henningsen returned to Rivas, and ordered the cannon, foundry, and ammunition to be destroyed, by breaking the trunnions, and sawing through the carriages of the former, by breaking up the steam-engine, fan, and cupola of the foundry, and throwing the ammunition and powder into the arsenal-yard wells. " In this manner were destroyed," acccording to Henningsen's report, " in the arsenal, two twelve-pounder brass howitzers, three six-pounder iron guns, four light iron twelve-pounder mortars, four brass guns taken from the enemy, viz. : one four-pounder, and three five-pounder guns ; in the ordnance office, fifty-five thousand cartridges, three hundred thousand caps, fifteen hundred pounds of powder. There remained undestroyed : fifty-five shell, three hundred and twenty twenty-four-pound shot—fired into Rivas by the enemy—two hundred and forty six-pound shot, of iron cast from the enemy's shot, from bell-metal, or from lead."

While Swingle and Potter were, under Henningsen's direction, executing the orders for the destruction of the articles in the arsenal and ordnance, Walker sent for the surgeon-general, Coleman, and informing him of the agreement made with Davis, instructed him to remain in charge of the hospital, and see that the sick and wounded were properly cared for. He then made out a list of the officers who were to accompany him on board the St. Mary's, and notified them to prepare forthwith to proceed to San Juan del Sur. The officers thus selected were, Henningsen, Hooff, Brady, Natzmer, Waters, Henry, Swingle, Rogers, Tucker, Kellum, McAllenny, West, Williamson, McEachin, McMichael, Hankins, and

Bacón. About five o'clock in the afternoon, Commander Davis, with Zavala, arrived at Walker's quarters; and Henningsen and Davis repaired to the Plaza, where all the troops of the garrison were formed. The order of the day, containing the agreement between Walker and Davis, was then read to the troops, and the garrison was delivered to the commander of the St. Mary's. The state of the garrison, when given over to the United States officer, was: Wounded and sick in and out of hospital, surgeons, and hospital attendants, 173 ; prisoners, 102 ; officers, non-commissioned, and privates, exclusive of the 16 going to San Juan, 148 ; employees of departments and armed citizens, 86 ; native troops, 40. While Henningsen was turning over the garrison to Davis, Walker, accompanied by the officers he had selected, and by Gen. Zavala, rode out of Rivas, and took the road for San Juan del Sur. On the night of the first of May, a few hours after leaving Rivas, the Nicaraguan officers were aboard the St. Mary's.

Commander Davis did not reach the St. Mary's until the morning of the 2d. Soon after he came aboard the sloop he proposed to Walker that the schooner Granada should be given into his hands without the use of force. Of course the proposal was rejected. He then said to Walker that the latter might keep the arms and ammunition on the schooner if he would give up the vessel. This was a proposition to sell the Granada, with all the glories of the 23d of November, for the paltry cargo aboard of her ; and there was not a lieutenant in the service of Nicaragua who would not have rejected it, with scorn and contempt for the officer, so far forgetful of his own honor as to utter the proposal. Just before dinner, on the 2d, Davis went ashore, leaving written orders with his first lieutenant to take the schooner. The log of the Granada, for the 2d, says: " At 4 P. M. Lieut. Maury came on board the schooner, and requested me to turn over the schooner to Capt. Davis. I asked why I should do so. He answered that Capt. Davis considered it his duty to seize her if I did not give her up, as he looked upon her as included in the treaty between himself and Gen. Walker. I refused to give her up." Then Maury returned to the St. Mary's, and requested Walker to give an order to Fayssoux to turn over the schooner to him. Walker replied he would not give the order, unless there was a demonstration of overwhelming force on the part of the St. Mary's. Maury brought the broadside of the sloop to bear on the Granada, and then he received the order of surrender. The log continues: " He (that is Maury) returned in half an hour, with an order from Gen. Walker to turn her over to the United States ; he was accompanied by 100 armed men and a howitzer. At 4.30 P. M. the Nicaraguan flag was hauled down, and the United States' run up in its place, and my crew sent on shore." Finally, on the 4th of May, the Granada was turned over to Costa Rica, and the person who received her for that republic was an aid of Cañas, a Jamaica negro, known by the name of Captain Murray.

This was a fit conclusion to the combined efforts of the British and United States naval forces to get the Americans out of Nicaragua. The descendant of revolutionary ancestors,* bearing in his own name of Irvine

---

* The paternal grandfather of Captain Fayssoux was chief surgeon of the Carolina forces during the war of Independence ; his maternal grandfather was General Irvine, who commanded a division under Washington at the crossing of the Delaware.

that of a grandsire who was a general officer in the war
of Independence—himself fitted by the purity and integrity of his character to adorn the service of any power
on either continent—was forced to give way to a negro
subject of Her Britannic Majesty holding a commission
from the Republic of Costa Rica. The poet could not
have imagined aught more striking or more characteristic.

Thus have I, during a leisure thrust on me against
my will, tried to tell clearly and concisely the story of
the rise, progress, and close, for a time, of the War in
Nicaragua. Doubtless many brave deeds and some
worthy names have escaped the notice they deserve, for
I have been obliged to write almost entirely from memory, with few papers or documents to refresh my recol-
lection of events now some time past. My main effort
has been to trace as distinctly as I could the causes of
the war, the manner in which it was waged, and the
circumstances attending its conclusion. As I said in the
last general order published at Rivas : " Reduced to our
present position by the cowardice of some, the incapacity
of others, and the treachery of many, the army has yet
written a page of American history which it is impossible to forget or erase. From the future, if not from the
present, we may expect just judgment." That which
you ignorantly call " Filibusterism " is not the offspring
of hasty passion or ill-regulated desire ; it is the fruit of
the sure, unerring instincts which act in accordance with

laws as old as the creation. They are but drivellers who speak of establishing fixed relations between the pure white American race, as it exists in the United States, and the mixed Hispano-Indian race, as it exists in Mexico and Central America, without the employment of force. The history of the world presents no such Utopian vision as that of an inferior race yielding meekly and peacefully to the controlling influence of a superior people. Whenever barbarism and civilization, or two distinct forms of civilization, meet face to face, the result must be war. Therefore, the struggle between the old and the new elements in Nicáraguan society was not passing or accidental, but natural and inevitable. The war in Nicaragua was the first clear and distinct issue made between the races inhabiting the northern and the central portions of the continent. But while this contest sprang from natural laws, I trust the foregoing narrative shows that the stronger race kept throughout on the side of right and justice ; and if they so maintained their cause in Central America let them not doubt of its future success. Nor kings nor presidents can arrest a movement based on truth and conducted with justice ; and the very obstacles they place in the way merely prepare those who are injured for the part they are to play in the world's history. He is but a blind reader of the past who has not learned that Providence fits its agents for great designs by trials, and sufferings, and persecutions. " By the cross thou shalt conquer" is as clearly written in the pages of history as when the startled emperor saw it blazing in letters of light athwart the heavens. In the very difficulties with which the Americans of

Nicaragua have had to contend I see the presage of their triumph. Let me, therefore, say to my former comrades, be of good cheer: faint not, nor grow weary by the way, for your toils and your efforts are sure in the end to win success. With us there can be no choice; honor and duty call on us to pursue the path we have entered, and we dare not be deaf to the appeal. By the bones of the mouldering dead at Masaya, at Rivas, and at Granada, I adjure you never to abandon the cause of Nicaragua. Let it be your waking and your sleeping thought to devise means for a return to the land whence we were unjustly brought. And, if we be but true to ourselves, all will yet end well.

THE END.